FRANK MILLER'S

SIN CITY

EXT. MANSION BALCONY - NIGHT

A beautiful woman. Standing over an estate balcony. A party goes on inside.

                    MAN
                    (vo)
          She shivers in the wind like the last leaf on a dying tree. I
          let her hear my footsteps. She only goes stiff for a moment.

THE MAN appears behind her.

                    MAN (CONT'D)
          Care for a smoke?

                    WOMAN
          Sure. I'll take one.

Her hand stretches out to the pack.

                    WOMAN (CONT'D)
          Are you as bored by that crowd back there as I am?

                    MAN
          I didn't come here for the party. I came here for you.

She readies her cigarette for a light.

                    MAN (CONT'D)
          I've watched you for days. You're everything a man could
          ever want.

He pulls out a lighter.

                    MAN (CONT'D)
          It's not just your face, your figure, your voice.

Click. The flame burns bright in her green eyes.

                    MAN (CONT'D)
          It's your eyes. All the things I see in your eyes.

She turns away, giving him her bare back.

                    WOMAN
          What is it you see in my eyes?

MAN

I see a crazy calm. You're sick of running. You're ready to face what you have to face.

The words dig into her.

MAN (CONT'D)

But you don't want to face it alone.

WOMAN

No. I don't want to face it alone.

She turns back. Their eyes meet.

MAN
(vo)

The wind rises electric. She's soft and warm and almost weightless. Her perfume a sweet promise that brings tears to my eyes.

Backlit raindrops sweep through the air. The couple embraces. He whispers to her.

MAN (CONT'D)
(vo)

I tell her that everything will be alright. That I'll save her from whatever she's scared of and take her far, far away.

They kiss.

MAN (CONT'D)
(vo)

I tell her I love her.

PFFT.

MAN (CONT'D)
(vo)

The silencer makes a whisper of the gunshot.

We look down on the couple as they lower to his knees. An endless embrace.

MAN (CONT'D)
(vo)

I hold her close until she's gone. I'll never know what she was running from.

She expires.

                    MAN (CONT'D)
        I'll cash her check in the morning.

We pull up. Up into the sky until we are looking down onto a SIN CITY.

TITLE sequence:

FRANK MILLER'S

SIN CITY

THE MAKING OF THE MOVIE

by FRANK MILLER and ROBERT RODRIGUEZ

Design by KURT VOLK

TROUBLEMAKER
PUBLISHING

DIMENSION
FILMS

INTRODUCTION BY FRANK MILLER

You've got no damn idea how you wound up in this godforsaken place.

Maybe you fell asleep on the train, rode past your stop. Landed in this dump. Maybe you're coming off one hell of a bender. You've got no damn idea.

At least you've still got your wallet. From the looks of the locals, the ones who are still vertical, that's a miracle.

It's a hot night on a street that feels like it's never seen sunlight. Since there's nothing else to do, you walk. You step over some wino who's passed out in his own vomit. A newspaper rides a gust of wind and flaps against your leg. It's a tabloid, the trashy kind. Blood's dried on it.

The street's gutter is a symphony of cigarette butts.

The next bum you step over has a knife stuck into what used to be his eye.

Maybe you've died and gone to hell. Maybe that's it.

Then the roar of a V8 engine blasts the night to bits. You turn and watch a gleaming, showroom-slick '53 Cadillac El Dorado rip past you, leaping a good ten feet off the ground. Vintage. Magnificent. It fishtails out of sight.

Blocks away, glass shatters and some old-fashioned burglar alarm goes jangling. Some maniac laughs. You don't want to know.

You keep walking.

You reach the corner and you see them. Hookers. A whole lot of hookers, flagging down pickup trucks and squad cars alike. But these hookers, they aren't the sad, hard, weary, drug-soaked women you'd expect. They're proud creatures. Each of them as confident and beautiful as a goddess. Dressed to the nines.

Most of them pack heat. One of them tosses you a smile you can feel in your pocket. They astonish. Out of this world.

You walk. You walk and maybe you light up a cigarette yourself. The old kind. Unfiltered. Hard on the throat. You catch a coughing fit and toss the butt away to join all its brothers and sisters in the gutter.

You're getting there. You're on your way.

You walk. You don't really have anywhere in particular to go. So what the hell. You could use a brew. You spot a half-blind neon sign for what looks to be the seediest saloon in the world. You go to the door and the bouncer eyeballs you like you smell bad, but he lets you in. And there's no cover charge.

You're in.

The joint reeks. Smoke. Urine. Puke. It's the worst.

There's a guy with blood for a face mashed into one booth, an asshole pleading to his wife to forgive him for whatever in the next. Some guy just plain face down in the third. This place is bad.

So you belly up to the bar and order some lameass Texas brew. Some Lone Star crap. And then you see it. The stage. Your heart sinks.

The place has a goddamn stage. Like for dancing. Exotic dancing.

Your heart stays sunk. This is gonna be just plain awful. Some hard-muscled, hard-headed, hard-hearted bitch-of-a-bitch skank, shaking what she's got for a bunch of hopeless losers.

The music goes quiet. Slow. Sad. Country. The good kind.

And the crowd goes silent as an angel wafts across the stage.

She's a cowgirl angel, slowly swinging her lasso, moving like a dream. Her eyes are sad, her smile sweet. Her figure is a fantasy come to life. For that moment, you'd swear there's nothing ugly anywhere on earth.

Welcome to Sin City.

-Frank Miller
2005

For twelve years, this was my *Sin City* experience: I'd walk into a comic book store, gravitate towards the Frank Miller section and thumb through a *Sin City* graphic novel. I'd buy it, take it home, only to find I'd already bought that same book *three times*. There's something oddly alluring about Frank's books. The visuals grab you first, but then you read the stories and find they are just as lurid and appealing. I love film noir and had always wanted to make one. What I loved about *Sin City* was that there was nothing nostalgic about it. It was modern...savage.

2003 rolls along and I had just finished making several effects-heavy movies, doing my own digital cinematography and lighting, and learning a lot. My next movie had to be challenging in those areas to take full advantage of all that I'd learned. I bought my tenth copy of *Booze, Broads, and Bullets*, looked at the cover and realized, "I can do this now...the technology has caught up to Frank Miller."

The heart started pumping. I thumbed through all seven volumes of *Sin City* in succession. I grabbed my hot-rodded digital cameras, went to my green screen and shot a test. I worked on the final look with my effects company, Troublemaker Digital. It looked cooler than

I thought possible. I had to hunt down Frank. Not easy. Frank hears "the movies" are calling, and the last thing he'll do is pick up the phone. I don't blame him. But I knew he'd like this. I found him...in a Hell's kitchen saloon.

The reason I had to make this movie was because of how the comic was created. Frank was burned out by Hollywood and as a reaction he wrote *Sin City*. He made a book that was the ultimate *anti*-movie. Something that could never be made into a traditional movie, it could only exist in comics. Something that pure is hard to come by. That's why I had to have it. I wanted to make an "anti-movie," something not even meant for the big screen. It was a completely renegade work of dangerous art, with no compromises for what people tend to think movies should be. The words didn't sound like screenplay dialogue, the story didn't move in traditional story arcs. It did its own damn thing and didn't apologize for it. To me, that's a movie worth making.

While in that saloon, I opened a laptop and showed Frank my first test footage. His reaction was, "That's powerful stuff, mister." "Those images are straight from your books, Frank." I pointed out. I told him I wasn't interested in adapting *Sin City*. I wanted to "translate" it to the screen. Frank nodded his head, the kind of nod that said he'd never expected to hear that in his lifetime. "First, I'll send you a script. Then we'll shoot the opening sequence as a test, and on my dime. If you like it, we make a deal and move on. If you don't, it'll be a nice short film you can show your friends."

Frank said, "You're on."

Black and white movies really aren't black and white, they are mostly gray and white. So many mid-tones get introduced that images go flat. That's why when most people think of a black and white movie, to them that equals: dull. But as the photographer, I shot the movie completely on green screen, so that I could isolate the actors from the backgrounds and each other. Sometimes lights were even in frame to get the best position, to be removed later digitally. This is what allowed me to get that punchy, stark black and white look of the books, with very little grey tone except to add some modeling to a beautiful (or ugly) face. Since it was shot in color, I could then bring back colors later as needed throughout my editing process.

I could go on and on about the making of the movie, and will eventually, but for now hear from some of my awesome crew people that worked on this groundbreaking movie (It was groundbreaking the moment Frank's ink hit the page, and the movie just took it to the next level).

This was such a renegade picture, I had to break a lot of rules along the way to get this made, including resigning from the DGA so that Frank Miller could direct alongside me. But that's what it takes sometimes to make an anti-movie. In the end, all I can say is, "Fair trade."

Enjoy.

-Robert Rodriguez
2005

ELIZABETH AVELLÁN ON PRODUCING *SIN CITY*

My excitement level was high as we flew to New York so Robert Rodriguez could meet with Frank Miller about *Sin City*. Robert had been trying to set up a meeting with him for a couple of months, but Frank was hard to pin down.

Now that I know Frank's prior experience in the Hollywood machine, I find his decision to take the meeting with Robert as a very brave move. Almost as brave as when he made the decision to put this crazy, wonderful, complex world of *Sin City* on paper all by himself with such a unique artistic vision.

Robert and I are producing partners. He decides on the project and I carry out the logistics. He chooses the cast, and I take care of making the deals. In addition, I make sure the cast has a great experience working with us while they are in Austin. He makes the creative decisions, and I figure out how to make it happen within the budget that we are given.

I consider myself one of the luckiest producers in the movie business because I work with one of the most decisive, knowledgeable, creative filmmakers in a business where time usually equates to money. We get as much information as possible, as fast as possible, then we make our decisions.

Sin City was a completely different experience for me, a huge challenge. We had two directors and a "guest director." There was a large cast with many big stars who worked anywhere between two to fifteen days out of a fifty-day shooting schedule. Our cast was huge, with so many major players that the biggest challenge for me was putting together the great big puzzle of the schedule and making it with a very tight production budget. One of the major things that we had in our favor was the fact that 95% of the movie was shot in our green screen stage. That gave us total control over the weather, the ability to work long hours, and not having to move the company to different locations.

The work that Line Producer Bill Scott, Unit Production Manager Ron Schmidt, and First Assistant Director Brian Bettwy did to help me make Robert and Frank's vision a reality was invaluable. I truly can say that I could not have done it without them. We all worked together to make sure that the actors and the crew had everything they needed to make it happen on time and on budget...actually *below* budget!

Our crew, based out of Austin, has worked with us on several movies. Going back all the way to *The Faculty* (1998), we have consistently had a great time working with our local crew. They are a mature, experienced, diverse group who have worked together for so many years that they are like family.

Sin City was a welcome change of pace for many. For years we were doing the *Spy Kids* movies, and now we had bloody limbs, wild language, and scantily-clad women all over the place. That made for an interesting return to production, considering I was coming to set with a newborn everyday.

Post-production also proved challenging and interesting, as we were entering uncharted visual effects territory. This movie was all about recreating the look of Frank's work, so getting the visual effects right was critical and if I thought budgeting all those actors was trying, it was easy compared to making sure all those shots happened.

RANK MILLER ON THE ORIGINS OF SIN CITY

...on Comics

My mother tells me that when I was six years old I walked into her kitchen and announced—holding sheets of typing paper that I had folded over and stapled in the middle and drawn all over—that I was going to be doing comic books for the rest of my life. And it's about the only job I was ever able to keep. I stuck with it. Obsessive kids tend to know best.

...on the Big City

I was a country kid. I grew up in rural Vermont, and I always fantasized about the big city. I grew up reading comic books, and eventually graduated from superhero comics to Mickey Spillane novels, and Raymond Chandler and all that, and fell in love with film noir and the whole crime scene. When I finally started making

my way as a comic-book artist, I showed up in New York with a bunch of samples for work that I wanted to sell to the comics publishers. My stuff was all guys in trench coats and beautiful women in vintage cars, and the publishers not too politely told me that all they did was people in tights hitting each other, and I had to learn how to do that. And I did do that for years, and had a great time. But when I got popular enough to have the freedom to do what I wanted to do, I went right back to the stuff I had been doing when I was fourteen (although with a bit more polish to it): It was still vintage cars, hot babes, and guys in trench coats.

Sin City started as the fantasies of a country kid. It was almost as if I had been born to live in New York, because when I moved there, I immediately fell in love with the

city and just about everything about it. Well, not the bums, but just about everything else. At the time—this was the late '70s—there was great late-night TV in New York that showed movies from the '40s and '50s—all the stuff I essentially ripped off cold for *Sin City*—that I watched on this crappy little black-&-white television I had.

...on Crime Stories

I've always loved crime stories. I've loved the romance of the big city, the tough guys and beautiful women, the cars and guns, and all of that. But mostly what keeps me involved in crime stories, the reason I go back to them, is that under the surface, these are all morality tales. Times of great stress are clarifying times, and the genre, because it is so much about good and evil, delves deeply into evil. It's got the virtue of melodrama, which is not nostalgic at all. We have our ups and downs in real life, but in melodrama things are taken to extremes. Hitchcock said, to paraphrase, "melodrama is real life with all the boring parts taken out." In good melodrama, and good adventure, and in good crime fiction, there is a fierce clarity in which each person makes his moral decisions. It's also the motif of crime fiction—à la Chandler, Spillane, or Hammett—that the virtue, the heroism of these characters is disguised. They are blood-caked knights. They don't let on that most of them are compulsive do-gooders. That's Dwight for instance. He's a compulsive do-gooder. He's fiercely loyal—he's trying to make things better, but you'd never know that when you hear him talk.

...on California and Sin City

I had been living in New York for fourteen years when I moved to California to see what that was like, and it was during that period that I formulated *Sin City*. So *Sin City* was clearly inspired by New York at the beginning, but I also think there's an existential aspect to Los Angeles, that it's such an illusion of a city. It's so beautiful but everybody knows it's really just a desert with stuff built on it and growing there. And there's a sense of randomness and madness to the violence there. But there's also a real sweaty romance to that city because of the weather, because of how beautiful the women are, and because of the sheer beauty of the city. So, with *Sin City* being, of course, a collection of things I like to draw, I was quick to bring those palm trees in, and use those cars that never rust because of the climate and everything else right down to the terra cotta tiles on rooftops.

...on Film Influence

Comics and films have been doing an interesting dance the past few years. The two fields have always been related: They're both visual forms and they share a lot of the same dynamics. Unfortunately, up until very recently, the relationships have been enormously one-sided. Comics have been the retarded second cousin of movies begging for scraps. Historically, the first thing usually done in developing a comic-book movie is to throw out the original material and start from scratch. The results generally are predictably horrible. It's only recently that there's been an attempt actually to translate the content of comics to film rather than treating comics like some crappy genre for slumming actors to act goofy in. *Sin City* is far and away the most faithful translation of a comic book to film, and we're finding that a lot of things that filmmakers have often said can't translate from comics, the particular kind of dialogue, the very abrupt jump cutting—from image to image, and from moment to moment—sure seems to edit out sweet. So I think people are going to be quite surprised.

The thing people most often get wrong about film noir is that they think it just looks spooky, missing the fact that the spookiness of the look is a reflection of what's going on behind the eyes of people. If there is some real emotional darkness, it doesn't matter how dark the film is, with shadows and blinds behind them, and all these other things that are metaphors for the torment, or the rage, or the self-hatred, or the despair the character's going through. So drawing a comic book like *Sin City*, or shooting a movie like *Sin City* is a matter of making the entire picture part of the character's mind, while still keeping it a real place with real dangers. The dark images aren't just there for looks.

...on Comic Influences

When I originally tried to figure out how to draw *Sin City*, I knew I wanted it to be black and white first off. I wanted it to be a one-man show and to see if I could really pull it off. I studied a lot of the comics and movies of the past, and I could give you a list of influences as long as your arm, but I can name three cartoonists in particular who were the biggest influences to *Sin City*. Certainly Will Eisner who brought the crime genre to comics in the '40s with his spectacular *The Spirit*. Two other ones who aren't quite as well-known but were extraordinary in how they were able to think in black and white—not just do all this complicated stuff of psychology, but also make everything look gorgeous—were Wallace Wood and Johnny Craig. Both were known for their work for the legendary EC Comics line. Both did horror and crime stories, and with their work just the sheer romance of the genre really came to beautiful fruition in the '50s. After that there was a long time when no crime comics were done at all. When I came in to do mine I didn't want to ape them, but I sure as hell learned a lot from their examples. I learned how much was involved in making the images themselves tell the story, and to let the lines fall away so that the reader creates the lines for me. The mind gets very excited by an unfinished image, the same way when you move from one of the panels of the comic book to the next, there's a white gutter between the two where your brain makes up a hundred images. That's my job—not to be there when it counts.

...on Stories Colliding

My citizens do tend to bump into each other a lot across stories. Some of the characters come up with scenes of their own. Sometimes a scene will call for Shellie to walk in, and other times I'll have a feeling that a scene I did before should happen in the background of a scene that I'm doing now to give you a sense of how all these characters interconnect. How if you walked into Kadie's bar on a given day you could walk out at a different time, and into a completely different story. A lot of the time that I unintentionally set up these scenes, I throw a line in without even knowing why I threw it in, and realize later that I'm working on a story and that it relates, and that it would be this character who does this or that. So, an awful lot of it just seems to be happening somewhere in a subterranean cavern somewhere inside my head.

-Frank Miller

RR: This is the most faithful adaptation of a graphic novel ever produced in Hollywood, and for anyone to ever duplicate that, they'd have to break all kinds of Hollywood rules, including leaving the DGA, because the only way to do a movie this faithful to a graphic novel like *Sin City* would be to have someone like Frank Miller co-directing with me.

the comic book store, they always just stand out. Then when you read them, the stories grab you. One of the funny things I mentioned to Frank was that I would go to a comic book store, pick one up, buy it, go home and realize I already had three copies. I just kept re-buying his material. Back in the early '90s I remember thinking about a movie version of *Sin City* and thinking, 'How could I ever adapt it? It would just become a regular

of adapting the comic to cinema, we can turn it around, and bring the comic to life, and really just translate it to the screen. That was my whole pitch to Frank. But when I finally tracked him down and got to meet with him, he originally thought it was going to be another Hollywood tale.

FM: I was hard to find.

Opposite: Frank Miller and Robert Rodriguez on the set of *Sin City*; Above from left: Mort's suicide from *A Dame To Kill For*, camera operator Jimmy Lindsey against greenscreen, a preliminary color-correction test by Troublemaker Digital

I got the idea to do this movie back in September of 2003 because after doing the *Spy Kids* movies, which had a lot of high technology, a lot of lighting and special effects tricks, I wanted to stay in that vein and use what I learned on some other, bigger challenge. I think it was about September 2003 that I was looking at the *Sin City* books again. I had been buying those for the past twelve years since the first one came out. When I go to

movie. It wouldn't have the same feel as the comics.' Now, knowing what I know about effects and lighting, I started looking at it differently. Instead of trying to turn it into a movie that would be terrible, let's take cinema and try to make it into this book. And that was what got me. Using the technology that I know how to use—technology, and lighting, and effects—we can make it look and feel like the original comics. Instead

RR: Unlike most movies, where so much of the time is spent developing the project, I told Frank that for this movie, there is no development. He'd already developed this over twelve years. We were just going to start shooting. If changes needed to be made it'll be a question of finding the right actor, but once we've got it cast it's already up on stage. At that point, having reread them with a movie in mind, I'd already come to think

that these comics are the best shot, written, directed, lit, and edited movies that people have never seen, just on paper. So the idea was to take a work, acknowledge that it's already a valid graphic, visual storytelling with character, and just change the medium, because the mediums of film and comics are really very similar. These are just snapshots of movement, and I really didn't see anything that different. Frank is a natural storyteller, he's a visual storyteller, and I thought that he had a different approach to it. I didn't think someone from the comic world like Frank, who does what Frank does, could come into Hollywood and move his way up from the bottom. I thought he should be right at the same level doing what I'm doing. He's adept with graphics, and with character, and with visuals, and just creating and telling stories. So I thought he should just be co-directing the movie. And that in doing so, he would find the similarities between the two mediums to be striking.

Because I used to be a cartoonist, I used to draw as well, and I told Frank in the beginning that moviemaking is very much like drawing.

FM: That was the real shocking lesson. I mean he said it to me, but you really have to get your hands dirty with this sort of thing. The process by which Robert puts these movies together, using the green screen and everything, greatly resembles drawing. It's really a matter of creating elements and moving them about. So a lot of the things that I've learned over my career as a cartoonist applies well to this process, and for me, it was a revelation because I'd had encounters with production before. I'd been in positions where the director seemed to show up in a headdress with a couple of rattles and shake them around. Director as witch doctor. Robert's the great "demystifer." He explains things in a very coherent way, both as a natural

teacher, and also as a very honest guy. He breaks things down, and basically tells you it's not quite as difficult and magical as everybody says it is.

RR: It's kind of like the ten-minute film school. Frank got something like a twenty-minute film school and then was directing on the set. It was as easy as pulling a curtain rod. Look, I'd say, that's what is behind the curtain right there, that's all it is. And he picked it up so quickly.

FM: The crash course.

RR: Frank just jumped right up into the highest tech level possible and picked it up like that. It's not well-known material we're doing, we're pretty cutting-edge down here. And he got right in on the cutting-edge technology very quickly.

Speech bubble in panel: "IT TURNS OUT I'M GOOD AT KILLING. AND I LIKE IT. I LIKE IT A LOT."

FM: Robert is a persistent guy. Up until meeting Robert several times, I just didn't want *Sin City* in the process of movies, I didn't want to put my little baby in the river and say goodbye and leave her vulnerable. I didn't want to be in a situation where the characters that I'd lived with and worked on for years on end would suddenly be subjected to somebody's whim, or to the latest focus group. So it took some convincing for me that anybody would be willing to do something this faithful. And also that it was possible to do something visually that would relate to such a stylized piece. But when Robert showed up for our first meeting, he opened his laptop and he'd already done some test shots of how he wanted to photograph actors and stage things. It really was damn good.

RR: Frank's reaction was great. He looked at that and went, "That's some pretty powerful stuff, mister." The shots were straight out of his books. I lined up the frame right from the original panels, so that it was the shot from the comic, but it was moving. It hit Frank immediately as something from *Sin City*.

FM: I also remember saying, "Who's that actress? She's beautiful," and Robert saying, "Oh, that's my sister."

So from there I was intrigued but still very protective, because this is my baby, and it's my home. *Sin City* is where I always go back when I'm not doing something else. I always return to *Sin City*.

RR: And I understood that, because if someone goes and makes a bad movie out there, it's ruined. You can't go back. They remember it because it was a bad movie, and then you have thrown your baby out the window. As someone who creates his own material, I knew I had to track him down and convince him personally, because I knew already what he was thinking. I mean I just opened the book and it says, "Written by Frank, drawn by Frank"—essentially directed, edited, chopped, shot, scored by Frank. I think I know this guy. I think I know how to convince him, and I think I know how to do the book.

FM: I didn't even let anybody else letter the thing.

RR: So I understood, because we're cut from the same cloth. If I can track him down, I can convince him. I don't want to make Rodriguez's *Sin City*, I want to make Frank Miller's *Sin City*, because I love that material so much. I keep buying it, there must be something I'm connecting to. How could I rewrite it? Yeah, I could rewrite it and change it completely and turn it into something else, but why? You're not making it better,

you're just making it different. And it was so good the way it was. I thought this would be a great movie as-is on screen before there's even the input of the actors, which is always going to bring something. So I just thought we needed just to start moving, that the pre-production was already done, the development was already done. And so I just started shooting.

FM: It's characteristic of Robert—when he has an objective—he simply moves toward it as if all systems are go whether they are or not. And it's like reality follows along behind.

RR: There is a trajectory. There is a snowball effect that happens. If you just start moving, everyone just falls right in. "Oh," they say, "he's going somewhere, there's a train leaving the station, I think I want to be on it. It looks cool."

FM: Then, of course, there was what Robert still laughingly refers to as "the test." Robert said, "Look, why don't I just have you out to Texas and we'll shoot a little three-page story with one of your books. It won't take long, and we'll see how you feel. And if you don't want to do it, we'll have a cool little short movie, and if

you do want to do it, we'll do it." That's kind of hard to turn down, you know. But I thought if he's going to do three pages, why has he only got me there for a couple of days? And of course, he shoots it in ten hours, and it looks great, and this little test, by the way, featured not only Marley Shelton and Josh Hartnett, but it was also the first day of principal photography.

RR: I did warn Frank in advance that once we got started and shot this little test, he was going to wish we could have just kept going. And we got there, and we realized that now we had to go cast the rest of the movie, and he said, "This is going to work." I didn't just want to show Frank, but I wanted to prove it to myself too. I thought, I'll pay for it. Usually the artist takes all the risk. When an artist gives his material away, he's taking all the risk. He's giving it to someone hoping that it'll be good. I wanted to reverse that process to where I would take all the risk. I'll go pay for the test. I'll bring my guys together, and I got my own stages and camera, so we'll shoot it ourselves. I'll do the effects in my effects company. And if he was not convinced to do it by then, I did not deserve his business anyway. That was my approach to it, and so I really wanted to prove to myself it could be done, and of course, if it comes

out okay, there's the opening. And it became a great sales tool to take around to show all the other actors, because we were moving so fast. We could say this is the book, and this is what we're going to do. In fact, here's the opening into the credits, and we show the sequence to people like Bruce Willis—and it already had their name in the credits.

FM: Robert already put his wish list into the credits.

RR: We put our wish list in the credits, and we ended up getting all those people. So they could already picture themselves being in this movie because they could see the opening scene. And that was actually a real revelation, too. I think I should do that more often. Make a nice short film, and you'll know if your ideas work.

FM: They know if they can hook into it because it creates such a coherent sense of the world. The production of that little job I'll never forget because I was sitting watching the whole thing, actors just standing against green, and I was thinking, "You're gonna do what?"

TROUBLEMAKER DIGITAL ON PREVISUALIZATION

...on Troublemaker Digital

"The artists are there as a creative spark for Robert to help him conceptualize his vision. We use drawings and 3D animatics to layout a blueprint of the entire film. This process helps the crew to actually see what Robert is thinking. Throughout production and post-production, we continue the process to flesh ideas out by integrating what the production crew has shot to help the VFX vendors do their jobs."

...on the previsualization process

"The previsualization for previous films like the *Spy Kids* movies consisted of not only look, concept and shot design, but also choreography and animation. We would figure out what the camera would be doing in addition to the action of the elements of the scene. Therefore, the process consisted of a lot of animation and trying to figure out the flow of the action. *Sin City* was mainly trying to figure out the look of each frame instead of worrying about what the next shot should be."

...on Sin City from start to finish

"*Sin City* was all shot in color. On set they were able to tweak the lighting, but pretty much kept it neutral so there was enough information to play around with in post. We didn't want to do too much processing in camera because then it would limit us later on. Once we got the plates in, the team started doing rough composites; turning them black and white, getting the contrast levels right, making sure the skin looked right and the eyes didn't get too dark. Then it was just a matter of getting the actors integrated with the CG backgrounds we were designing. From that point, it was just a balance of stepping back to look at the picture compositionally to make sure the overall shot wasn't too black or white and that the live action plate was embedded realistically in the shot. In fact, when we started out, the look was really graphic, almost no gray at all. I originally thought an audience would have a hard time following the story with such a visually contrasting style between the actors and the CGI. Although we entertained the idea of pushing the live action imagery to more of a graphic toon-shaded look, we started to take the whole thing in a more realistic direction."

-Chris Olivia
Previsualization Supervisor

...on the black and white look

"One of Frank Miller's trademarks is his use of black and white, negative and positive images. So it became one of Troublemaker's biggest challenges to find a way to translate that look to film without it becoming distracting. Certain shots, like Lucille's bathroom or Kevin's tiled room, went through maybe twenty different versions before matching what Robert saw in his mind."

"There's a shot near the beginning of the film where two people are standing on a rooftop and the frame goes completely negative. What would normally be white is black and vice versa. Fans of the comics will notice shots like this are pretty much exact recreations from the books."

"In other shots, the look is less literal, but the overall spirit of the drawings remains. For instance, in the books, Frank draws the grout between tiles as black. But when a character casts a shadow on it, the grout turns white - it becomes a negative. It's a unique look, and something Robert had us spend a lot of time fine tuning."

-John Ford
Visual Effects Artist

Opposite: Animatic version of Hartigan torture scene by Troublemaker Digital; This page clockwise from upper right: Marv from *The Hard Goodbye*, man and woman on rooftop from *Booze, Broads and Bullets*, animatic by Troublemaker Digital, Marv and Lucille from *The Hard Goodbye*, animatic with high-contrast grout, animatic with low-contrast grout

THE WIND RISES, ELECTRIC.

SHE'S SOFT AND WARM AND ALMOST WEIGHTLESS. HER PERFUME IS A SWEET PROMISE THAT BRINGS TEARS TO MY EYES.

I TELL HER THAT EVERYTHING WILL BE ALL RIGHT. THAT I'LL SAVE HER FROM WHATEVER SHE'S SCARED OF AND TAKE HER FAR, FAR AWAY.

25

Clockwise from above: Animatic of Mimi's Motel by Troublemaker Digital, the finished shot from the film by The Orphanage, Mimi's Motel from *That Yellow Bastard*; Opposite: Animatic of Marv's mom's staircase by Troublemaker Digital, Marv's mom's staircase from *The Hard Goodbye*

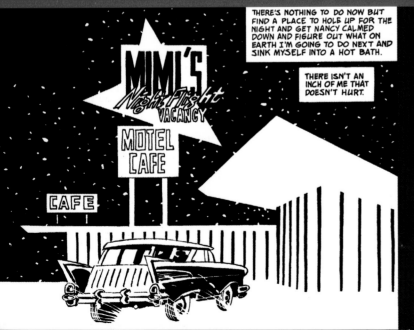

THERE'S NOTHING TO DO NOW BUT FIND A PLACE TO HOLE UP FOR THE NIGHT AND GET NANCY CALMED DOWN AND FIGURE OUT WHAT ON EARTH I'M GOING TO DO NEXT AND SINK MYSELF INTO A HOT BATH.

THERE ISN'T AN INCH OF ME THAT DOESN'T HURT.

...on Sin City's look

"Robert was really open to seeing different ideas, but I know that he had something very specific in mind. Primarily he just wanted us to look at the panels and create slight variations on them. So it ended up that whatever Frank Miller drew was pretty much what we tried to establish. On the previous Troublemaker movies, we basically had a blank canvas. Here, Frank Miller's comic book was our bible and our jumping off point for every shot. Since the film is so close to Frank's books, I guess you could say Frank Miller did most of our previsualization for us."

"The challenge was then to make the images work in a 3D environment where there's perspective. When you see things in 3D, they change a little bit. Something very graphic that works in a 2D panel can get confusing once it starts moving. The stark contrast, the black and white, trying to translate that to 3D and moving a camera through it can get a bit tricky sometimes."

-Rodney Brunet
Visual Effects Artist

...on the early stages of adaptation

"I remember during the filming of *Spy Kids 2* when Robert showed up with the *Sin City* graphic novel. It had post-it notes all over it. He was so excited about the look of it. The black and white, the composition, the feel. He was like, 'Wouldn't it be cool to make a movie just like this?' A couple of years later and *bam*, the rebirth of the novel into film."

"Robert was very adamant about the visual quality from very early on and 'the look' started to show up in the animatics. Marv climbing the stairs is a good example of how we started to integrate the look of the comics into the animatics. Troublemaker Digital's previsualization work, along with the opening prologue with Josh Hartnett, were the foundation that Hybride, CafeFX and The Orphanage used to build and finalize the amazing look of what is *Sin City*."

-Alex Toader
Visual Effects Artist

...on the visual evolution

"The first thing I knew about the project was from the early Troublemaker Digital tests. Robert took that footage to his digital artists to make them look like pages from the novels; the silhouettes and the high contrast, straight black and white look with no grays at all and only some select isolated color. Then Robert evolved the style toward what we did on the opening scene, which consists of more grays, still very black and white, but a lot more photorealism. From there the various VFX houses took what we provided and went into their own direction. We knew there would be room for the houses to have their own art direction, so for continuity's sake, we had one VFX house assigned to each story, so each one could have their own look, but it would be for each story. For instance, Hybride's (*The Hard Goodbye*) and CafeFX's (*The Big Fat Kill*) look became more photo-real than The Orphanage's (*That Yellow Bastard*) sequence, which occurs later in the film. Robert was okay with their look being more graphic and closer to the look in the novels, increasing the use of more contrast black and whites."

...on color

"*Sin City* is extraordinarily violent. But there are certain places, for example in *The Big Fat Kill*, where the violence is not supposed to be horribly graphic. The scene where Jackie Boy and his Goons are killed is comical in a sense. If you really watched someone stab swords into heads or cutting hands off, it would be too gross and there would be no way for us to show that in the theatre. But the fact that the blood isn't red and it glows white makes the scene more palatable. The audience can get that Frank really just wanted the scene to be crazy obscene. So we were able to make that campy, violent look stylistic - like

the novels. The MPAA basically said that we would have had to cut many scenes if the movie had been in color, but because the film is in black and white, we can get away with more graphic violence."

...on simple solutions to complex problems

"We also were presented the challenge of trying to figure out how to pull off the 'glowing blood' that appeared in the shadows of Frank's illustrations. At first the idea was to animate the blood and then we realized that it would be too expensive and complicated. We then came up with using fluorescent paints and black lights to create the glow."

"If we had done CG snow throughout the entire *Yellow Bastard* sequence, it would have been a lot more expensive. We approached The Orphanage for this sequence because of the great snow work they did on *The Day After Tomorrow*. Instead of relying on all CG, The Orphanage built a miniature set and used baking powder for snow. So a lot of their shots where you are seeing snow in the environment, you are looking at baking powder and matte paintings. I thought that it was cool of them to come up with a really amazing look that was not in the direction they were expected to go in the first place."

-Keefe Boerner
Post Supervisor / Visual Effects Producer

...on title design

"Out of the dozens of films that I've worked on, *Sin City* has to be my favorite, in terms of visual effects. Robert is a strong, inspirational force as a director. Even though Robert has a firm vision on what he wants, he is very open to creative input from Troublemaker Digital. For

the main title design, I thought it would be great to use the comic book image of each character as a backdrop to match each actor's name. The title design also uses the juxtaposition of negative light and shadows that is inherent in Frank Miller's images. Robert made it even better by refining it, changing the timing, and cutting it to his music."

...on color timing

"In addition to title design, I was also the color timing supervisor. Since this task is normally Robert's, I was basically acting as Robert's extra pair of eyes. There just wasn't enough time for him to do both the final music mix and supervise the color timing. Because, as part of the Troublemaker Digital team involved with the initial creation and tests of the *Sin City* prologue, I knew exactly the look that Robert was going after. The final color correction of every frame and shot of the movie is a long, arduous, yet rewarding task. I would color correct a reel (ten to fifteen minutes of the movie) at a time at 501 Post in Austin, take the HD tape to Robert's house to get feedback, then go back and make corrections the next day. This went on for 2 weeks, and that was just the initial pass on an HD monitor. Then I would fly to Los Angeles and do it all over again, but this time with a full 2K digital projection on a theatrical-size screen at Efilm. My eyes were always bloodshot at the end of each day, but I loved every minute of it. The best way to describe color-correction on a film like *Sin City* is that of an artist's dream of being able to paint on thousands of giant canvases, because the color and composition on each frame of *Sin City* is so unique, graphic, and powerful by itself."

-Eric Pham
Digital Color Timing Supervisor

Clockwise from above: Animatic by Troublemaker Digital of Hartigan's jail cell, the finished shot by The Orphanage, Hartigan's cell from the *That Yellow Bastard*

THE HA

GOOD

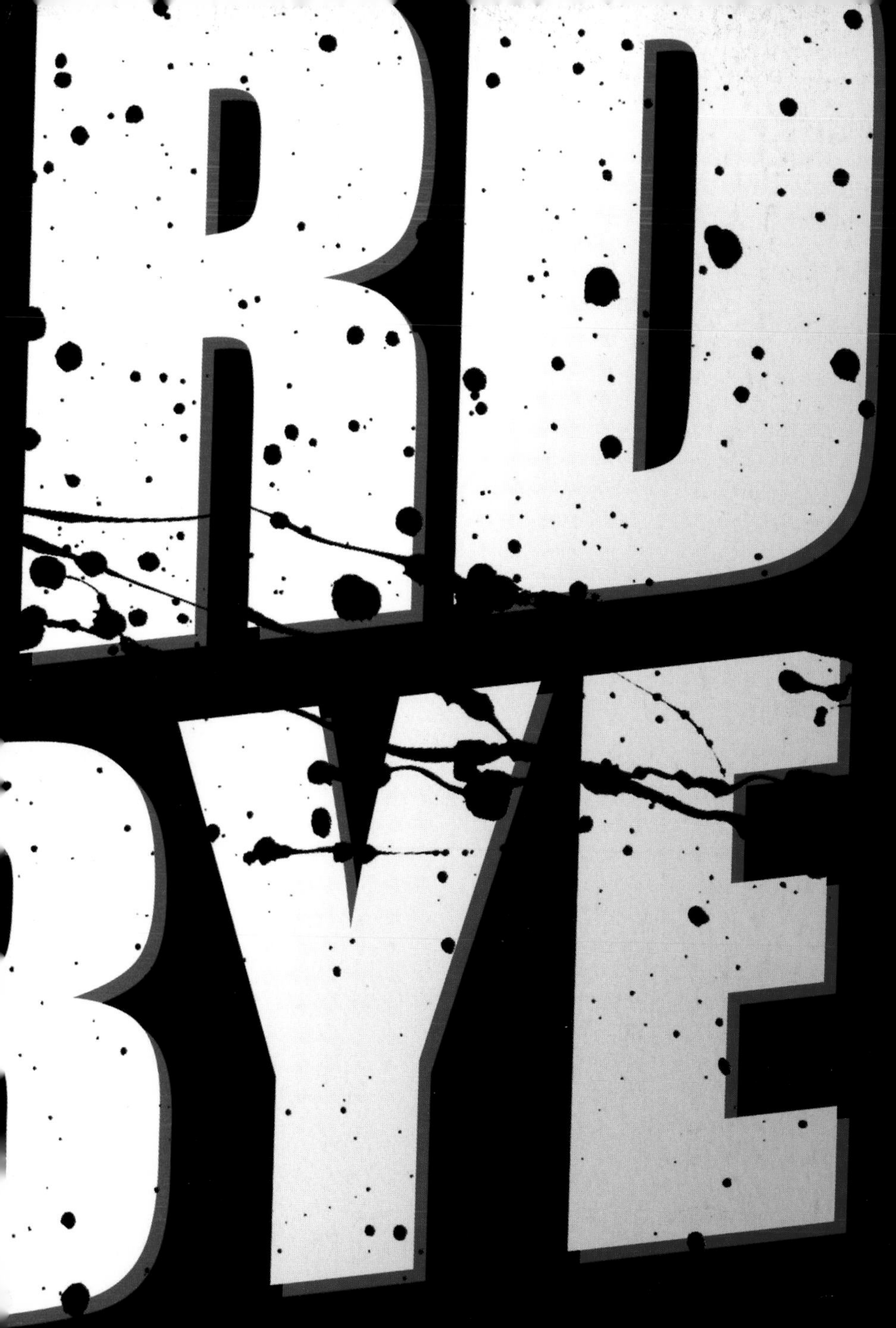
RD
YE

OM - HEART SHAPED BED - NIGHT

ls by the window. Chugging a bottle.

> MARV
> (vo)
> e night is hot as hell. It's a lousy room in a lousy part of
> ousy town.

wrapped in sheets before him.

> MARV (CONT'D)
> (vo)
> staring at a goddess. She's telling me she wants me. I'm
> t going to waste one more second wondering how it is I've
> tten so lucky.

> MARV (CONT'D)
> (vo)
> e smells like angels ought to smell. The perfect woman.
> e goddess.

love.

y from the heart shaped bed.

> MARV (CONT'D)
> (vo)
> ldie. She says her name is Goldie.

OM - HEART SHAPED BED - NIGHT

> MARV
> (vo)
> ree hours later my head's feeling several sizes too big
> d that cold thing happens to my stomach and I realize
> ldie is dead.

FRANK MILLER ON MARV

"THE DAY I CAME UP WITH HIM I WAS STANDING AT MY DRAWING BOARD AND THINKING ABOUT *SIN CITY*, AND LOOKING TO CRACK THE NUT OF WHAT THIS SERIES WAS. I HAD A HOST OF CHARACTERS, BUT I KNEW I WANTED TO START WITH SOMETHING THAT WOULD BE STRIKINGLY DIFFERENT THAN WHAT PEOPLE WOULD EXPECT. AND THE FIRST WORDS I WROTE DOWN WERE 'CONAN IN A TRENCH COAT.' THE IDEA BEING TO BRING THE KIND OF BARBARISM THAT YOU GET IN A CONAN STORY TO AN URBAN SETTING, AND FROM THAT CAME THE PART THAT MICKEY ROURKE IS PLAYING SO WELL. A BARBARIAN IN OUR WORLD, A SAVAGE. HE'S NOT A BAD GUY, AND HE'S NOT A KNIGHT IN SHINING ARMOR. HE'S A MAN FROM ANOTHER ERA. HE SIMPLY DOESN'T UNDERSTAND CIVILIZATION. HE BELIEVES THE PROPER THING TO DO WHEN YOU'RE UP AGAINST AN OPPONENT IS TO KILL THEM IN THE MOST INHUMANE WAY POSSIBLE. HE DOES HAVE A CODE. HE PROTECTS WOMEN, HE HONORS HIS WORD, BUT HE JUST NEVER UNDERSTOOD THE WAY WE ALL BEHAVE."

Angle.

> MARV (CONT'D)
> (vo)
> Not a mark on her. You'd have to check her pulse or notice those perfect breasts of hers aren't moving like they woul[d] if she was breathing. And there's nothing telling me it wasn't just a heart attack in her sleep... nothing but that cold thing in my gut getting colder...

Angle.

> MARV (CONT'D)
> (vo)
> ..And it's been too damned many times across too damned many years for me to even question that feeling. She was murdered and I was right here when it happened, lying nex[t] to her, stone drunk just like she was. Damn it, Goldie. Who were you and who wanted you dead? Who were you besides a[n] angel of mercy giving a two-time loser like me the night o[f] his life? God knows why. It sure as hell wasn't my looks...

Angle. Marv lights a cigarette. We see his face.

> MARV (CONT'D)
> (vo)
> Why the kindness, Goldie?

Angle on street as Cop cars approach.

> MARV (CONT'D)
> Cops... they're telling me too much, showing up before anybody but me and the killer could know there's been a murder. Sin City cops have had their hands on me before. This time they won't make the mistake of letting me live. Damn.

He pulls on his coat.

> MARV (CONT'D)
> (vo)
> No reason at all to play it quiet. No reason to play it any way but my way.

He leans over the bed and holds Goldie's hand.

MARV (CONT'D)
Whoever killed you is going to pay, Goldie.

Cops charge up the steps. In RIOT gear.

MARV (CONT'D)
(vo)
We're supposed to call them Cops-- but everybody knows who they're working for and what it takes to keep them happy. Somebody paid good money for this frame...

Close on Marv pulling out a pills and popping a couple.

COPS
Open up! Police!

MARV
I'll be right out.

INT. BUILDING - STAIRS/HALLWAY - NIGHT

SHRKKKKK! Marv tears through the door.

MARV
Graa!

COPS
Oh no!

A bullet blasts through Marv's shoulder and hits the wall beside him. Marv crushes a cop's skull into the other wall.

Marv dives head first over the hand rail as cops shoot and miss.

Another cop tries to shoot him on his way down, misses.

Marv catches a rail on the way down and pulls himself over to the stairs.

COPS (CONT'D)
Up there!

Marv rushes down the hall. Bullets give chase.

EXT. BUILDING - NIGHT

KASHH! MARV CRASHES OUT THE WINDOW. Falls into a pile of trash bags and bums.

A cop car pulls up in front of him.

Marv plays leap frog with the car, hopping over its hood. Feet first planting through the windshield. SKAK!

Marv throws out the cop and drives away in the cop car.

EXT. DOCK - NIGHT

> MARV
> (vo)
> I don't know why you died, Goldie.

The cop car flies off the dock.

> MARV (CONT'D)
> (vo)
> I don't know why and I don't know how I never even met you before tonight, but you were a friend and more when I needed one and when I find out who did it, it won't be quick or quiet like it was with you.

INT. UNDERWATER - NIGHT

Underwater, Marv swims away from the car.

> MARV
> (vo)
> It'll be loud and nasty, my kind of kill. I'll stare the bastard in the face and laugh as he screams to God, and I'll laugh harder when he whimpers like a baby.

Close on Marv's shattered bloody face as he swims.

> MARV (CONT'D)
> And when his eyes go dead the hell I send him to will seem like heaven after what I've done to him. I love you Goldie.

He continues his swim. Marv climbs into a sewer pipe. He rises up as his last breath fades.

EXT. SEWER PIPE - NIGHT

                    MARV
          KHAKK! Khoff... bastards...

He climbs out of the sewer.

EXT. CITY ALLEY - NIGHT

He hides between two walls as a cop passes.

                    MARV
                    (vo)
          I have to get to Lucille. She knows what I need and she's got
          it. She's always got it.

EXT. LUCILLE'S APARTMENT - NIGHT

Marv scales a building. He walks the ledge.

INT. LUCILLE'S APARTMENT - BEDROOM - NIGHT

Lucille wakes with a start.

                    LUCILLE
          Claire?

She thinks. Grabs a gun. She hears the "KOFF" outside her window. She stalks. Aims.

                    LUCILLE (CONT'D)
          Oh, it's you.

We see Marv. White tape bandages all over his face and body.

MARV
Don't worry, Lucille. I was just grazed. Got any beers around this place?

INT. LUCILLE'S APARTMENT – BATHROOM – NIGHT

CLOSE ON MEDICINE CABINET OPENING.

LUCILLE
There's no way I'm giving you any alcohol. Besides, that's not what you came here for anyway, is it?

MARV
No...

She finds a bottle. Tosses it to his massive, bandaged hand.

MARV (CONT'D)
(chewing pills)
Thanks. You're the best.
(vo)
Lucille's my parole officer. She's a dyke, but God knows why. With that body of hers she could have any man she wants. The pills come from her girlfriend who's a shrink. She tried to analyze me once but got too scared.

LUCILLE
Haven't seen you like this in a while...

MARV
Yeah, I had to fight some cops...

Angle.

LUCILLE
You didn't happen to kill any of them, did you?

MARV
Nah, I don't think so. But they know they been in a fight, that's for damn sure.

LUCILLE
And how the hell do you suppose I'm going to square this with the board? Ow!

CARLA GUGINO ON LUCILLE

"I THINK SHE'S GOT A BIT OF A SAVIOR COMPLEX. I THINK THAT SHE IS OBVIOUSLY IN LOVE WITH WOMEN, BUT MEN ARE LIKE BROTHERS TO HER. SHE JUST WANTS THEM ALL TO BE OKAY, AND IT SEEMS LIKE THE MEN THAT COME INTO HER LIFE ARE MEN THAT HAVE A HARD TIME TAKING CARE OF THEMSELVES, SO SHE'S GOING TO TRY TO DO IT FOR THEM. SHE'S ONE OF THOSE WOMEN WHO, IF SHE'S FIGHTING FOR SOMEONE, SHE'LL TAKE IT TO THE END."

He grabs her.

                    MARV
There's no squaring it, babe. Not a chance. Not this time.

Over her onto his menacing chopped face.

                    MARV (CONT'D)
This isn't some barroom brawl or some creep with a gas can
looking to torch some wino. This is big and I'm right in the
middle of it, and there's no place I'd rather be.

                    LUCILLE
Settle down, Marv. Take another pill.

Angle.

                    MARV
There's no settling down. It's going to be blood for blood
and by the gallons. It's the old days... The bad days. The
all-or-nothing days. They're back. There's no choices left
and I'm ready for war.

Over him onto her.

                    LUCILLE
Prison was hell for you Marv. It'll be life this time.

                    MARV
Hell is waking up every god damn morning and not knowing
why you're even here, and I'm finally out. It took somebody
who was kind to me getting killed to do it, but I'm out. I
know exactly what I'm doing.

EXT. CITY - NIGHT

He leaps into the night. Across building tops.

                    MARV
                    (vo)
Now for Gladys. Sweet Gladys.

INT. MOM'S PLACE - STAIRS - NIGHT

He climbs the stairs.

>   MARV
>   (vo)
>   But I'll have to sneak past Mom. And her ears have gotten a
>   whole lot better since she went blind.

INT. MOM'S PLACE - NIGHT

He takes off his shoes and sneaks through the house.

>   MARV
>   (vo)
>   Mom still hasn't changed a thing in this room. Every week
>   she dusts it all off so it looks like it was only yesterday I
>   moved out.

INT. MOM'S PLACE - MARV'S ROOM - NIGHT

Top angle, from above the hanging airplane, Marv sits on his bed. Going
through a suitcase.

>   MARV
>   (vo)
>   And every time I come visit she has me sleep in here and the
>   old smells make me cry like they do right now. I knew Gladys
>   would be safe here.

He pulls up his 45. A smile stretches across his face.

>   MARV (CONT'D)
>   (vo)
>   I stole her off the toughest guy I ever messed with. I call
>   her Gladys after one of the sisters from school. She's almost
>   lived up to the name.

He swings the gun around.

>   MARV (CONT'D)
>   (vo)
>   For a while we just get the feel of each other back, good as
>   ever. I tell her about Goldie and what we have to do.

KREEE. The door opens.

           MOM
Marvin? Is that you, baby?

           MARV
Yes, Mom. Sorry I woke you up.

Angle on Mom and Marv.

           MOM
Oh, I couldn't sleep for the worry. There were men who came
looking for you. They weren't police.

           MARV
That was about my new job. I got a new job. It's night work.

           MOM
        (feeling his face)
And what have you done to your face?

           MARV
I cut myself shaving.

           MOM
You're getting confused again, aren't you?

           MARV
Mom, I feel better than I have in years.

EXT. CITY STREETS - NIGHT

MARV walks the streets at night.

           MARV
         (vo)
I've been framed for murder and the cops are in on it.
But the son of a bitch who killed Goldie, he's out there
somewhere, out of sight. So all I got to do is send the
bastard an invitation. He'll come or he'll send somebody and
if I don't get dead I'm bound to wind up with one or two more
puzzle pieces.

Close on Marv.

A SEQUENCE WITH MARV AND HIS BLIND MOTHER WAS SHOT
FOR THE MOVIE, BUT NOT INCLUDED IN THE FINAL EDIT. IT
WILL BE COMPLETED AND REINCORPORATED INTO THE DVD
RELEASE.

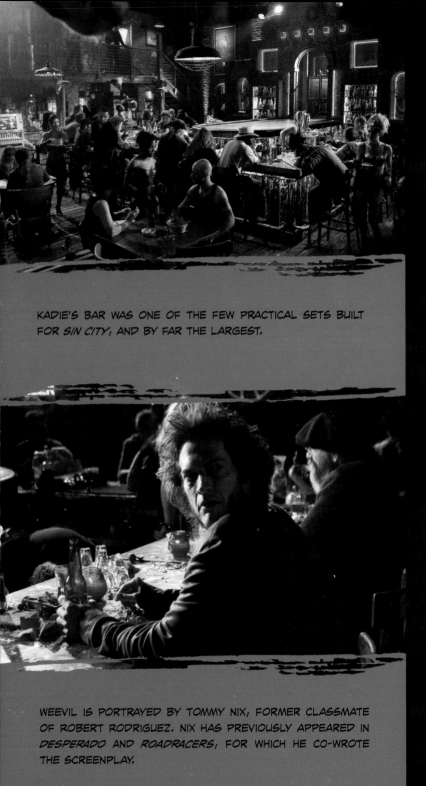

KADIE'S BAR WAS ONE OF THE FEW PRACTICAL SETS BUILT FOR *SIN CITY*, AND BY FAR THE LARGEST.

WEEVIL IS PORTRAYED BY TOMMY NIX, FORMER CLASSMATE OF ROBERT RODRIGUEZ. NIX HAS PREVIOUSLY APPEARED IN *DESPERADO* AND *ROADRACERS*, FOR WHICH HE CO-WROTE THE SCREENPLAY.

EXT. KADIE'S CLUB - ALLEY IN BACK - NIGHT

> MARV
> Walk down the right back alley in Sin City and you can find anything.

Marv walks up the alley to the back door of an establishment. We hear the WHUMP WHUMP of someone getting their ass kicked right on the other side of the door.

The door kicks open and the bouncer throws out a beaten man.

> BOUNCER
> And you--- your coat looks like Baghdad. So's your face. Take off.

Marv grabs him by the face and sinks his thumbs into his eyes. YAAAA! Krnch Marv shoves the bouncer inside.

INT. KADIE'S CLUB - NIGHT

> LARGE WAITRESS
> He's new here, Marv. He didn't know.

He walks through.

> MARV
> (vo)
> Kadie's is my kind of joint. Country, and I don't mean that touchy feely "you put me on a natural high" garbage they're passing off as country these days. No, at Kadie's it's the old stuff. Songs to drink to and to cry to.

NANCY dancing on stage.

> MARV (CONT'D)
> (vo)
> Nancy's just getting started with her gig but already the crowd's breathing hard.

Marv lights a smoke and watches Nancy from afar.

> MARV (CONT'D)
> (vo)
> Plenty of nights I've drooled over Nancy, shoulder to

shoulder with all the other losers like me. But that's not what I'm looking for tonight.

Close on his eye. Weevil turns around.

Close on Marv's gritting teeth. THUMP! AAAK!

> MARV (CONT'D)
> Take it easy, Weevil. I'm here to do you a favor. It's money in your pocket.

Wide angle of the bar. Nancy in the center, Marv pinning Weevil to the floor.

> MARV (CONT'D)
> Spread the word. And get good cash for it because it's worth it.

Close on Marv.

> MARV (CONT'D)
> Tell them I've been hitting the joints, drunk off my butt, shooting off my mouth, crying over some hot babe name of Goldie.

> WEEVIL
> Ghakk!

Weevil runs away after his release.

> SHELLIE
> What'll it be. Marv?

> MARV
> A shot and a brew, Shellie. Thanks.

More angles on Nancy.

INT. KADIE'S CLUB - NIGHT

A gun sticks in Marv's back as he drinks his beer.

> MAN
> Show's over, Buddy. Drink up.

NANCY, THE MAIN ATTRACTION AT KADIE'S BAR, IS ONE OF THE THREADS WHICH STITCHES *SIN CITY* TOGETHER, APPEARING IN TWO OF THE THREE CHAPTERS.

                    MARV
        Now that is one fine coat you're wearing there. Urpp.

Marv is escorted back out the way he came.

                    MARV (CONT'D)
                    (vo)
        I love hit men. No matter what you do to them, you don't feel
        bad. Fact is, the worse you do, the better it gets.

EXT. KADIE'S CLUB - ALLEY IN BACK - NIGHT

They're in the alley.

                    MARV
        Must've set you back five bills. That coat, I mean-- damn it
        if it isn't one fine piece of work.

                    HITMAN
        You shut up.

                    MARV
        And here I thought they stopped making decent coats back in
        the fifties-- like cars, you know? OOF!

Trip. Thud. CHUDD. Huh?

                    MAN
        Stan-- he's got me!

BLAM! GHAA!! CHUDD CHUDD CHUDD!

The men lie bleeding against the wall.

                    MARV
        Take it off.

                    HITMAN
        What?

                    MARV
        Fine coat like that and you're bleeding all over it.

```
                    HITMAN
        All right. Okay. It's all yours. Oh, God...


                    MARV
        Thanks.

BLAM! Marv takes off his own coat.


                    HITMAN
        Don't kill me, Man... gaa.

Marv whacks him in the teeth with his gun butt.


                    MARV
        I already killed you, you jerk. Wise up!  But even though it
        feels like Niagara Falls down there, you'll be a damn long
        time dying and I can make it quick or I can make it worse...
        I don't hear you giving me any names jerk. Guess when I shot
        you in the belly I aimed a little too high...

                    HITMAN
                    (tears flowing)
Nooooo.

BLAM!

                    HITMAN (CONT'D)
OOOOOAAGGGG


EXT. KADIE'S CLUB - ALLEY IN BACK - NIGHT

Marv is lying back against the wall now. Casually lighting a cigarette.
Hitman is slumped even lower.


                    MARV
        You keep holding out on me like this and I'm going to have to
        get really nasty.


                    HITMAN
        It was Telly Stern passed me the order. Runs the tables over
        to the Triple Ace Club.


                    MARV
        Thanks again.
```

STUNT COORDINATOR JEFF DASHNAW ON MARV AND MICKEY ROURKE

"MY FAVORITE CHARACTER WAS MARV. MICKEY ROURKE WAS PERFECT. IT WAS FUNNY TO WATCH BECAUSE HE DEFINITELY WAS MARV, TO ME. HE GOT SHOT A MILLION TIMES, HE GOT STABBED, HE GOT THE CRAP BEAT OUT OF HIM, AND HE JUST KEPT COMING BACK TO FINISH THE JOB. AND THEN WHEN HE KNEW EVERYTHING WAS RIGHT, HE CHECKED OUT."

BLAM! The Hitman's brains make a quick exit.

Marv pulls on his new coat and leaves.

> MARV (CONT'D)
> (vo)
> For a second I smell that angel smell that belonged only to
> Goldie. Just need my medicine, is all.

A BLONDE stands in the shadows. Holding a gun.

> BLONDE
> Bastard. You're going to pay for what you did to me.

EXT. CITY - NIGHT

Marv beating the hell out of an informant.

> INFORMANT
> Noooo... GHAGG no more!...

> MARV
> (vo)
> The instincts take over, white hot, the animal in me I tried
> to drown in booze and bloody brawls, he's back and he's
> howling, he's laughing out loud, he's crazy with the pure
> sweet hate of it all...

INT. BATHROOM - NIGHT

Marv shoves Tommy's face down the toilet.

> MARV
> Feel like talking yet, Tommy?

> TOMMY
> Glakk!!

EXT. CITY - NIGHT

Marv leaps through the city.

MARV
(vo)
Sin City. She's a big, bad broad flat on her back begging
for it and I take her for all she's worth and then I take her
again and still she's begging. Damn. It's good to be alive.

XT. STREET - CAR (MOVING) - NIGHT

Marv dragging another informant across the asphalt as he drives with his
ar door open.

MARV
I don't know about you but I'm having a ball.

NT. CHURCH - CONFESSIONAL - NIGHT

MARV
(vo)
Then I go to church. Not to pray.

PRIEST
And what have been your sins, my son?

MARV
Well, padre, I don't want to keep you up all night... so I'll
just fill you in on the latest batch.

Close on Marv in the confessional.

MARV (CONT'D)
These here hands of mine, they got blood all over them -- I
don't mean really. I wouldn't come to church without wiping
it off.

PRIEST
You're speaking figuratively.

MARV
I knew there was a word for it. You're one smart guy. Myself,
I'm not so bright. When I need to find something out, I just
look for somebody who knows more than me and I go and ask
them. But sometimes I ask pretty hard.

FRANK MILLER AS "THE PRIEST." HIS PREVIOUS ROLES INCLUDE
"MAN WITH PEN IN HEAD" IN *DAREDEVIL* (2003), WHICH WAS
LOOSELY BASED ON HIS RUN OF MARVEL COMICS' *DAREDEVIL*,
AND "FRANK THE CHEMIST" IN *ROBOCOP 2* (1990), FOR WHICH
HE WROTE THE SCREENPLAY.

Close on priest. Listening intently.

                  MARV (CONT'D)
By way of a for instance, I killed three men tonight. I tortured them first. You might say I been working my way up the food chain. The first two, they were minnows, small time messengers -- but it was Connelly - the money man - who fingered you, padre.

The padre starts to rise. ChkChak.

                  MARV (CONT'D)
You know what that sound means. Sit down.

                  PRIEST
Dear Lord, Man, this is a house of God.

                  MARV
Just give me a damn name.

                  PRIEST
Roark.

                  MARV
Roark? You are really pushing your luck, trying to feed me garbage like this. It can't be that big.

                  PRIEST
Find out for yourself, you sorry bastard! There's a farm out at north cross and Lennox. It's all there. Find out for yourself--- and while you're at it---

Marv listens.

                  PRIEST (CONT'D)
Ask yourself if that corpse of a slut is worth dying for.

BLAM!

                  MARV
                  (vo)
Worth dying for. Worth killing for. Worth going to hell for.

BLAM BLAM BLAM!

MARV (CONT'D)
Amen.

EXT. CHURCH - NIGHT

He walks out of church lighting a cig.

MARV
There isn't much better in life than a smoke when you
haven't had one in a while. Like after a movie. Or after
church.

Close on keys in Marv's hand. He unlocks the door.

MARV (CONT'D)
His keys say the padre drove a Mercedes or at least what
they're passing off as a Mercedes these days. Modern cars.
They all look like electric shavers.

HNNH? Marv spins at the sound of a speeding convertible. He aims. He sees
the driver.

MARV (CONT'D)
Goldie?

WHUMP!! Marv is hit square. He flies over the car.

High angle as he lies in the street, and Goldie maneuvers her car around to
go at him again. She does. WHUMP!!!

MARV (CONT'D)
Goldie?

WHUMP! Then she aims her piece. BLAM BLAM BLAM SPAK SPAK.

The car speeds off. Marv, bloody as hell, rises and makes it to the Mercedes.

MARV (CONT'D)
No... couldn't have been Goldie.

INT. MERCEDES (MOVING) - NIGHT

He drives. He pops more pills.

49

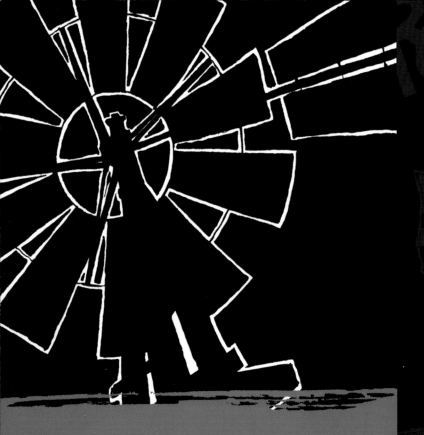

MARV
(vo)
It's my own fault and nobody else's that I got confused. I've
been having so much fun I forgot to take my medicine. That
wasn't Goldie back there. Goldie is dead and that's the whole
reason I've been doing what I've been doing.

He swallows.

MARV (CONT'D)
(vo)
When you've got a condition it's bad to forget your medicine.

EXT. FARM - WOODS - NIGHT

He makes his way through the farm. Cutting through the woods.

KAKK KAKK. The sounds of the farm keep him alert.

MARV
(vo)
That cold thing. It creeps into my gut and tells me one more
time it won't let go. This is a bad place, this farm. People
have died here. The wrong way.

RRRR. Marv turns. A big dog snarls and barks.

MARV (CONT'D)
I don't want a fight, pooch.

The dog leaps and digs teeth into Marv. KUNK! Rowr! Marv swings and
good punch. Knocked out cold.

MARV (CONT'D)
(vo)
No way I was going to use my gun on you, buddy. And besides,
it's whoever owns you I'm curious about.

Close on Marv. A shadowy, glasses-wearing figure behind him.

MARV (CONT'D)
(vo)
Because there's blood on your breath and I think I know what
kind.

FRANK MILLER ON THE FARM

"I'VE ALWAYS LOVED THE CITY AS A VENUE, AND I LOVE THE
FACT THAT THE CITY FORCES PEOPLE INTO CLOSE CONTACT.
THIS IS WHY I MAKE A BETTER NEW YORKER THAN AN
ANGELENO—I'D RATHER WALK THAN DRIVE, AND I'D RATHER
SEE PEOPLE IN CLOSER CONTACT, AND SEE HOW THEY
INTERSECT. SO I LOVE THE CITY, AND THE CITY IS WHERE I
LOVE TO SET MY DRAMAS; BUT I GREW UP A COUNTRY BOY IN
VERMONT, AND I KNOW WHAT THE COUNTRY'S LIKE AS WELL.
AND THERE'S NOTHING LIKE A CITY PERSON WHO'S OUT IN
THE COUNTRY. THEY CAN'T SLEEP. THEY HEAR CRICKETS AND
IT'S SCARY. THEY HEAR FROGS AND IT'S SCARY. GUNSHOTS
THEY'LL SLEEP THROUGH BUT SILENCE DRIVES THEM CRAZY.
THERE IS SOMETHING SCARY ABOUT THE DARK THINGS THAT
CAN HAPPEN AWAY FROM THE CITY BECAUSE THERE ARE
THINGS THAT NOBODY CAN SEE. YOU KILL SOMEBODY IN THE
CITY, SOONER OR LATER SOMEBODY'S GOING TO KNOW THAT
SOMEBODY GOT KILLED. BUT HERE I AM ON A FARM, WHO'S
GOING TO KNOW?"

The figure comes up behind Marv.

                    MARV (CONT'D)
                    (vo)
          So I sniff around to see what's buried. Here we go.

Marv pulls up a femur bone.

                    MARV (CONT'D)
                    (vo)
          This didn't come out of any coyote.

He pulls up a woman's shoe. Close on sneakers.

                    MARV (CONT'D)
                    (vo)
          Impossible. Nobody can sneak up on me. Nobody.

WHUNGG! BLAM KRAK! THUK! Several kicks and sharp nail scratches to the face
and hands.

                    MARV (CONT'D)
                    (vo)
          I go blind. Not a sound. Nobody's that quiet. Nobody except
          the one who snuck into that hotel room two nights ago...

The man with glasses steadies a sledgehammer.

                    MARV (CONT'D)
          It was you, you bastard! You killed her! You killed Goldie!

KUDD! Marv is smashed. Blackness.

INT. FARM - TILE ROOM - NIGHT

                    MARV
                    (vo)
          I blew it, Goldie. I found your killer but he was better than
          me, too quiet and too quick, a killer born. He took me out
          like I was a girl scout. Why didn't he finish the job? A smell
          hits my nostrils, hard, burning, antiseptic.

He lies in a tile room. A drain near his head on the floor. He sees a rose.
Then the placement of it. A tattoo on a woman's face. Wider angle.

51

WOMEN'S HEADS MOUNTED ON THE WALL.

                LUCILLE
He keeps the heads. He eats the rest.

                MARV
Lucille?

                LUCILLE
It's not just that wolf of his. The wolf just gets scraps.
Bones. It's him. He eats people.

                MARV
You're in shock.

                LUCILLE
He cooks them first.

                MARV
You got to settle down, kid. You're in shock. Here, let's get
you warm.

He drapes his coat over her naked body.

                LUCILLE
He cooks them like they were steaks. And now he's got us.

                MARV
It's all right. Take a nice, slow breath...

                LUCILLE
Son of a bitch kept smiling that damn smile and made me
watch him suck the meat off my fingers. Son of a bitch. He
made me watch.

She covers her bandaged stump.

                MARV
Oh Jesus.

                LUCILLE
HE MADE ME WAAAAAAATTTTCCCHHH

Outside of the grate above their heads stands the Man in Glasses. Smiling
that damned smile.

Marv holds her.

> LUCILLE (CONT'D)
> ... Christ, I could use a cigarette.

> MARV
> (vo)
> Dames. Sometimes all they got to do is let it out and a few buckets later there's no way you'd know.

Marv tries to pull off the bars.

> LUCILLE
> You've brought us some big trouble this time, Marv. Whoever's behind all this has got his connections -- right in the department. Any leads?

> MARV
> One guy I talked to told me it was ROARK running the show.

> LUCILLE
> Well, whoever it is, he knew I was checking out that hooker almost before I did.

> MARV
> What hooker?

> LUCILLE
> The one you've been obsessing over. The dead one. Goldie.

Close on Marv.

> MARV
> I didn't know she was a hooker. It doesn't make any difference about anything. But I didn't know that.

> LUCILLE
> She was high-class stuff. She must've shown you quite a time.

> MARV
> Tell me about him. The bum who snuck into my room and killed Goldie and did what he did to you.

He pulls on the bars. WHUFF. Damn...

ELIJAH WOOD ON KEVIN

"BEYOND THE FACT THAT HE'S PSYCHOTIC, AND A MURDERER, AND A CANNIBAL, KEVIN'S SORT OF PHILOSOPHY IS ACTUALLY WRAPPED UP IN SPIRITUALITY. HE FINDS PEACE, AND LOVE, AND GOD'S LOVE IN THE KILLING AND THE EATING OF PEOPLE. SO THAT'S WHAT MY CHARACTER'S ABOUT, AND THERE'S SOMETHING INCREDIBLY CALM AND PEACEFUL ABOUT HIM."

                    LUCILLE
        I was walking to my car. That's all I can remember. Then I
        was in his kitchen. Paralyzed. I smelled meat cooking. He'd
        cut it off before I woke up. My hand, I mean. Then he made me
        watch.

Shot from across the heads on the wall.

                    MARV
        Quiet. There's a car coming.

EXT. FARM – TILE ROOM – NIGHT

Shot from outside the grate. The man in glasses stands off to the side. HONK
HONK!

                    MARV
        V-8 engine. Coming fast.

                    VOICE
        Kevin! Kevin come quickly!

Man in Glasses reacts. Walks to the car. Marv watches.

                    MARV
                    (vo)
        All I've got is a face. And a name.

Close on Marv.

                    MARV (CONT'D)
                    (vo)
        See you later, Kevin.

EXT. SKY – NIGHT

Shots. Helicopter in the sky. KUNK. KUNK.

EXT. FARM – NIGHT

The farm. A hatchet in a stump. Kunk!

EXT. FARM - TILE ROOM - NIGHT

Down the stairs. To the big metal door. Kunk!

INT. FARM - TILE ROOM - NIGHT

Marv hits the ground after hitting the door again. He charges yet again.
KUNK! Various angles. CRASH! The bolts rip loose. The door flies off its
hinges.

                    MARV
          Let's go.

EXT. FARM - TILE ROOM - NIGHT

RAKKA RAKKA RAKKA. Police chopper lowers to the ground.

                    MARV
                    (vo)
          The wind off the desert goes cold. Lucille's a kitten under
          my arm, soft and weightless and warm. But I know Gladys will
          be cold. Cold and ready and begging for it.

He grabs the gun from the ground.

                    MARV (CONT'D)
                    (vo)
          Sweet Gladys.

Several cops, one with a painted face step out of the chopper.

                    MARV (CONT'D)
          They're done checking the house. They're coming this way...
          bastards. I'll show them...

He's aiming the gun. But LUCILLE is holding a rock over his head. KUDD! She
knocks him out.

                    LUCILLE
          You're not going to get either of us killed, Marv.

She yells to the men.

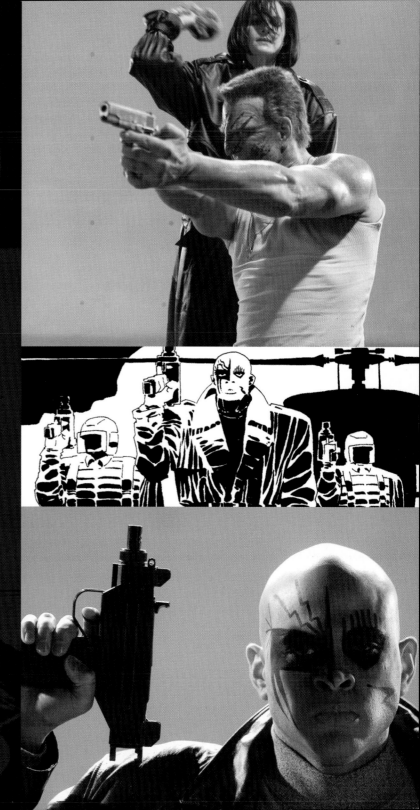

FRANK MILLER ON MICKEY ROURKE

"WHEN ROBERT MENTIONED HIS NOTION OF HAVING MICKEY ROURKE PLAY MARV, I HADN'T SEEN ANY OF MICKEY'S RECENT WORK AT ALL, AND ALL I COULD THINK WAS THAT SKINNY GUY FROM *BODY HEAT*. THEN ROBERT SAID, 'STAY WITH ME ON THIS, WE'LL MEET HIM, AND TAKE A LOOK.' SO I MET MICKEY. AND HE LUMBERED INTO THE ROOM, PRACTICALLY TAKING OUT THE DOOR JAM AS HE CAME IN, AND WE SAT AND TALKED FOR ABOUT HALF AN HOUR, AND THE ONLY NOTE I WAS ABLE TO WRITE DOWN WAS, 'MET MICKEY ROURKE, HE IS MARV.' HE COMPLETELY INTEGRATED THE CHARACTER, AND ABSORBED IT. GREG NICOTERO AND HIS PEOPLE DID AN AMAZING JOB OF MAKING HIM LIKE THE CARTOONS WITH THEIR PROSTHETICS. SO IT'S A STUNNING PERFORMANCE."

LUCILLE (CONT'D)
No! Don't shoot! Please listen to me... I'm his parole officer. He's unconscious and unarmed. So there's no reason to kill him.

EXT. FARM – HATCHET STUMP – NIGHT

Close on the hatchet. Marv's shadow approaches it.

PAINTED COP
Yes, there is, Ma'am. Once he's told us who else he's spoken to.

Lucille is filled full of lead. Marv witnesses the kill.

COPS
Excuse me, Captain, but the target -- There's no sign of him.

MARV
Here's a sign.

Marv digs the hatchet into the cop's back. PUNT! He kicks another one into a third. BREKK!!

He charges. CHAKK! Brekk! Ghugg! CHAK! He kills them all. Captain Dry fires his empty gun at Marv. Corpses of the other cops at their feet. Captain lowers his useless gun.

MARV (CONT'D)
That there is one damn fine coat you're wearing.

He chases Captain. Laughing maniacally.

EXT. FARM – HATCHET STUMP – NIGHT

Time Cut. Marv wears Captain's coat.

EXT. DARK RAIN - NIGHT

                    MARV
                    (vo)
          Rain doesn't come to Sin City real often.

EXT. BRIDGE - NIGHT

Shot of a bridge in the rain. Marv walking across.

                    MARV
                    (vo)
          Most people hate the rain when it's nasty like this. But
          me, I love it. It helps me think. I keep coming back to that
          cop I just killed and what he told me. I was pretty steamed
          about what he done to Lucille so I took my time with the son
          of a bitch. It wasn't until I showed him all those pieces of
          himself that he said it. I figured that priest was jerking my
          chain. But hearing it from the cop I knew it couldn't be a
          coincidence. Just a name. Roark.

EXT. STATUE - NIGHT

Marv stops before a GIANT STATUE OF A SAINT.

                    MARV
                    (vo)
          Roark. Patrick Henry Roark. "Saint Patrick," They call him
          but it's a just a nickname. The Pope hasn't gotten around
          to making it official. Not yet anyway. The Roark family has
          owned Sin City since the days of wagon trains and six-guns.
          Over the generations their millions have grown to billions.
          They're kind of like our own Royal Family. This particular
          generation produced a United States Senator, a State
          Attorney General--- and Patrick Henry Roark. Cardinal
          Roark. Man of the cloth. War hero in the medical corps.
          Philanthropist. Educator. Could've become President but
          he chose to serve God. And along the way he just happened
          to become the most powerful man in the state. He's brought
          down two mayors and gotten governors elected. And here he's
          going to get killed in the name of a dead hooker. I'm getting
          used to the idea. More and more I'm liking the sound of it.

JAIME KING ON WENDY

"WENDY, TO ME, IS THE PROTECTOR OF GOLDIE. WHEN I WAS THINKING ABOUT THESE CHARACTERS, I SAW GOLDIE AS THIS CHILD THAT WAS ALWAYS AMBITIOUS, WHO HAD THIS HEART OF GOLD, AND THAT WENDY WAS THE CHARACTER THAT THROUGHOUT THEIR LIVES HAD TO PROTECT HER SISTER. AND WENDY IN THIS STORY IS ACTUALLY KIND OF LIKE A COP. SHE AND A GROUP OF OTHER WOMEN RUN OLD TOWN AND PROTECT THE OTHER PROSTITUTES, SO SHE'S NOT ACTUALLY A PROSTITUTE. SHE'S A STRONGER CHARACTER, AND WHEN SHE FINDS OUT THAT HER SISTER'S DEAD, THAT'S WHEN SHE GOES AFTER MARV TO AVENGE HER DEATH, AND ENDS UP FINDING OUT THAT HE'S THE ONE THAT'S GOING TO AVENGE IT FOR HER."

Back view of Marv.

> MARV (CONT'D)
> (vo)
> I love the rain. It helps me think.

Marv aims Gladys at the statue's head. BLAM.

KUNKK! The bullet makes a pit right between the eyes.

> MARV
> Good Girl.

Marv falls to his knees.

> MARV
> (vo)
> Then it hits me like a kick in the nuts. What if I'm wrong? I've got a condition. I get confused sometimes. And with Lucille dead I can't get my medicine. What if I'm imagining things? What if I imagined all of this? What if I've finally turned into what they always said I was going to turn into. A maniac. A psycho killer?

Close on Marv. Face in shadow but the eyes and teeth.

> MARV (CONT'D)
> (vo)
> Can't kill a man without knowing for sure you ought to. I've got to know for sure.

EXT. OLD TOWN - NIGHT

CLOSE ON WOMAN'S BODY.

> MARV
> (vo)
> The rain's sputtered to a stop and the streets have come back to life by the time I make my way to Old Town. Old Town is why nobody calls this burg "Basin City" like it says on the maps. It was Saint Patrick's great-grandfather who made it happen. Gold rush town on its way to becoming a ghost town. Then old man Roark got himself an idea. He spent every silver dollar he had, importing top hookers from France and places like that. Word got out and pretty soon Sin City was the hottest stop in the west. Old Town's kept its

traditions, handed down from gorgeous mother to gorgeous daughter. For an hour or so I ask around about Goldie. I don't get any answers but I know I'm bound to. Lucille said Goldie was a hooker and if she was she has roots here. Friends. Maybe even family.

BLAM! A bullet bites into Marv's shoulder.

>   MARV (CONT'D)
>   You can't be Goldie! You can't! Goldie's dead!

The BLONDE shoots another one. Marv's forehead is struck.

Marv falls into darkness.

INT. OLD TOWN - ROOM - NIGHT

He wakes. Bandage over his shoulder. He lifts his head.

>   MARV
>   KOFF. Goldie. Yeah sure. Right.

BLONDE stands before him. A cigarette dangling from her lips.

>   MARV (CONT'D)
>   It's okay, Goldie. I got nobody to blame but me. I haven't had anything to eat or gotten any sleep or taken my medicine for days now. No wonder I'm seeing things.

She strikes him in the face with a gun.

>   BLONDE
>   BASTARD!

KRAKK!

>   MARV
>   Ha ha ha ha ha...

We see that he is surrounded by Old Town girls.

>   BLONDE
>   Son of a bitch.

MICKEY ROURKE ON RODRIGUEZ

"I THINK NUMBER ONE, WHICH IS RARE, IS THAT ROBERT'S A REALLY GOOD GUY. HE'S A NICE GUY, HE'S A REALLY DOWN-TO-EARTH GUY WHO'S GOT HIS HEAD ON REALLY SQUARE. HE'S EARNED MY RESPECT, AND I'M VERY IMPRESSED WITH HIM. HE'S JUST A GOOD DUDE. AND THAT FILTERS DOWN WITH THE WHOLE CREW. I DON'T CARE IF IT'S A GODDAMN GREEN SCREEN, OR PINK SCREEN, OR WHATEVER, HE MAKES IT WORK. I'VE NEVER DONE A MOVIE WITH GREEN SCREEN BEFORE WHERE I'VE GOT NO SET, OR SOMETIMES NO OTHER ACTORS TO WORK WITH, BUT HE MAKES IT VERY CLEAR FOR ME. HE'S VERY PREPARED. WE GET DONE SHOOTING A TWELVE, FOURTEEN-HOUR DAY; WHATEVER IT IS, AND HE GOES HOME AND HE'S WORKING AGAIN FOR ANOTHER FOUR OR FIVE HOURS. IT'S NOTHIN' BUT A JOY TO WORK WITH THE GUY."

GIRL
He's crazy.

GIRL 2
He's faking it. Hit him again, Wendy. Harder.

KRAKK!

MARV
You shouldn't ought to hit me that way, Goldie. With the barrel, I mean. You'll knock it out of whack and the gun'll be useless. Do it right and use the handle.

KRAKK! She hits him again.

MARV (CONT'D)
Wait a minute. Just hold on a second. Why'd she call you "Wendy?"

WENDY
Cause that's my name, you ape! Goldie was my sister! My twin Sister!

MARV
I guess she was the nice one.

KRAK KRAK KRAK. Close on the faces of the other girls.

WENDY
You're going to die, mister. But first you're going to talk. Goldie and the other six -- where are they? What did you do to them?

MARV
You crazy God Damn broad! Just take a look at this mug! Look at it! Would any of you dames let me get close enough to you to kill you?

Close on him yelling.

MARV (CONT'D)
Damn straight you wouldn't! None of you would but Goldie. And she only did because she thought I could protect her. But I got too drunk so I couldn't. And I'll bet the cops didn't do a damn thing about those other girls, did they? But as soon as they had me for a fall guy they showed up guns blazing!

Over him onto her. His bloody face in camera.

                    MARV (CONT'D)
     But they didn't get me and I been killing my way to the truth
     ever since and I'm getting damn close to it. So go ahead,
     Doll. Shoot me now or get the hell out of my way.

Close on all their faces.

                    GIRL 2
     Oh nuts.

                    MARV
     Okay. I'm glad we got all that sorted out.

He stands. The ropes broken long ago.

                    WENDY
     What the hell...

                    GIRL 2
     I tied those knots -- and that's my specialty!

                    WENDY
     You sat there and took it -- when you could've taken my gun
     away from me any time you wanted to...

Marv pulls a cig.

                    MARV
     Sure. But I thought I might be able to talk some sense into
     you -- and I probably would've had to paste you one---

He lights the cig.

                    MARV (CONT'D)
     ... And I don't hurt girls.

INT. OLD TOWN - BATHROOM - NIGHT

He stumbles to the bathroom. He grabs his coat, gun, hatchet.

INT. OLD TOWN - ROOM - NIGHT

               MARV
   I need a pair of handcuffs.

               GAIL
   What style you want? I got a collection.

               WENDY
   Just give him the ones you've got with you, Gail.

The handcuffs are tossed in close-up.

INT./EXT. PORSCHE (MOVING) - NIGHT

The Porsche tears down the street. Wendy drives.

               MARV
   It was a farm boy name of Kevin who killed Goldie. But it's
   Cardinal Roark who's behind it and I don't know why. I know
   that sounds crazy.

Close on both from above.

             MARV (CONT'D)
   No, it doesn't. Goldie worked the Clergy.
               (vo)
   "Goldie worked the clergy." Just like that a whopper of a
   puzzle piece falls smack in my lap. I'm too dumb to put the
   whole picture together yet, but... she fires up two cigarettes
   and hands me one and I taste her lipstick on it and suddenly
   my heart's pounding so loud I can't hear anything else. I
   want to reach over and touch her and taste Goldie's sweat
   one more time. But she isn't Goldie.

She hits a trash can and almost swipes a Jeep. She cuts off another ca
she swerves. SCREEECH.

               WENDY
   She was my sister and I loved her. So I'm in this one to the
   end. But why are you willing to go up against Roark for
   somebody you barely know?

               MARV
   She was nice to me. She gave me something I didn't know

existed. I wasn't never even able to buy a woman, the way I
look.

INT. STORE - NIGHT

STORE: Marv examines a hacksaw.

> MARV
> Yeah, this'll do. I'm also gonna be needing a dozen two-
> foot lengths of rubber tubing and a spool of razor wire and
> those special gloves that'll let me handle the wire.

INT./EXT. HILLS OF SIN CITY - PORSCHE (MOVING) - NIGHT

Driving over the hills of Sin City.

> MARV
> (vo)
> I take my mind off her and then crawl back inside myself.
> It's almost killing time and I better get sharp. Kevin's
> faster and better than I am. I got to use every dirty trick I
> know.

Close on his face. Then on each object.

> MARV (CONT'D)
> (vo)
> I check the list. Rubber Tubing. Gas. Saw. Gloves. Cuffs.
> Razor wire. Hatchet. Gladys. And my mitts.

EXT. PORSCHE - FOREST - NIGHT

Pulling through the forest.

> MARV
> We're close enough. Pull over.

> WENDY
> Yes, Marv.

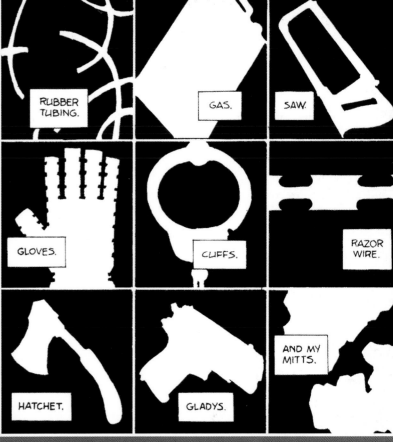

EVEN WITH THE GLOVES ON I GOT TO BE CAREFUL WITH THE RAZOR WIRE.

I LOVE THIS STUFF. IT CUTS THROUGH MEAT AND BONE LIKE THEY WAS BUTTER.

KEEK

WENDY HAD ENOUGH MONEY FOR IT SO I THOUGHT IT WAS WORTH TRYING, ONCE I GOT THE IDEA.

EXT. FOREST - PORSCHE - NIGHT

He pulls the supplies out of the trunk.

> MARV
> Keep the engine running. If I'm not back in twenty get the hell out of here and don't look back.

> WENDY
> Kill him for me, Marv. Kill him good.

He walks away.

> MARV
> I won't let you down, Goldie. I promised.

EXT. WOODS - NIGHT

Running through the woods.

> MARV
> (vo)
> I'm gambling that none of them think I'm dumb enough to come after them. They told Kevin to sit tight and figured I bugged out of town.

EXT. FARMHOUSE - NIGHT

He unrolls the razor wire.

> MARV
> (vo)
> I love this stuff. It cuts through meat and bone like they was butter.

He stretches the wire between several trees. Close on his face. Watching Kevin in the house.

> MARV (CONT'D)
> (vo)
> Heading downstairs to the kitchen. Getting himself a midnight snack. And I can guess what kind.

CHIKK! He lights the rag dangling from the Gas tank. He throws the tank.
KRASHHH! Into the house it goes.

KASSSH!!! Out leaps Kevin, tearing out of the house as it

EXPLODES. POOM! BOOM BOOM! Marv lets Glady sing.

> MARV (CONT'D)
> Like that, Kevin?

Kevin lands like a cat as bullet hits fly around his feet.

> MARV (CONT'D)
> Come on, Boy! Don't be scared!

He pulls out the handcuffs.

> MARV (CONT'D)
> (vo)
> Come on, come on come on... you son of a bitch. Don't look
> down, boy.

Kevin runs right toward the wire. Stops. Sees. Leaps through it.

> MARV (CONT'D)
> (vo)
> Damn he's slick.

Marv leaps to Kevin, who is fighting with Marv's discarded coat. A savage
fight. Kevin smashes into Marv's face with his foot. Marv raises his bloody
head.

> MARV (CONT'D)
> Is that the best you can do, creep?

Another face smashing kick. Fists in gut.

> MARV (CONT'D)
> (vo)
> That's right... get personal. Get close. I can take it.

Kevin has his sharp nailed hands poised in deadly poses. He snaps the cuff
onto Kevin's wrist. Kevin leaps and kicks at Marv's face with both feet.

> MARV (CONT'D)
> Go ahead. I can take it. And blood in my eyes or not I can
> find you.

ELIJAH WOOD ON FIGHT SCENES

"THERE'S ACTUALLY A LOT OF FIGHTING. IT WAS FUNNY,
MIDWAY THROUGH THE FIGHT SEQUENCE ROBERT SORT OF
LOOKED OVER TO ME AND HE SAID, 'WOW, THIS IS A REALLY
PHYSICAL ROLE. IT'S LIKE SOMEHOW I FORGOT, BUT THERE
WERE ALL THESE FIGHT FRAMES WHERE YOU'RE SUPPOSED
TO BE KICKING, AND JUMPING IN THE AIR. I THOUGHT YOU
WERE JUST GOING TO STAND HERE AND LOOK KIND OF, YOU
KNOW, EVIL FOR THE ENTIRE TIME.' SO IT'S BEEN GREAT. I'VE
BEEN UP IN A HARNESS, AND DOING ALL SORTS OF JUMP
KICKS. IT'S BEEN FUN."

Marv is handcuffed to Kevin, and with his free hand he lets loose a strong right cross that lays Kevin out cold. Smashing a lens in his pair of glasses.

> MARV (CONT'D)
> (vo)
> I try to slow my heart down and breathe the fire out of my lungs. My muscles make me a thousand promises of pain to come. It'll be a rough morning if I'm alive to see it.

Wendy approaches. Kevin out cold on the grass.

> WENDY
> (pointing gun)
> Let me do it, Marv. She was my sister. Let me finish him.

> MARV
> You wasn't supposed to come this way, Wendy.

> WENDY
> But I.. OOF!

He swats her. Knocking her out.

> MARV
> (vo)
> Sorry, kid. But I haven't even started with this creep and I don't want you watching the rest. It'd give you nightmares.

EXT. FOREST - PORSCHE - NIGHT

He carries her to the car. She's asleep in the passenger seat. We hear voices

EXT. WOODS - NIGHT

The camera pushes through the woods to find the voices.

> MARV
> I'll tell you, I am good and bushed. And it wasn't our fight that did me in, either. It was all that sawing and tying. It's not as easy as it looks.

We settle on the scene. Marv sitting relaxed by a pair of severed legs. Hacksaw in hand. The legless Kevin propped up.

MARV (CONT'D)
It would've been a mess around here if I hadn't had tubing
for the tourniquets. I got to admit there was a spurt or two.
To get the scent in the air. To get a friend of yours to come
running.

The wolf shows up. GRRRRRR.

MARV (CONT'D)
Well what do you know. Here he comes. Let's see what happens
if I loosen up one of these.

He unwraps a stump. The wolf stalks. RRRRR.

Close on Kevin. Smiling strangely. Even as the wolf eats.

MARV (CONT'D)
Good dog. Good dog.

Marv squatting and smoking as the wolf dines.

MARV (CONT'D)
(vo)
He doesn't scream. Not even when the mutt's had his fill and
Kevin's guts are lying all over the place and somehow the
bastard is still alive, still staring at me. Not even when I
grab the saw and finish the job. He never screams.

Marv is holding the severed head in his hand.

EXT. NANCY'S APARTMENT STAIRS - NIGHT

MARV
(vo)
I put in a call to Kadie's and ask Nancy to get her clothes
on and meet me at her place. She says yes, like always.

Marv carries Wendy up a flight of stairs.

MARV (CONT'D)
Hi, Nancy. Got any beers?

NANCY
Sure, Marv. Who's the babe?

THOUGH MICKEY ROURKE AND JESSICA ALBA WERE NEVER ON SET AT THE SAME TIME, A COMPOSITING EFFECT ALLOWED THEIR CHARACTERS TO TALK FACE TO FACE.

INT. NANCY'S APARTMENT - NIGHT

> MARV
> (vo)
> There isn't much of anything Nancy wouldn't do for me. Not since a year back when a frat boy roughed her up and I straightened him out but good. It really gets my goat when guys rough up dames.

Nancy bandages Marv. He inhales an ice cold long neck.

> MARV (CONT'D)
> (vo)
> By my fifth beer she's up to speed.

> NANCY
> So what do you want me to do with her?

> MARV
> Your best bet is to drive her all the way to Sacred Oaks. Put her on a plane there. She'll kick up a fuss but tell her said she owes me one. It's not true, but she'll believe it.

Close on Marv. Drinking the beer.

> NANCY
> What about you? Are you leaving town?

> MARV
> Hell, No. I like it here. *URP*.

EXT. STREET - NIGHT

A CAB barrels down the road.

> MARV
> (vo)
> I hot-wire a parked cab and stay under the speed limits so as not to get any attention. The wind is warm on my face an everything's simple and clear. I can't help smiling.

EXT. CAB - HILL ABOVE OLD MISSION - NIGHT

The car is parked on a hill above an old Mission.

>   MARV
>   (vo)
> The Mission. "Fortress Roark." Is what some people call it
> and if you ask me they aren't wrong. Roark's been holed up
> there for years. Surrounded by a squad of armed guards,
> sitting pretty while mayors and senators and governors
> come, hats in hand, begging favors from mighty Saint
> Patrick. I'd like to blow the whole damned place sky high
> and leave a crater big enough to suck in all the money and
> lies of all the generations of the Royal Roark family. But
> that's just enthusiasm talking. I've got to play this sneaky.
> Sneaky and very nasty.

EXT. OLD MISSION - FRONT GATE - NIGHT

He races down the hill. A guard patrols the front gate.

>   GUARD
> Corporal Rivera, checking in. Quiet as a grave here. No sign
> of target.

>   VOICE
> We copy, Corporal. Stay on your toes. Central out.

SNAP! Marv attacks silently from behind.

>   MARV
> Sleep tight corporal Rivera.
>   (vo)
> Guards, hell. These bums are a death squad-- From the same
> bunch that killed Lucille. So there's no reason at all to be
> nice about this.

EXT. OLD MISSION - ROOFTOP - NIGHT

Marv leaps to a rooftop. Attacks a guard on the roof.

>   GUARD
> What the hell-- no--

PUNT! Marv kicks another guard off the tiled roof.

                    MARV
                    (vo)
          A few more go down, without much trouble.

CHUDD! He cracks another guard's face. Runs past him.

INT. OLD MISSION - STAIRS - NIGHT

Marv stalks up the stairs.

INT. OLD MISSION - ROARK'S ROOM - NIGHT

The light creeps into Roark's bedroom as Marv opens the door.

                    MARV
                    (vo)
          Finally. Roark. Patrick Henry Roark.

Roark wakes at the light. Shadows playing on the wall. Sees Kevin standing
in the shadows. Light plays across his face.

                    ROARK
          Kevin?

Marv steps up from the shadows, revealing he's merely holding Kevin's head
up.

                    MARV
          What's left of him, anyways. The dog ate the rest.

Marv sits and places the head on the floor.

                    MARV (CONT'D)
          Don't scream or I'll plug you.

Cardinal Roark lifts the head. Examining it.

                    ROARK
          .. Oh God. You monster! You monster!

MARV

At least I don't go around eating people.

ROARK

You don't understand him! You don't know anything about him! You probably think he couldn't talk.

ark cradles the head. Marv lights up a cig.

ROARK (CONT'D)

He had a voice like an angel. But he spoke only to me. And now he's dead-- and all because of one stupid whore!

MARV

It's not a real good idea for you to talk about Goldie that way while I'm around. Just give with the scoop. The whole story. If you don't I'll start with your fingers.

ROARK

He was just a boy when he first came to me --- a tortured soul. Tormented by guilt.
(rising up)
But the eating. It filled him with WHITE LIGHT -- with love for every living thing. Tearful, he swore to me that he felt the touch of God Almighty.

lls smokes. Roark paces.

ROARK (CONT'D)

At first, I thought he was insane. I tried to counsel him. But, as years passed, Kevin's voice grew more certain-- until it filled me with pleasure. Just to hear him speak. To share in his ecstacy...

Roark.

ROARK (CONT'D)

In time, I began to envy him. I could no longer stand to the side while he touched heaven.

in.

ROARK (CONT'D)

He didn't just eat their bodies you pig! He ate their souls! He loved them in a way that was absolute and clean and perfect. And I joined in. The women were nothing. Whores. Nobody missed them. Nobody cared. And then that one girl-

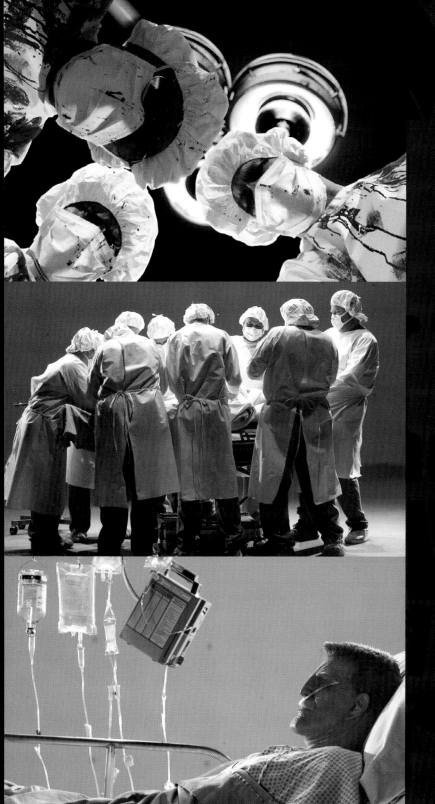

- your GOLDIE--- almost ruined everything. She must have
suspected something, after the first few girls. Perhaps she
saw one of them getting into my limousine... She followed us

On Marv smoking as Roark talks.

> ROARK (CONT'D)
> Kevin was... engrossed, when she found us. She made it to her
> car and escaped. She stayed in public places. Then with you.
> You were so convenient. Nobody would believe a thug like
> you. You'd broken a man's jaw that same night! Kevin killed
> her. I ordered the police in for you. But you -- you wouldn't
> be caught. And you wouldn't stop -- and now Kevin is dead
> and you're here to kill me. Will that give you satisfaction,
> my son? Killing a helpless old man?

> MARV
> The killing, no. No satisfaction. But everything up until the
> killing will be a gas.
> > (blows a smoke ring)
> You can scream now if you want to.

Police guards climb the stairs.

> MARV
> > (vo)
> It's beautiful, Goldie. It's just like I promised only better.
> It's not quick or quiet like it was with you. It's loud and
> nasty. My kind of kill. I stare the bastard in the face and I
> laugh as he screams to God for mercy. He spurts and gurgles
> and life is good.

Close on Marv as the quivering dying hand of Roark rises into frame.

> MARV (CONT'D)
> > (vo)
> And when his eyes go dead, the hell I send him to must seem
> like heaven after what I've done to him.

> COPS
> FREEZE! Oh my God!

BREKK BREKK BRAKA! Marv is filled with lead.

INT. HOSPITAL - ER - NIGHT

Marv's POV of doctors working furiously on him.

                    MARV
                    (vo)
          Jerks! They should have shot me in the head -- and enough
          times to make sure. It's stupid. Everybody knows what's
          coming. But they go through the motions anyway. What a
          waste of time.

INT. HOSPITAL - MARV'S ROOM - NIGHT

Marv in a hospital bed. Tubes connected.

                    MARV
                    (vo)
          Months fall off the calendar while I breathe and eat through
          tubes. Night after night I wait for somebody to come and
          finish me off. After a while I realize it's not going to be so
          easy as that.

INT. INTERROGATION ROOM - NIGHT

Marv tied up in a chair getting beat.

                    MARV
                    (vo)
          I'm on my feet for about ten minutes before the cops kick
          them out from under me. They don't ask me any questions.
          They just keep knocking the crap out of me and waving a
          confession in my face. And I keep spitting blood all over it
          and laughing at how many fresh copies they come up with.

A cop drags an attorney away from the interrogation room.

                    MARV (CONT'D)
                    (vo)
          Then along comes this worm assistant district attorney
          who turns the recorder off and says if I don't sign their
          confession they'll kill my mom. I break his arm in three
          places and sign the confession. From then on it's the circus
          everybody wants it to be. They nail me for the works. Not
          just the people I did kill but even Lucille and the girls
          Roark and Kevin ate. And even Goldie.

73

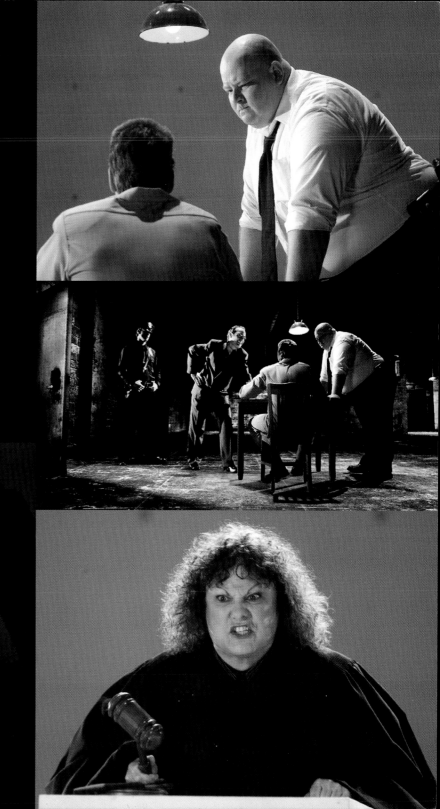

GOLDIE.

SHE SAYS
HER NAME
IS GOLDIE.

INT. COURT - NIGHT

The judge rants and raves, slamming the gavel repeatedly.

>   MARV
>   (vo)
>   The judge is all fire and brimstone when she hands down
>   the sentence. Midnight and my death are only a few hours
>   away when I get my first surprise in eighteen months.

INT. MARV'S CELL - NIGHT

He looks up at the grate.

>   MARV
>   (vo)
>   My only visitor. I'm ready for anything but that scent.

>   MARV (CONT'D)
>   I got them for you good, didn't I, Goldie?

Wendy steps in.

>   MARV (CONT'D)
>   I'm sorry Wendy. I got confused again, seeing you like this.

>   WENDY
>   It's all right, Marv. You can call me Goldie.

She kisses him.

>   MARV
>   (vo)
>   She smells like angels ought to smell. The perfect woman.
>   The goddess.

Camera high looking down at their bodies in the window light.

>   MARV (CONT'D)
>   (vo)
>   Goldie. She says her name is Goldie.

INT. HOT SEAT – NIGHT

                    HOT SEAT
Marv is strapped into the electric chair.

                    MARV
                    (vo)
They fix me a pretty decent steak for my last meal.
They even throw in a brew, the first I've had since
back at Nancy's. Then they shave my head and fix me
with a rubber diaper and get to it. And it's about
damn time, if you ask me.

                    PRIEST
Though I walk through the valley of the shadow of
death...

                    MARV
Could you get a move on? I haven't got all night!

                    JUICER
You heard the man. Hit it.

                    COP
Yes, sir.

Handle is pulled. We have X-RAY vision of Marv's Skull as he's given
the first jolt. He slumps.

                    MARV
Keff. HA Ha HA Ha... that the best you can do... you
pansies?

The switch is thrown again. Blood pours down his head.

They listen to his heart. CAMERA pushes into MARV.

                    JUICER
He's dead.

Push in tight on his eye... the reflection is Marv and Goldie lying
peacefully on the heart shaped bed.

                              CUT TO BLACK.

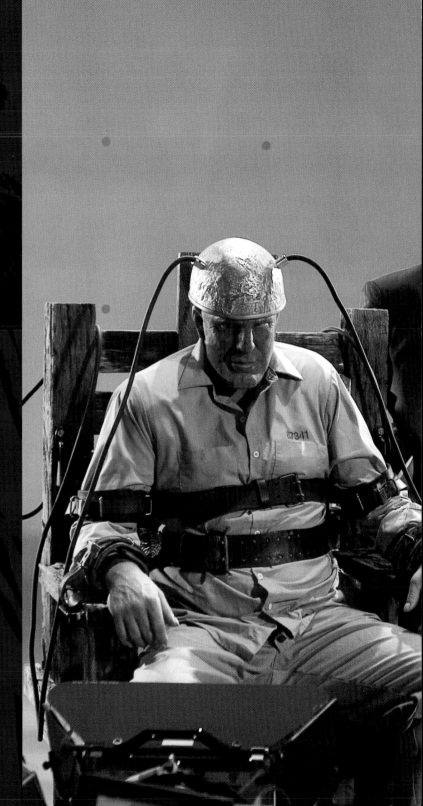

ART DIRECTOR AND PROPERTY MASTER STEVE JOYNER ON APPROACHING SIN CITY

"When Robert first contacted me about the job he said, 'You're gonna love it. The storyboards are completely done for every frame.' I'm like, 'Robert, what are you talking about? How can the storyboards be done, there are six hundred pages?' He said, 'I've got the three books. Just take 'em, look through them, we're going to shoot it exactly like that.' So it makes it very easy for me, and the art department, and the property department to put together the sets and the props for the actors. It also makes it easy for the costume designer, Nina Proctor, to put the costumes together because we're being very, very faithful to Frank's original drawings. I think people that are fans of Frank Miller's work will see him in every shot, even though this is a Rodriguez movie."

"Speaking from a property point-of-view, working with the drawings that Frank Miller's done has been really amazing because he draws based on life, but everything has a basic *Sin City* twist to it. It's Frank's own world, so it's slightly unreal. We manufactured pretty much everything. There's probably not a single off-the-shelf prop in the movie. The time period of the movie really has kind of a 50's feel to it, but it's also modern, so we span a lot of time trade, and combine them into Frank Miller's own world."

"Mostly *Sin City* is about booze, broads, and guns, so we have a lot of guns that Frank's drawn in the books. Because of the 50's nature of Frank's drawings, the characters in the books use a lot of revolvers, usually WWII. Colt Pistols, very classical designs. However, Frank contributed to some of the *Robocop* films, and he drew in the Robocop pistol in some of the scenes. So we had to go to Gibbon's Entertainment of Burbank and find the manufacturer of the *Robocop* guns and bring them in for Frank, and he was amazed to see them after so many years, back in action. But again, we're matching the story panels exactly to the movie. So what he's drawn, we're bringing to life."

FRANK MILLER ON PROPS

"The precision Caylah and Steve are bringing to the props is astonishing. They will look at a drawing I did in a few brush strokes, find out it's a Mongolian Bow and bring it in. Miho flips through the air holding the bow that I drew, but it's also a real functioning bow from a different part of the world. They created everything right down to the arrowheads—a lot of which I made up— and the throwing stars and such. I'm now seeing these in three dimensions. I'll tell you, I'm going to walk away from this production with a lot of souvenirs."

"Research is a passion of mine, anyway. I call it a hobby, but it's part of my job. So I collect little metal cars, and all kinds of martial arts weapons, and even things like toy plastic guitars in case I might want to draw a guitar sometime. I've essentially got a studio that's full of stuff that most people regard as junk, but it's all materials because cartooning is essentially drawing, and drawing is fundamentally finding out what things really look like. Nothing ever looks like you imagine it to. I often tell a novice that the first thing you've got to do is just look at things. For instance, if you need to draw a shoe, take your own shoe off and put it on your drawing board, and discover that shoe until it doesn't look like you think it does. Things look much weirder and much more interesting than we imagine they do. A gun is not an L-shaped thing; there's an elegance to where the grip goes. As you become comfortable with the process of research and the rediscovery of what things really look like, you become addicted to it. You start not feeling right about faking even a coffee cup. You've got to grab one and draw it. Then you find out the handle is just a little different than you thought."

"I've seen the same type of research going on with Steve and Caylah, hunting things down and then building them. But they're doing it completely in three dimensions, making things that are sort of functional. It's stunning, but it's also a little creepy. In a lot of ways this movie is quite literally like having a dream come true."

PROPERTY MASTER CAYLAH EDDLEBLUTE ON MIHO'S BOW AND ARROW

"'That's a Mongolian bow,' said David 'Bowwiz' Lynch when I brought the BFK Miho storyboard into Archery Country, just down the road from our shop. 'Can you get me one?' 'No, they're not made in this country.' A call to prop houses came up with zilch. I'd rifled through their cluttered bins before on other shows. We didn't want anything bashed up, used and faded. We wanted something heroic. Bowwiz suggested going online. Several sites came up. One called back promptly. Kimberly Coleman, proprietor of Washington-based Seven Meadows, placed an order through a gentleman in Hungary named Toth Anita who makes Mongolian bows. The price was reasonable, so I ordered one, with arm and finger guards, a pouch and four-dozen arrow shafts, no tips. We were making the tips ourselves, to match Frank's ink. Kimberly made the arrows, including six of aluminum tube. We gave them to Special Effects supervisor John McLeod so his team could rig them to fly."

"The least poundage bow made was rated at thirty-five. This refers to the pounds of resistance required to pull the bow back and give it its force. Steve and I had walked this road before, during *From Dusk Till Dawn,* when Juliette Lewis wielded a bow against some badass vampires. The challenge is getting someone not experienced in archery to pull the string back on one of these things not once, but for many takes, without their arm falling off in a quivering puddle of fatigue. There is plenty of force behind the pull, even at thirty-five pounds. The bow arrived in about four weeks. I kept the mailing label; fascinated by exotic writing I could not read, but found its way through continents, oceans and Customs to my office. It's funny the things that intrigue you along the way."

"Even at thirty-five pounds of pressure, the bow's pull was too great. Stevie J knew exactly what to do. We had an authentic bow in our hand, a reference for size, scale, feel, that indefinable tactile quality that makes a good prop. We could proceed and make our own stunt version, lightweight, easy to pull, modeled after the real thing. We cut two stunt bows from Lexan, wrapped them with leather to match, and added the stitching embellishments with a scenic touch. Miho was able to do take, after take and all the parts worked."

"Another scene through the pipe. A small victory."

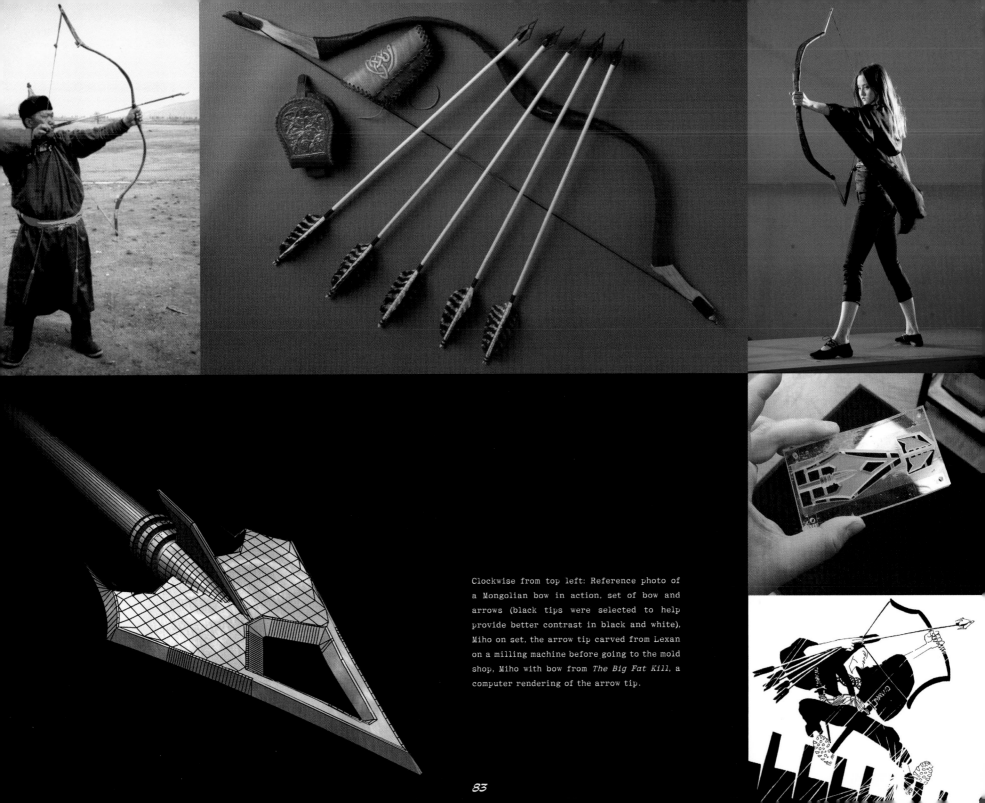

Clockwise from top left: Reference photo of a Mongolian bow in action, set of bow and arrows (black tips were selected to help provide better contrast in black and white), Miho on set, the arrow tip carved from Lexan on a milling machine before going to the mold shop, Miho with bow from *The Big Fat Kill*, a computer rendering of the arrow tip.

STEVE JOYNER ON MIHO'S SWORD

"IN *BIG FAT KILL* WE HAVE A CHARACTER NAMED MIHO, WHO'S A FEMALE ASIAN MARTIAL ARTIST. ROBERT'S BROTHER, QUENTIN TARANTINO, JUST DID ANOTHER SMALL MARTIAL ARTS FILM. I WORKED ON THAT AS WELL, AND WE DREW QUITE A BIT FROM *KILL BILL* FOR MIHO TO USE IN *BIG FAT KILL*. IN FACT, IF YOU LOOK CLOSELY, MIHO'S SWORDS ARE CRAZY 88 SWORDS, WHICH ACTUALLY CAME FROM QUENTIN'S GARAGE. CAYLAH CALLED HIM UP AND SAID, 'QUENTIN WE NEED TO BORROW THE SWORDS.' AND QUENTIN WAS LIKE, 'YOU NEED TO DO WHAT?' SHE SAID, 'IT'S FOR ROBERT.' QUENTIN SAID, 'OH, OKAY.' SO THAT'S HOW WE ENDED UP BRINGING *KILL BILL* TOGETHER WITH FRANK MILLER AND ROBERT RODRIGUEZ."

"WHEN WE SHOT *KILL BILL*, WE MADE A HUNDRED AND EIGHTEEN DIFFERENT STYLES OF SWORDS, AND SPENT SIXTY-FIVE THOUSAND DOLLARS MAKING THE FIGHTING SWORDS. THAT WAS THE SWORD BUDGET ALONE. ALL OF THESE WERE MADE IN JAPAN AT A MARTIAL ARTS FACILITY IN SIKI CITY, WHICH IS THE CITY FAMOUS FOR ITS KNIFE STEEL, AND WE HAD A LOT OF COLLATERAL FROM THOSE SWORDS. WE GOT *KILL BILL* VOLUME ONE AND TWO OUT OF IT, AND NOW WE HAVE *SIN CITY*. SO THEY LIVE ON, AND THEY'LL PROBABLY LIVE ON IN THE FUTURE HERE BETWEEN ROBERT AND QUENTIN."

DEVON AOKI ON PROPS AND WARDROBE

"Miho has so many props. She is always loaded up with different things. She has a belt with two swords and has all sorts of throwing stars. In fact, she even uses her earrings as weapons. I think the prop department did an incredible job. They even made up some katana swords made out of bamboo. They look unbelievably real. I walked around with them at my hotel, because I had to practice, and people were scared of me. I tried to say, 'Don't worry, it's bamboo. I'm not going to cut you with it.'"

"But the props look incredible, and as far as the wardrobe goes, they also did a great job. It's so real. They kept so close to what it really was in the book, even down to the details of the shoes."

"They really paid attention to all the details, and that's what makes her outfits so killer. People are really going to enjoy the visual aspect of Miho's character."

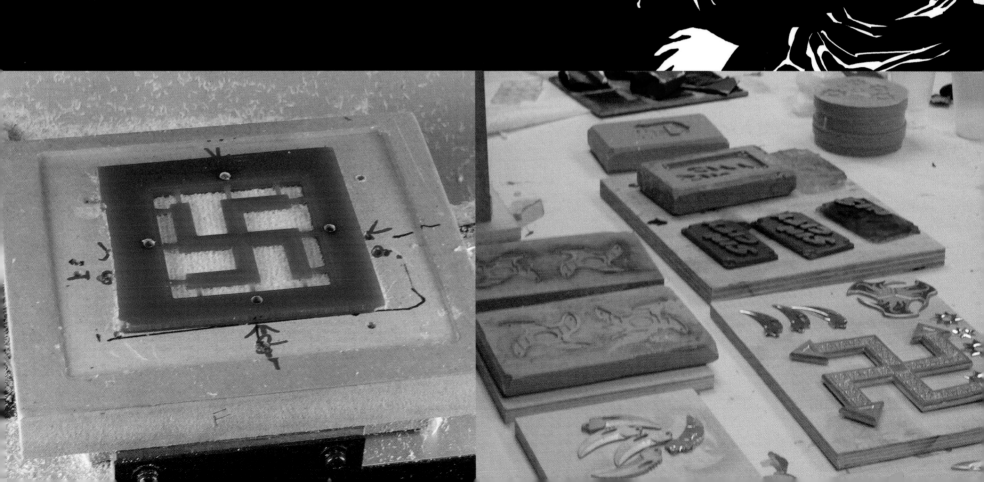

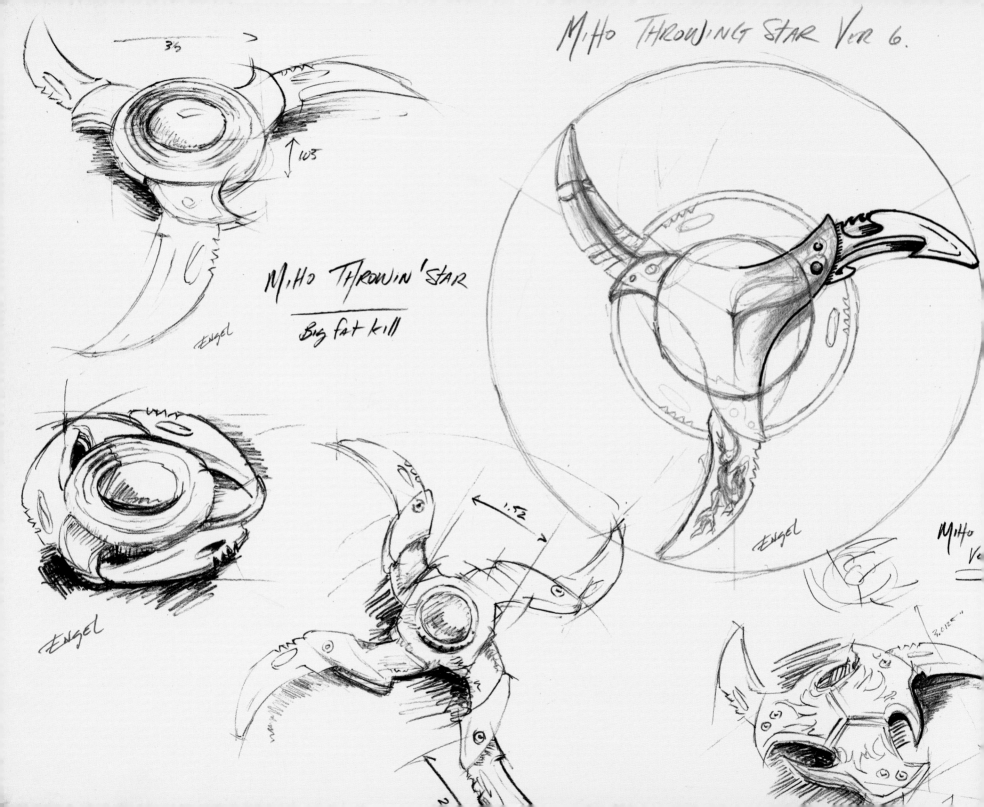

MiHo THROWING STAR Ver 6.

MiHo THROWIN' STAR

Big fat kill

EDDLEBLUTE ON MIHO'S THROWING STARS

"'Miho is all about weapons,' Frank said early on. 'I want something that can attach to her costume with a clip or a hasp.' He wanted gear to magically appear from all parts of Miho. In larger context, that would mean adding scenes not in his series. You make it, even though you may never get to shoot it. Rarely do you get to add shots, especially on something like this, where the storyboards in the graphic novel are so clearly laid out. Usually you're looking at what shots you can cut. Still, I went to a local martial arts store and picked up an off-the-shelf three-bladed throwing star and gave it to Troy. 'Like this, only smaller, with our own design.' That was all the direction he got. A visit across the hall to costume designer Nina Proctor was in order, to look at the fabrics she was considering for Miho. Purples. Blues. Reds. Silver. Whew. We were thinking along the same lines. Troy came up with a number of renderings, but this one with the flame pattern mirrored the fluid nature of Miho's garment. This prop is made of twenty-two parts. We made 'hero' pieces for close up shots and cast the blades as well as the filigree in sterling silver. We didn't want to mess around with chrome paint, which is a notorious pain, time consuming, and always requires lots of touch up."

"You won't find this prop in the movie. Time, as always, remains the great barrier. And Miho had plenty to keep track of with her double samurai sword rig. Yet when the director asks, you deliver. So here it is, for you to see."

JOYNER ON BECKY'S JEWELRY

"IN *BIG FAT KILL* WE HAVE A CHARACTER NAMED BECKY, WHO IS ONE OF THE TRAITORS IN THE STORY, AND FRANK HAS DRAWN HER IN SILHOUETTE WITH THESE AMAZING EARRINGS AND FLOWING NECKLACES. AGAIN, THAT STUFF DOESN'T EXIST IN REALITY. WE WENT TO AN AUSTIN JEWELER AND HAD HIM MANUFACTURE A LOT OF THE PIECES. OUR STAFF SHOP, WHICH IS BRANDON CAMPBELL AND MARCUS LAPORTE, THEN TOOK THOSE PIECES AND TURNED THEM INTO SEVERAL COPIES OF THE JEWELRY AND DESIGNED IT SO WE COULD PUT IT ON AND OFF OF HER IN ONE PIECE RATHER THAN LAYING IN EACH PIECE INDIVIDUALLY. SO TO GET BECKY'S JEWELRY TO MATCH FRANK'S DRAWING PROBABLY TOOK SOMEWHERE AROUND A HUNDRED AND FIFTY MAN HOURS OF MANUFACTURING. IT REALLY SHOWS, THOUGH. SHE LOOKS GREAT."

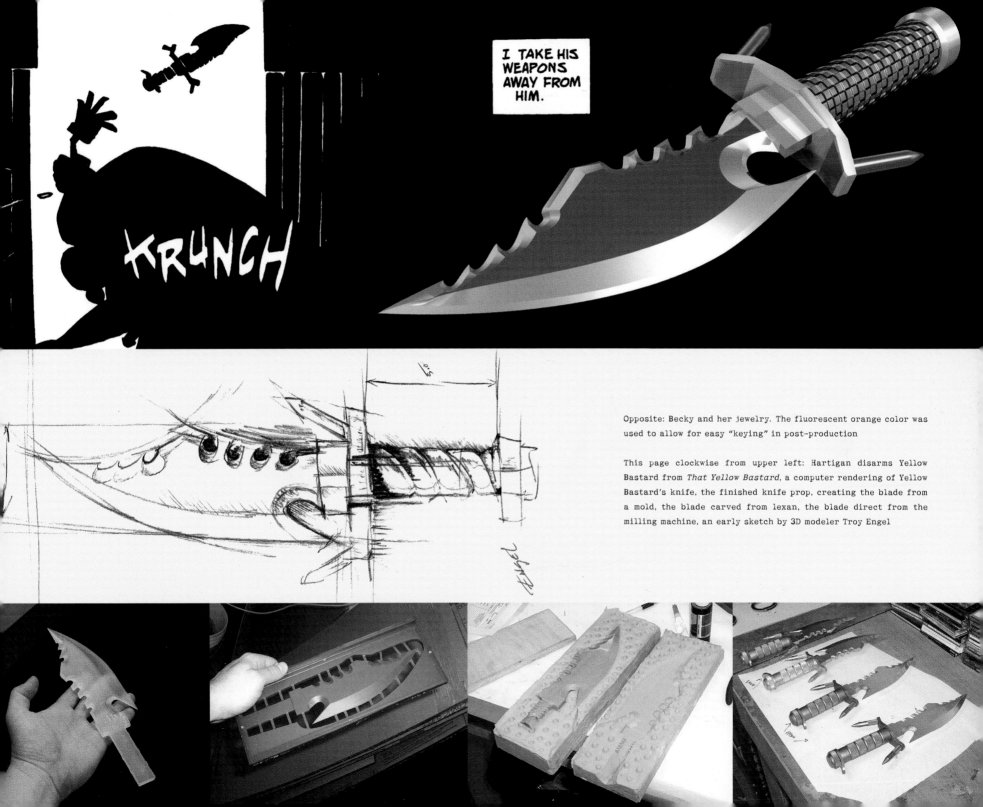

I TAKE HIS WEAPONS AWAY FROM HIM.

KRUNCH

Opposite: Becky and her jewelry. The fluorescent orange color was used to allow for easy "keying" in post-production

This page clockwise from upper left: Hartigan disarms Yellow Bastard from *That Yellow Bastard*, a computer rendering of Yellow Bastard's knife, the finished knife prop, creating the blade from a mold, the blade carved from lexan, the blade direct from the milling machine, an early sketch by 3D modeler Troy Engel

JOYNER ON NANCY'S LASSO

"A THREAD RUNNING THROUGHOUT THE THREE STORIES IS KADIE'S CLUB PECOS, THE BAR WHERE ALL THE CHARACTERS SORT OF MIX AND MINGLE, AND IN THAT BAR IS NANCY. ONE OF THE STORIES CENTERS ON NANCY AS ONE OF THE LEAD CHARACTERS, AND WE DID A VERY COOL WESTERN, RIGGED, DOUBLE BLACK HAWK PISTOL SET-UP FOR HER. ONE OF OUR DRIVER CAPTAINS, A GUY NAMED JOE LLANES, IS ALSO AN EXPERT TRICK ROPER, AND HE WORKED WITH JESSICA ALBA FOR SEVERAL DAYS AND TAUGHT HER HOW TO ROPE FOR REAL. SO WHEN YOU SEE JESSICA UP THERE WITH THE LARIAT, SHE'S DOING IT, AND SHE'S VERY GOOD AT IT. SHE LOOKS GREAT. NANCY'S AN ABSOLUTE HIT WITH THE CREW, AND SHE'S JUST THE HEART OF CLUB KADIE'S."

JOYNER ON GLADYS

"WE HAVE A SCENE THAT REALLY DEFINES MARV. HE GOES BACK TO HIS CHILDHOOD HOME WHERE HIS MOM STILL LIVES, AND GOES UNDER HIS BED AND FINDS HIS KEEPSAKES FROM WHEN HE WAS A CHILD. IN THERE HE'S HIDDEN HIS ONE GUN, A WWII COLT 1911 THAT HE'S KEPT AND IS SPECIAL TO HIM. FRANK HAS NAMED THE GUN 'GLADYS.' GLADYS IS KEY TO MARV, AND REALLY BRINGING GLADYS TO LIFE WAS OUR KICK-OFF FOR THIS MOVIE. FRANK WENT THROUGH THE COLT BOOKS AND WE SELECTED ONE VERY CAREFULLY, AND THAT BECAME GLADYS."

◀ OPEN

SELL BY JUNE 22

SPOUT

OPEN HERE

Be Good®

Be Good®

Be Good®

SELL BY JUNE 22

Be Good®

Whole Milk
VITAMIN D

milk

Whole Milk

MISSING

Kimberly Jane

Disappeared
January 02, 1952

Age: 7
Hair: Brown
Eyes: Hazel
Height: 4'0"

Last Seen
At her Momma's

milk

Whol

FAKE

HALF GALLON(1.98L)

FAKE

HALF GAL

0 14000 00502 6

Ultra-Pasteurized Vitamins A&D
37% Less Fat Than Regular Whole Milk
Rich in Calcium and Vitamin D
INGREDIENTS: ..UM MILK

PERISHABLE KEEP REFRIGERATED

PERISHABLE KE

EDDLEBLUTE ON WHY MILK MATTERS

"Looking back on it now, one of the recurring themes, as far as creating props went, was the concept of weight. Mass. All in Frank Miller's world has heft. The guns. The boots. The syntax. Nowadays, we drink from plastic jugs. They're weak and they buckle. *Sin City* lives in the era of the milk carton. A real container. A wax box. A pass through the storyboards with a green highlighter revealed a milk carton in the foreground of a trash-strewn alley scene. An image instantly came to mind. A 'Missing Child' graphic. Kimberly Jane, the little girl Frank drew in *Silent Night*, a short story in *Booze, Broads and Bullets*. Perfect. The slogan? Be Good. The milk I got as a kid at the corner store had an orange label. Orange would be fine. Enough contrast to read in black and white. This was not a prop integral to the scene, just a foreground piece. No one would probably even notice if we made it or not. But Frank provided great art, and we wanted to use it. So at our first 'show and tell,' the milk carton stood out. It was the first time we really met Frank, the first time we could get a feel for each other. He held the prop, and stayed with it for several moments, turning it from side to side. 'I let my editor know something strange was coming,' Frank said of *Silent Night*. And the milk carton I think let him know that we, in some small measure, understood his language."

EDDLEBLUTE ON BIG RED BUTTONS

"The cool thing about the grenades in *Big Fat Kill* is the source material from which they're created, a cylinder of aluminum raw stock. Basic, geometric, a building block. Turning this shape on the lathe remains one of those mind puzzles I admire. Like watching men who can still use a slide rule. Frank selected the exact grenade design, from a number of reference photos. The WWII Japanese Type 97 Standard Grenade, 'the standard workhorse of the Japanese Army Ordnance.' Not U.S. issue, since the characters equipping themselves were mercenaries from abroad. Made originally in black with a red cap and a copper fuse."

"Paul Steele, one of our crew, turns exceptional lathe work. It's an internal, zen-like craft, like welding a perfect bead. The hum is the right pitch, the pacing like a metronome. You can't hurry it. After Paul completed a single grenade, moldmakers Marcus LaPorte and Brandon Campbell poured and cast lightweight versions, since so many had to fit on the costume belt. Paul also turned three detonators, for a choice of sizes. We wanted that Cold War feel, big in the hand. Always big and caught in time, like rows of Steel Case desks in endless rooms where men with drafting tools built rockets. Big red button. You just can't say no to a big red button."

The prop department was dogmatic in its quest to bring Frank Miller's drawings to life in exact detail. 3D modeler Troy Engel scanned Zorro Girl's earrings directly from the original panel. The stars are not symmetrical, and the prop department wanted to retain the kinetic, hand-drawn quality of the drawings. They cut masters on a Roland CNC machine, then made soft rubber castings.

EDDLEBLUTE ON DALLAS & ZORRO GIRL

"Robert cast his sister, Patricia Vonne, to play a character we called Zorro Girl. When the director's sibling is in the movie, you want to make especially sure you don't screw up. We got a kick out of how she turned out."

"In *Big Fat Kill*, Frank and Robert combined the characters of Zorro Girl and Dallas (Dallas is a western belle who gets killed in a car crash while attempting Dwight's rescue from the tarpits). Although they don't exist in ink, Robert wanted to add a holster rig to Zorro Girl's costume. He wanted her to look cool."

"In Frank's drawings, Zorro Girl draws 45's. We changed these to stainless steel Ruger 44 Blackhawks - one of the rare times we strayed from the source material. These were the same guns we'd used for Nancy. They read so well in black and white and had the right flavor. Wild West. And no additional cost since we had them already. We cast many of our replica and stunt guns in our own mold shop. The paint and detail work Brandon Campbell and Marcus LaPorte achieved were spot on."

EDDLEBLUTE ON COOL TRASH

"It's one of the things we built that's exactly the tone of the movie. Very fifties, industrial, a real *Iron Giant* feel. Steve drew a sketch. Basin City Sanitation. This was the first and one of the few practical set pieces we made since most of *Sin City* existed, for the shooting crew, in the green sea of the digital world. We couldn't help but notice the theme of Basin City. Basin, for starters. Going down the drain. Lots of alleys. Lots of trash. It was our duty to make cool stuff that was true to Frank's pen stroke. The heaps of refuse were iconic."

"We bought six brand-spanking shiny new metal trash cans. Our crew drilled scores of bolt holes and assembled the parts. Things really came to life, as always, when we handed the cans to our extraordinary scenic department. Lead Scenic Tommy Karl shows us the love like no other. Shortly after 9/11 we went to an Austin mall and saw a backlit poster of Peter Fonda's *Easy Rider* Harley chopper, the one with the American flag painted on the gas tank. 'The Guggenheim' read the caption. That's how we felt about the trash can. It struck us as a visually strong, singular object. It might sound corny, but we call it our Guggenheim piece."

I DON'T KNOW WHY YOU DIED, GOLDIE.

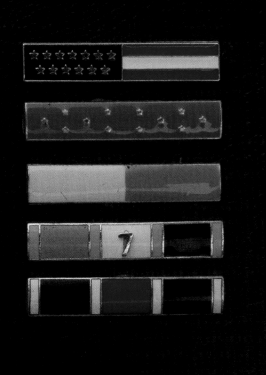

Medals. The bars men of distinction wear across their chest. The finishing touch. The prop department bought a selection from a military catalog, but they didn't measure up. Too short, cheap backings. Chincy. Besides, they didn't look substantial. They didn't "read."

Eddleblute called ISS, a Los Angeles rental house. Frank's medals were long bars with lots of color. The New York style medal. ISS sent the medals and the prop department inset them into the leather flap. The Patriot. The Medal of Honor. Wounded in Action. Iron Jack Rafferty.

Perfect.

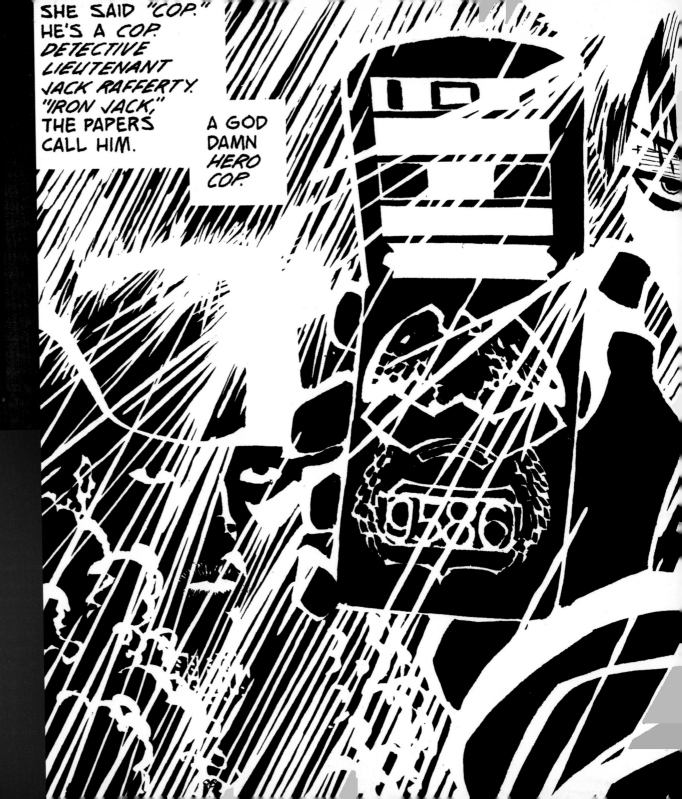

At one point, the shield saves Dwight's life, when he slips the badge into his own coat and it stops a bullet headed for his heart. The bullet rips through the leather and all the medals jut out, twisted, like buildings after a bombing. A war in your pocket, close to home, where it counts.

EDDLEBLUTE ON JACKIE BOY'S BADGE

"It's a tactile thing, creating an object by which a moment is measured. When we pile into the conference room for a production meeting, Steve and I bring one or two completed props. Something Robert can hold, think about, so his eyes don't completely glaze over while we review the finer points of the shooting schedule. We went into our *Big Fat Kill* meeting and brought Jackie Boy's badge. Robert opened the comic book and studied both the printed page and the real prop carefully. I sure was glad the badge number matched the storyboard."

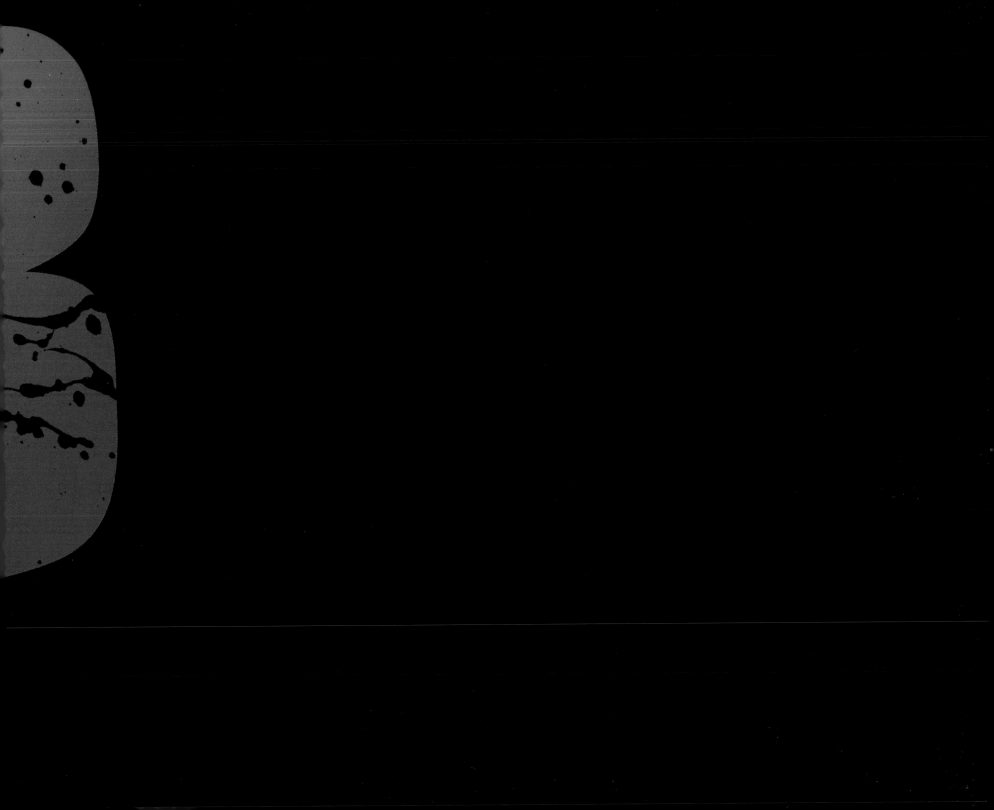

ON ROBERT RODRIGUEZ

"Watching Robert grow as a filmmaker from *Four Rooms*, and *From Dusk Till Dawn* through *The Faculty*, and all the *Spy Kids* films, and *Once Upon A Time In Mexico*, he has shied away somewhat from heavy prosthetic stuff in favor of more CGI and digital stuff because that's what has suited his stories. Now we're back in a room where prosthetics really do suit the story and propel the characters forward. So I was delighted at the challenge, and delighted at the opportunity to create Marv, and to create Yellow Bastard, and design Hartigan's make-up, and Jackie Boy. So it's been fun to do the prosthetics. I always feel like it's not high tech enough for Robert. He's always joked and he said, 'Oh, we're sort of going back to old school like rubber appliances, and pumping blood and tubing.' And when I agreed, he said, 'Yeah, but it's classic.' He loves all those 70's and 80's horror and sci-fi movies, so he has an affection for it. *Sin City* has been a film where the prosthetics played a really prominent role, and I'm delighted."

"Though KNB had done some work on Robert's segment in *Four Rooms*, *From Dusk Till Dawn* was our first time to be really in-the-trenches. The comparison between *Sin City* and *From Dusk Till Dawn* is that in *From Dusk Till Dawn*, none of the effects were really scripted, and Robert was like a kid in the candy store. He'd say, 'I'm gonna rip this guy's arm off,' or 'I want to slice this guy's throat and have a girl open out a fan and cut the guy's throat.' And I would say, 'Alright, great.' And then I'd run back to our little room, and we'd build it, and we'd come back to set and shoot it. Most of the gags in *Dusk* were improvised like that, with a combination of puppets, blood gags and character/creature make-ups. Robert and I have always shared an affection for the same types of films...*Jaws*, John Carpenter's *The Thing*, *Blade Runner*...films that inspired both of us when we were young. For *Dusk*, we wanted each vampire to have its own individual, distinct look, so we used headshots of the actors and played on their facial characteristics to design their vampire look. Quentin, Tom Savini, Cheech...all still looked like themselves, but a twisted, demonic version."

"From there we went on to design all of the creature effects for *The Faculty*, for which the film required a combination of practical and digital effects. I remember at one point in the scene where the 'lifecycle' of the alien organism is demonstrated in front of Elijah Wood, Jon Stewart and the rest of the class. Robert said, 'Well, we're going to do it digitally, but I want the actors to have articulated puppets to respond to.' We didn't have a lot of time for R&D. We built vinyl worms that had valves in them to which we would attach really tiny red tubing, and when we pumped water through the tubing, it would wave. At the time I said to Bill Scott, the unit production manager, 'We have so much work to do on the full size hydraulic creature and half scale puppet and transformation effects, shouldn't we concentrate on the that?' And the answer was, 'Robert wants it, he wants it there to get the performance from the actors.' And even on the *Spy Kids* movies, it was the same thing. We built all the Thumb Thumb and Shape costumes knowing Robert was ultimately going to replace them, but to him it was as important to have the physical object on set for the actors to react to and to act with. For *Spy Kids 3*, we built the hero costumes for Daryl Sabara and Alexa Vega. It's been great to wear a lot of hats with Robert. Given the fact that he and I have been friends for so long, I appreciate the fact that he trusts me enough that one movie we'll do prosthetics, and another movie we'll do gore effects, and another movie we'll do animatronics and puppets, and another movie we'll do costumes on the two hero kids. I think versatility has allowed my relationship with Robert to grow over the last ten years because he knows that he can come to KNB with anything, and I'll figure out a way to do it. If you look at Steve Joyner, Jeff Dashnaw, Nina Proctor and all the other people that Robert surrounds himself with, they're all the same way. You know, Steve Joyner will be on set at the drop of a hat to do anything, and same with Jeff. Robert has really cultivated his core crew of people that he relies on."

-Greg Nicotero
KNB

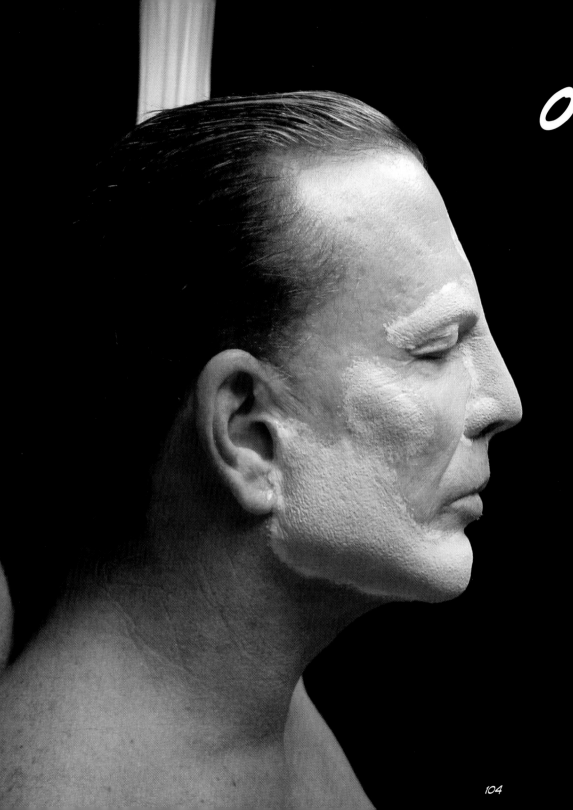

ON MARV

"Mickey's pretty notorious for not really enjoying the make-up process, and I remember kind of joking with Robert saying 'You know, Mickey's not real crazy about wearing make-up!' And he said, 'Yeah, yeah, yeah, it's gonna be great.' At that point, Mickey was already Marv in Robert's mind. We did a cyberscan of Mickey's head, and we created five different prosthetic looks because we wanted to explore a variety of make-up looks ranging from very subtle to extreme. We had three weeks to create the make-up for the Marv (*The Hard Goodbye*) segment. We tried to be faithful to the design and also incorporate some of Mickey. We didn't want to lose Mickey Rourke under a lot of rubber. What sort of turned the light on for me was a drawing Frank did of Marv's profile. In it you see his forehead and his nose, and then the nose cuts in, but if you continue drawing a semicircle his chin is literally in line with the semicircle. So Frank basically said, 'This is the way it works,' and he pulled out a piece of paper, and did a quick sketch of Marv's profile, a little semicircle and when he was done Frank said, 'That's classic Marv.' I looked at it, and right away I knew what he wanted. So we built out Mickey's chin, we accentuated the bridge of his nose. Up until two days before we started shooting we didn't know which make-up we were going to use. Nick Marra, Scott Stoddard and Jaremy Aiello worked on the variations of Marv's look, while Mark Boley, Jack Bricker and Ron Pipes created the signature military cut hair pieces. Once completed, we arrived in Austin and had Robert review the 5 prototype designs. His first question was, 'Greg, which one do you like?' And I said, 'Well, I like that nose and that chin.' He said, 'Let's test that one,' and that was the one we ended up going with. It was unbelievable. When Mickey stepped on set in character for the first time, I was watching Frank's face, because Frank has lived with these characters for twelve years, so he knows them personally. You'll always see crew people going up to Frank, 'What does this mean?' and 'Explain this to me,' and he'll say, 'Oh, well that's because in a previous story Marv pulled Manute's eye out.' Fun stuff like that. So Frank really knows these people intimately. We really had the luxury of designing the characters and going to Frank, asking the importance of the character design. And he would say with Marv it was the nose, with Hartigan it was the scar, and so on."

"Once we got the make-up worked out, Mickey brought it to life. He had a wig, a forehead/nose prosthetic that was one piece, and then the chin and jaw that was another piece. And it took about two and a half hours to get him in. Usually it took up to forty minutes to clean him up. Aside from the initial make-up, he went through thirteen different make-up changes. From the opening of the Marv segment, he goes through the windshield of a cop car, the cop car goes into the river, he comes out of the river, he's bleeding, and then he goes into his parole officer's apartment, and he tapes

himself up, so there's all these different stages that you had to follow. The cuts on his nose had to start healing while he was getting new cuts from his fight with Kevin, or hit with a sledgehammer, so everyday it was a little bit different. The way we shoot on this movie is they'll just refer to the storyboard and say, 'Okay, now we're doing top of page Marv 25, and then bottom of Marv 62. How long does it take him from stage two to stage five, and then back to stage four at the end of the day?' So you had to be on your toes every single second, and you had to listen to what the next shot was going to be or else they were going to fly forward, and you had to make sure that he stayed in the correct make-up stage. Chris Nelson applied Mickey's make-up while Gino Crognale, Kelly Mitchell and I handled the stunt doubles and on-set maintenance. We used regular red blood in that segment only because we really hadn't explored the idea of the fluorescent glow, and as the locomotive got rolling, Robert started getting a lot more creative with it; I think we probably would have used glowing blood on Marv as well if we would have gotten that far into it. But we just started shooting, and *boom*, all of a sudden within four weeks of getting the phone call, we were here filming. The trick was that there were two other segments that hadn't been cast, that hadn't been discussed. Our production meetings were four days before we would start shooting, so when you have questions about things, you're in the middle of shooting something else. So you don't want to interrupt the flow, or distract the director with a question that, as far as he's concerned, takes place a couple weeks away, when he's only worrying about what they're shooting right now."

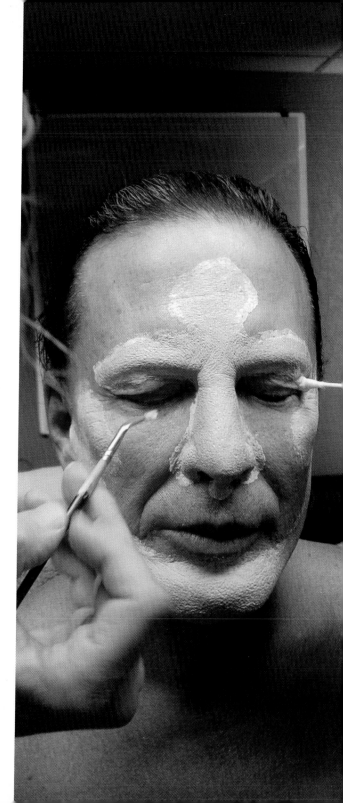

"The trick with Marv was that on *Sin City*, we were shooting digital, we were not shooting film. When you're shooting film, the director will call cut, and then the crew has got to re-light, or you move locations, to set up for the next shot, and you tend to have time between set-ups. Here, that time is gone. Here, they move a couple of lights and they're ready to start filming again. I really spent the four or five weeks of prep that we had on Marv studying the book, and getting the stages in my head so well that I would go to Brian Bettwy, the 1st Assistant Director, and say, 'If we're shooting this scene, he would be in this make-up.' So I was responsible for making sure that Marv was in the correct make-up stage for every shot, no matter how many changes per day. On top of that, we had two Marv stunt doubles that had their own prosthetics. Everyone's face is a little different, so we had to make-up stunt coordinator Jeff Dashnaw, who wore the same forehead and nose but a smaller chin, and then we had to make-up stuntman Mike Justus, whose face is thin and long, so we accentuated his jaw and his nose; those were all custom sculpts on each of those people. So we had three make-ups, three different wigs and, depending on what was shooting, we had to have each guy in the correct

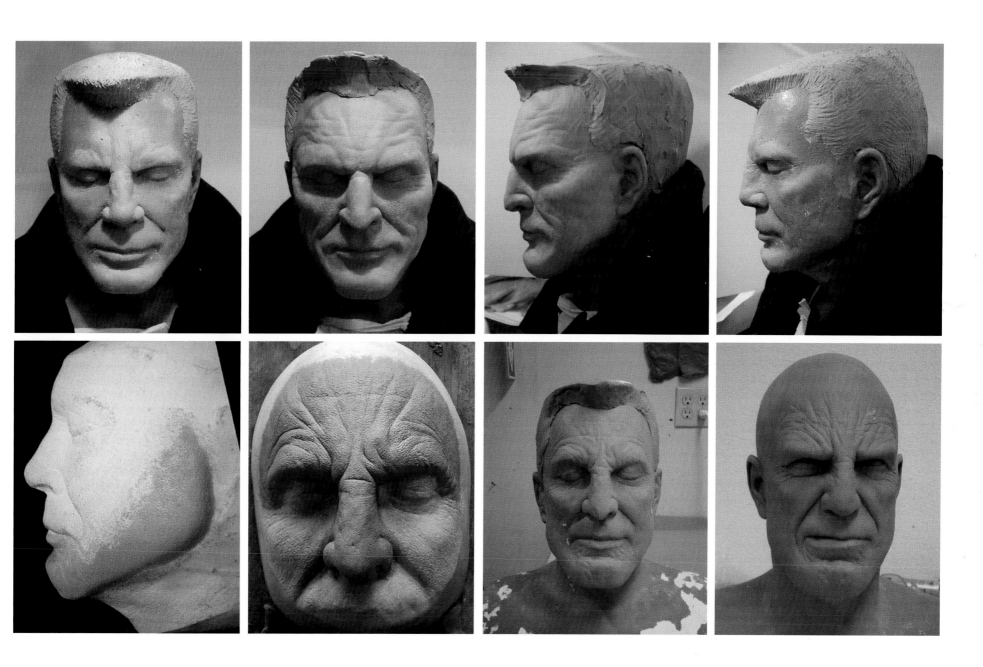

107

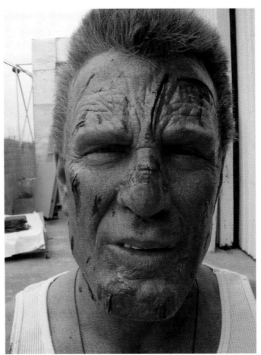
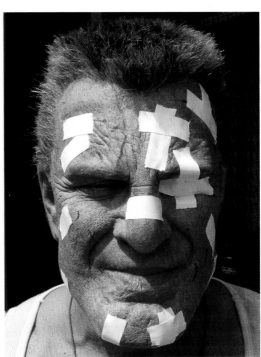

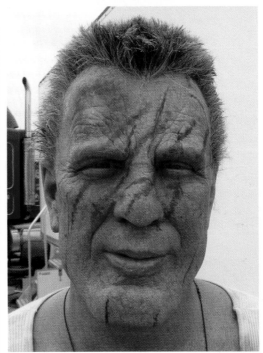
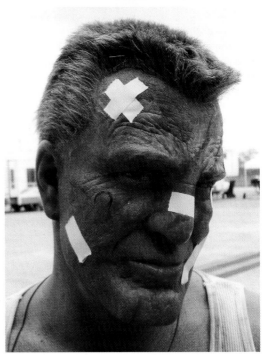

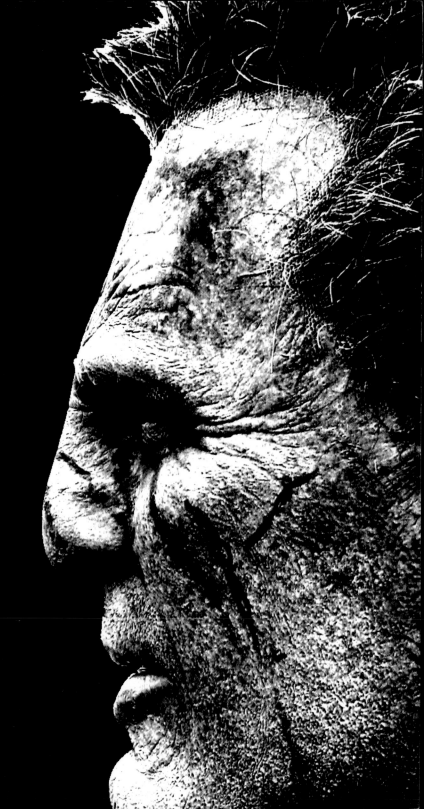

make-up stage for whatever he was going to be used for in that particular shot. So if sometimes we would have Mickey in one stage, and we'd have Mike Justus in another stage, and we'd have Jeff in the third stage, and then you had to keep track of what shot they're doing, and make sure that the stunt guys are in there. Brian was great because he would come to me with a preliminary call sheet and say, 'This is tomorrow's work. We need to go from stage two, to stage seven, to stage four, to stage eight, to stage six.' And I would say, 'Well change this order, put him in this stage, and this stage, and this stage first, and then we'll go back because it's easy.' So we had to do that everyday, having to carefully plan each day because we didn't have the luxury of long make-up change-overs. I think the longest make-up change we ever had was half an hour, or forty minutes at the most. So it was challenging. Mickey played fifteen days, so every single day we were the first ones there, and Mickey would go in, and one of the stunt guys would go in, and then it would be, 'We just hit set, what stage are we doing?' It was tough."

-Greg Nicotero
KNB

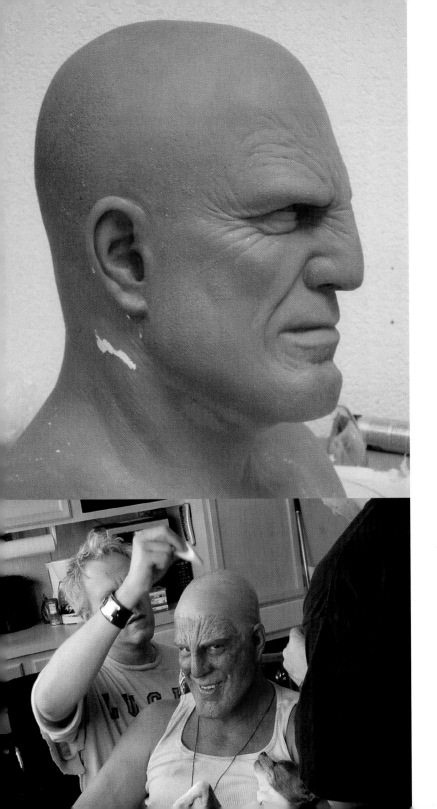

ON MILLER AND ROURKE

"The first time we came on set with Mickey Rourke, Frank was afraid. We did a camera test of the final Marv look, and Frank sat with Mickey, because Frank played a priest in one scene, and the two of them read lines back and forth. Robert was standing back and listening, and Frank just kept pulling him to one side, saying, 'God, when you hear his voice it's like rubbing gravestones together.' He said that he was terrified. Mickey's got this sort of untouchable presence about him anyway, and when he's in his mode, you don't want to have to walk up to him and say, 'Mickey, come here, I just gotta touch your blood up a little.' You just don't want to get near him because of the presence that he gives out, especially when he's in that Marv mode, and he's got the cigarette, and he's got the jacket on, and the gun. It's been interesting to watch Frank's knowledge of what I do grow because when we did the first make-up test on Marv at KNB in Los Angeles, he responded very positively. The first pass of the make-up was very subtle and kept most of Mickey's face and only slightly accentuated his nose and chin. Robert, after studying it, said, 'What if we tried more on the nose? And what if we brought the chin out more? Let's really go for it.' And Frank said, 'You mean we can go even further?' I think he assumed that would be it, when we really had so many other places we could go."

-Greg Nicotero
KNB

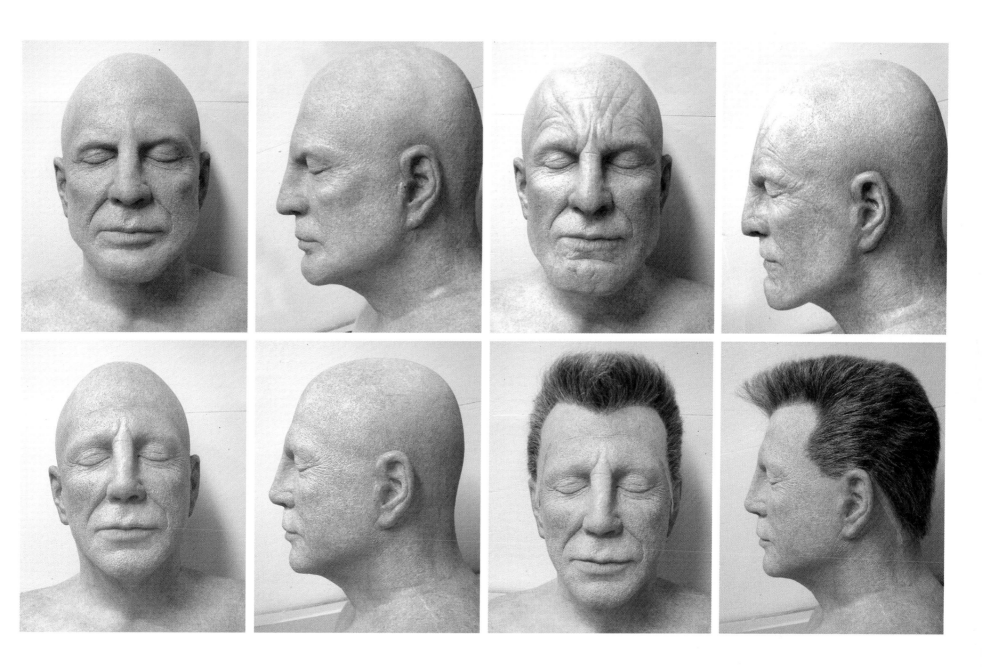

ON JACKIE BOY

"With Benicio, it was one of the first times I can ever remember where an actor came in for a head cast and looked at the graphic novel and said, 'I want to look more like the guy in the book. I think I need more.' I had flown from Austin to L.A. to meet with him because I wanted to make sure that we captured the spirit of Jackie Boy's character, and I said, 'Listen, I've spent two and a half months with Robert and Frank, and I know how to get into their heads now in terms of what they want. So in my opinion, if you want to look more like the book, let's square off your chin a little bit, let's give you a longer, thinner, more Roman nose. Those two pieces in conjunction with your hair down will make you look more like Jackie Boy.' And he just said, 'Great.' Jake Garber was on location for this segment, along with Mike McCarty and Gino Crognale. We had several other gore gags that played, along with the Jackie Boy effects. So we literally designed and built the prosthetics because the actor said he felt it was important to visually identify him as Jackie Boy. And boy did he bring it to life. Mitch Devane sculpted the make-up and corresponding fake heads."

-Greg Nicotero
KNB

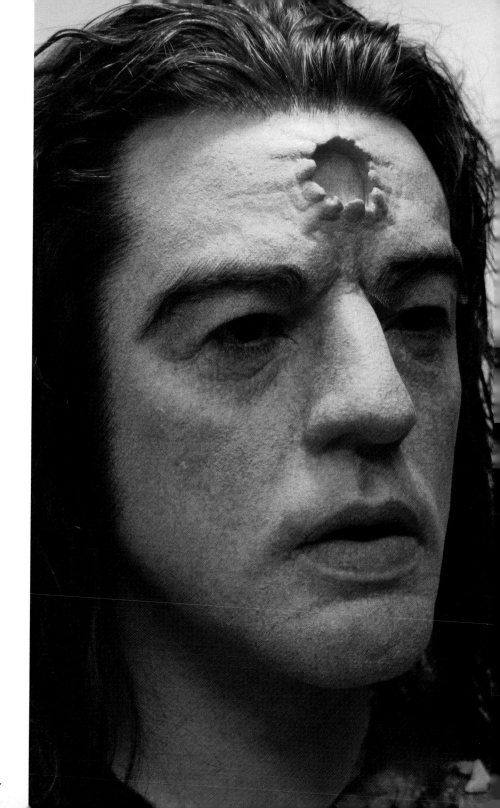

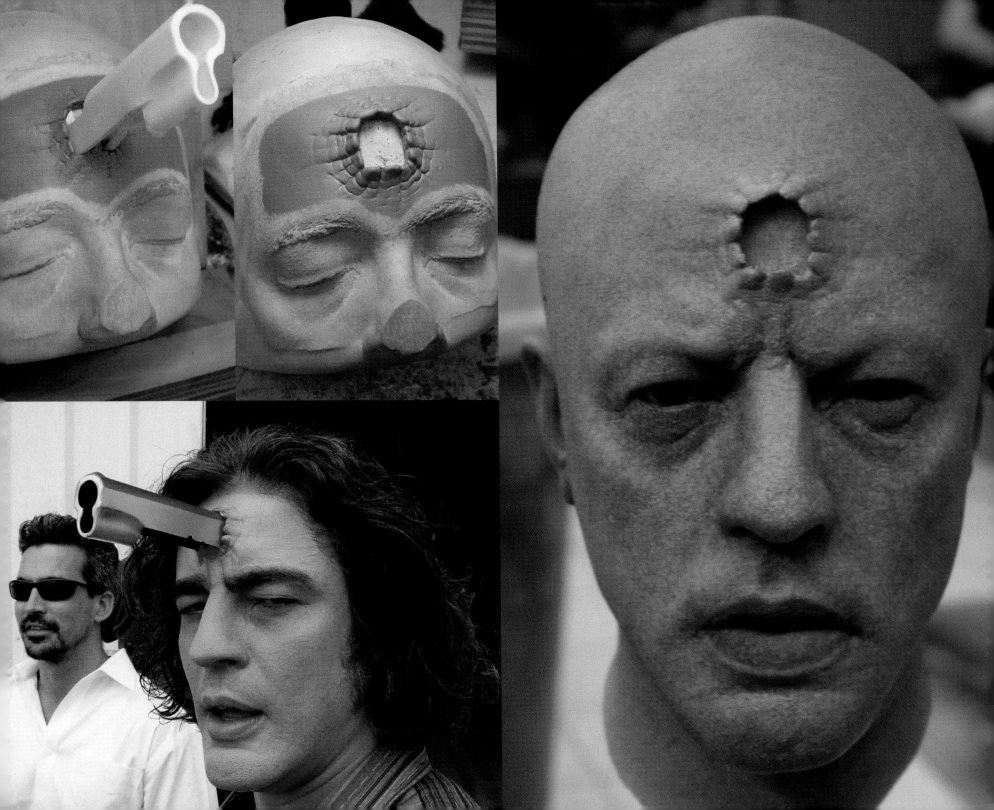

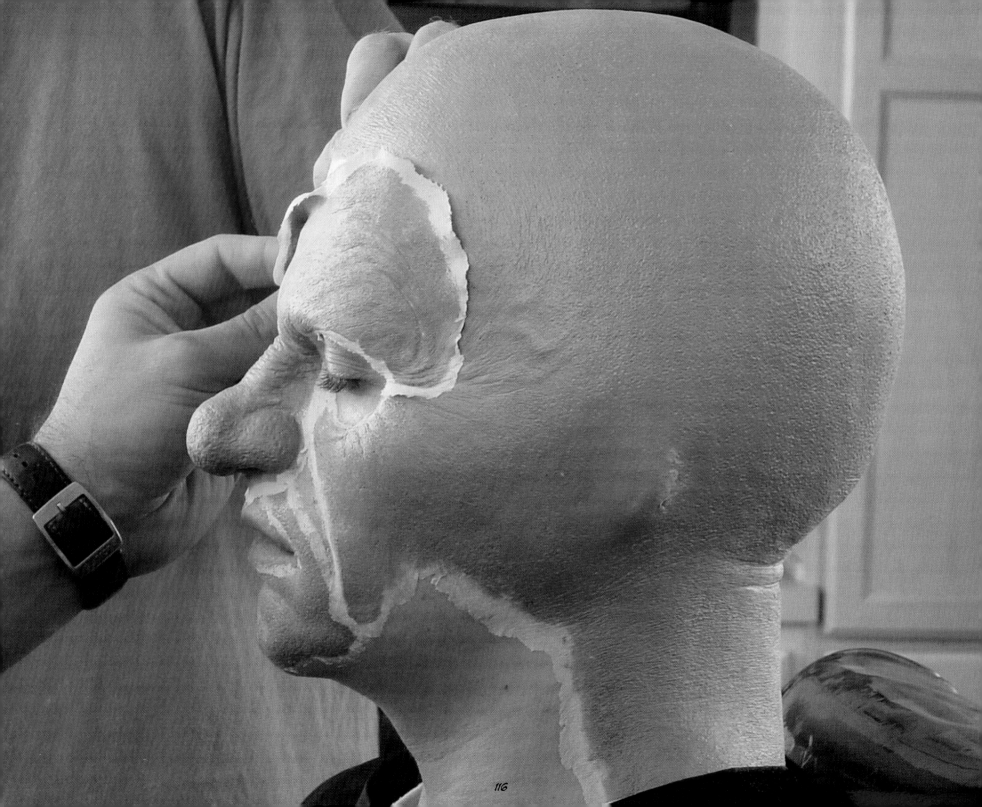

ON YELLOW BASTARD

"They talked about a whole bunch of different casting choices, and I thought we would get a jump on the Yellow Bastard character creating three 1:1 scale busts. Jaremy Aiello and Scott Stoddard worked up these prototypes. This way, Robert and Frank could look at the busts and comment on differences between the sculptures. We used drawings right out of the graphic novel, keeping an eye on details about the wrinkles under his eyes, the size and shape and positioning of his ears, and the shape of his nose. We really wanted to try to nail those details, and once we got our actor, we would then translate that approved make-up design to the actor's face."

"Ultimately, what ended up happening was that we got our actor on a Tuesday. It was Nick Stahl from *Carnivale*

and *Terminator 3*. He came to KNB, we literally left Los Angeles the following Tuesday, and that Thursday we were on set shooting Nick in the make-up. We had eight days to do a full head prosthetic which was a whole misshapen head, cheek pieces, nose, forehead, and ears, and then once we glued all that on, we flocked beard stubble and hair onto the make-up. Aside from the excruciating deadline, the other challenge was the color. In each segment there's one color that is saturated into the black and white. In *The Hard Goodbye* it's the red of Goldie's dress, and then in *Yellow Bastard*, the only thing that we see in color is his yellow face, hands, and ultimately his blood. So we did test after test of different colors to paint the make-up so that we would be able to digitally key off of it and get the exact sort of sickly yellow mustard color depicted in Frank's book. Rodriguez requested we paint him blue so he could get a good key and control the color later. We ended up literally painting him blue, and then we did a highlight and shadow, and they keyed off the blue and turned it yellow in post-production. So when you see the movie, everything will be black and white except for the Yellow Bastard character. So then, of course, at the end of the book, you see him almost completely nude.

And I remember saying to Robert initially, 'Well, we won't ever have time to do any body prosthetics 'cause we don't have an actor. But if we could, what would you want to see for that?' And he said, 'Well, I really want to see this gross distended belly.' So, aside from doing the prosthetics for just his face, we had Garrett Immel at KNB sculpt the whole chest and belly as a foam latex appliance that he put on like a vest—he put his arms through and he pulled it over his head. It was a five-hour process because not only did we have to glue the prosthetics on his face and body, but we then had to paint him blue from head to toe, and then highlight and shadow the musculature because you wanted to get the idea that he had this sickly, emaciated body where his ribs were exposed. The make-up was applied by Garrett, Gino and Greg. Nick Stahl's performance absolutely brought that character to life. We'd been unbelievably blessed with Mickey, Benicio and Nick. Those guys all brought those characters to life. You can only do so much when you glue rubber to somebody's face."

"All these guys really don't allow themselves to be inhibited by wearing rubber. When we were doing Nick's make-up, the back of the head would be glued

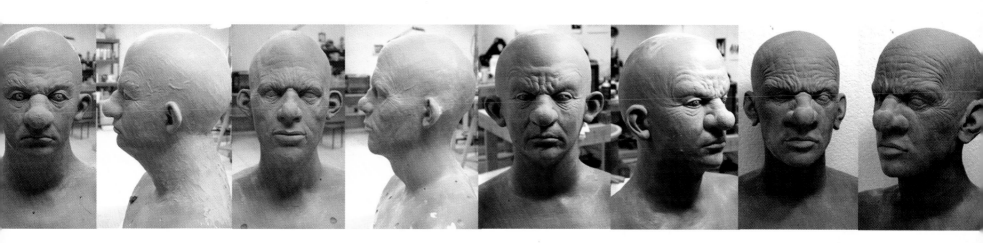

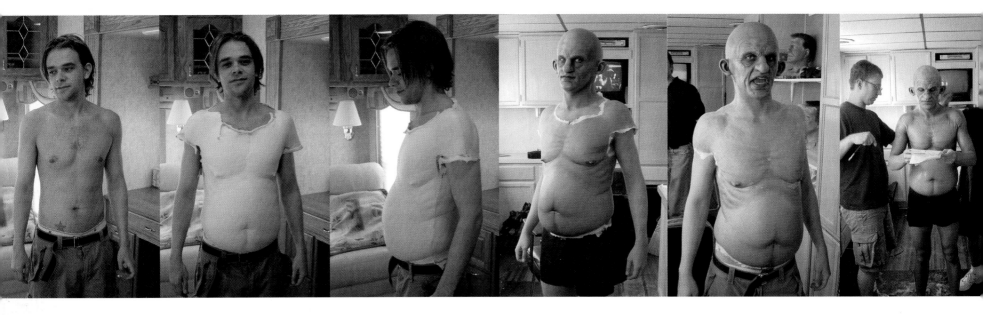

down right on the back of his neck. And the first couple times he put it on I would say, 'Nick, look over this way,' and he would turn his whole body toward me, and I explained to him that subconsciously he was turning his shoulders as well because his neck was all glued in. I told him that he'd really have to practice just holding his neck still and turning his head, and to really translate his movements so that the make-up came to life. And as soon as he had that full-body on, and he arched his shoulders, and he pushed his stomach, he was the Yellow Bastard. Nick weighs like, a hundred pounds; he's a thin guy, so we wanted to keep the look of the Yellow Bastard's scrawny, thin arms and the thin legs with this sort of weird belly. As a result, we purposefully exaggerated the belly, so that when he would arch his shoulders and push his stomach out, he

literally looked like the drawings in the book. It was astounding, really."

"Yellow Bastard is such a great character to begin with, just the way he was drawn and the way he was designed. I remember saying to Frank that the character gets his ear blown off, so wouldn't there be scars from when they tried to put the ear back on or something? And Frank said, 'No, no. They just messed this guy up.' It was as though they'd tried so much to just fix him that it's just procedure, after procedure, after procedure, and none of them work. Eventually they were left with this guy who, if he just walked into a room, everybody would say, 'Ooh, what is that horrible stench?' So, even in terms of the make-up design, I didn't want the ears to be incorporated into the back of the head because

I wanted to be able to place him. His ears were much lower than Nick's real ears were, which just helped translate that cartoony style, and add to the 'comic book style' of the characters. There's a couple shots that I took of Nick on set where he just looks like a creepy guy lurking in the shadows. Then there's other times when he looks like a really over-the-top character. But we come into our trailer in the mornings, and we see Nick, Mickey and Benicio without their make-up on. They go into KNB's trailer themselves, but when they come out, they're those characters."

-Greg Nicotero
KNB

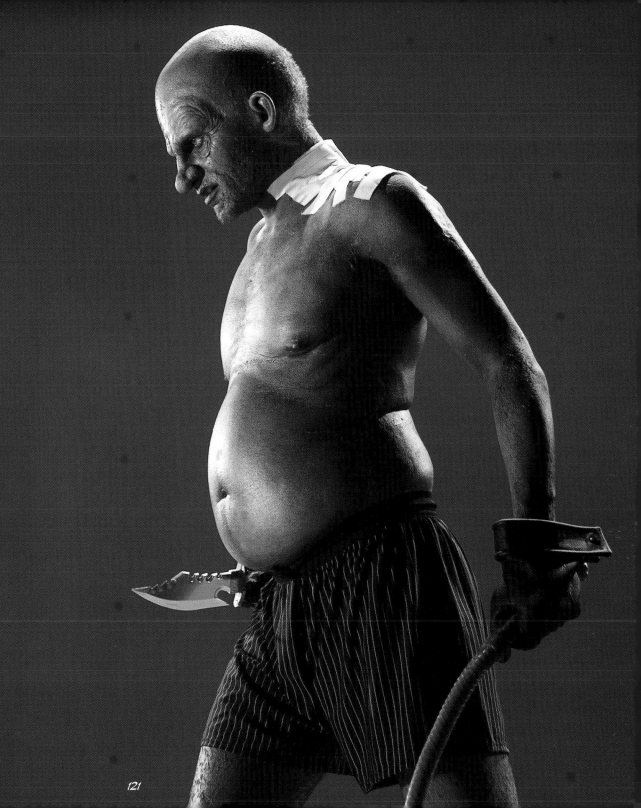

THE BIG FAT K

TITLE UP: THE BIG FAT KILL

INT./EXT. SHELLIE'S PLACE - NIGHT

We hear heavy knuckles BANGING on a door. SHELLIE paces past the window
we're peeking through. Draped in a man's shirt.

                    SHELLIE
          Forget it, man! You can bang on that door all NIGHT if you
          want to. There's no way in hell I'm letting you in.

                    JACKIE-BOY
                    (through door)
          I can't believe you're doing this to me, Shellie. Everything
          we've shared-- it has to mean something to you.

                    SHELLIE
          Oh yeah, it meant plenty. Plenty of nights holding an ice
          pack to my face where you punched it. Plenty of lost pay on
          account of how nobody wants to flirt with a waitress when
          her face is all swelled up and purple from bruises.

Close on Jackie-Boy. Standing outside her chained door.

                    JACKIE-BOY
          I know you're angry. And I forgive that, without you even
          asking me to. I know you think all those things you're
          saying are true. That's why we have to sit down and talk
          things through.

High angle looking down on Shellie. We can see that there is a naked man
standing in the shadows behind her.

                    SHELLIE
          There's a difference between getting honked off at a guy
          who's generally not so bad, and finding out you been sweet
          talked by a total jerk loser who skips out on a wife he
          doesn't even tell you about every time he gets himself
          drunk, which is way too often. Especially the kind of total
          jerk loser who's gotta beat up a girl to make himself feel
          like a man.

DWIGHT steps up slowly behind her.

FRANK MILLER ON DWIGHT

"ULTIMATELY, THE CHARACTER I IDENTIFY MOST WITH IS DWIGHT, BECAUSE HE'S THE ONE WHO TENDS TO GET IN THE MOST TROUBLE, AND HE DOESN'T HAVE THE SUPER HUMAN ABILITIES OF SOMEONE LIKE MARV. THE WORLD IS A CONFUSING PLACE TO HIM, AND HE KIND OF TRIES TO MUDDLE ALONG. SO I GUESS THAT'S THE CLOSEST I'VE COME TO MY HERO."

JACKIE-BOY
That hurt, Shellie. That was cruel. It's one thing for you to play hard to get. I can forgive that. But don't go trying to cut my NUTS off.

SHELLIE
I'm impossible to get -- for YOU. Do yourself a favor, Jackie-Boy, and get help. Like a shrink. Get HELP -- and get lost.

DWIGHT
Go ahead and open the door, Shellie. I'll take care of this.

She turns to Dwight. Worried eyes.

JACKIE-BOY
There's only so much abuse a man can take, baby. Just open the door. You'll see how wrong you've been about me...

DWIGHT
Oblige him Shellie. I'm ready.

SHELLIE
No, Dwight. If he knew you were here with me-- you don't know how bad this could get. This is my apartment and I'm telling you to stay out of this.

Close on Dwight.

DWIGHT
This clown's got a big, mean drunk on-- and he's got four friends out there in the hall, breathing hard and just as drunk as he is.

JACKIE-BOY
HEY! I could swear I heard somebody in there with you, just now. You got somebody with you, baby? You be honest with me!

SHELLIE
Somebody? Jackie-Boy, it's a regular African LOVE-FEST in here. I got me all five starters and half the bench of the Basin City BLUES keeping me company. You feel like taking THEM on?

Back outside with Jackie. The crack of light coming in from the slightly aja door lights his face.

JACKIE BOY

re teasing me, baby. I'm no racist... some of my best
nds... but you're really pushing my buttons. And the
e time you been doing me like this, I been too polite to
t out that any time I want to I can kick this damn door
linters. You know what I am, Baby. You know what I can

hishing dressing, his coat slipping on last.

SHELLIE

right, all right, just a second. OH CHRIST!

's PLACE - NIGHT

door. The whole GANG is in the door now.

SHELLIE

brought your whole pack with you! Don't any off these
s have lives they gotta hang out with you?

JACKIE BOY

re gonna love this, baby. You're gonna call up some of
friends who work the saloon with you and the bunch of
re going to hit every joint in town. It'll be great.

e.

BOZO 1

Guys! Beer!

BOZO 2

zos." Hell, I'd hit her.

SHELLIE

calling up nobody. I wouldn't wish you and your jerk
nds on my worst enemy.

the door.

BOZO 2

k friends." Begging for it is what she's doing. I'd hit
Hey. Stoli. Cool. Very cool.

FRANK MILLER ON BRITTANY MURPHY

"BRITTANY MURPHY PLAYS SHELLIE. SHE'S THE ONLY
CHARACTER WHO IS IN ALL THREE STORIES IN THE MOVIE.
SHE'S A FREQUENT CHARACTER IN SIN CITY, AND ONE OF
THE READER'S, AND NOW THE VIEWER'S, TOUCHSTONES
THROUGHOUT IT; SOMEONE WE SEE AT DIFFERENT STAGES
IN HER LIFE. DIFFERENT ADVENTURES AND MISADVENTURES.
SHE'S AN ABSOLUTE SWEETHEART, AND I'M REFERRING TO
BOTH THE ACTRESS AND THE CHARACTER, WHO IS A BIT OF A
SUCKER FOR A HARD LUCK CASE. THAT USUALLY GETS HER
INTO TROUBLE."

                            JACKIE BOY
Wait a minute. That's a man's shirt you're wearing, and it
sure as hell isn't one of mine!

He grabs her and pulls her close. Face to face.

                            JACKIE-BOY
You've got somebody's love stink all over you! I can smel
it! You've been with another man and you've been with hir
tonight! You invited me and my buddies in here just to ru
my nose in it! Just to humiliate me! Who is he?

                            BOZO 2
Hell, I'd hit her. (Glug)

                            SHELLIE
He's Superman. He flew out the window as soon as he hear
you were coming, cause you scare him so bad.

We see Dwight heading into the bathroom calmly.

                            JACKIE BOY
YOU THINK THIS IS FUNNY?! You think I've got no feelings
all?

We push in on the shadows playing against the floor.

                            SHELLIE
If you're going to slug me, go ahead and get it over with,
sick bastard!

                            JACKIE BOY
There you go lying about me again! Right in front of my
buddies. I never hit a woman in my life!

KRAK! He swats her good.

                            BOZO 2
That's showing her, man!

Jackie slams her into the kitchen counter, the knives fall over in

                            SHELLIE
God damn Bastard! God damn coward!

JACKIE BOY
There's no reason to be hostile, baby. Get in the swing of things. You, me, the guys-- we're all here to have a good time, right? I gotta take a leak.

Close on Shellie.

SHELLIE
I wish you'd dropped by earlier, Jackie Boy. You coulda met my boyfriend. You coulda seen what a real man looks like!

Jackie turns around.

JACKIE BOY
There you go after my nuts again. But I forgive you. I'm a generous guy.

BOZO 2
He is generous. Never a thought for himself. None of us guys ever have to pay for our drinks, not when big Jack's around. The man's a saint.

She spits blood. KHAFF. Bozo 2 leans down beside her.

BOZO 2 (CONT'D)
But that temper of his -- you never shoulda picked on him like you did. My temper, you don't have to worry about. I'm a gentle guy. A romantic. And you're the most beautiful creature I ever seen.

Shellie grabs a big knife. Backs up to the wall.

SHELLIE
Shut up and keep your hands to yourself or I'll cut your pecker off.

BOZO 2
Wooo. I been told.

Bozo 3 holds a gun up.

BOZO 3
Aw, you don't wanna hit the streets dressed like that, honey. It's a jungle out there. Besides. You got a couple phone calls you oughtta be making.

INT. SHELLIE'S PLACE - BATHROOM - NIGHT

In the bathroom. High angle. We see Jackie taking a leak, and Dwight behind the shower curtain.

                    JACKIE BOY
          And make sure you call that dancer. The one with the lasso--
          what's her name? Nancy, right?

                    BOZO 2
                    (off screen)
          Yeah, make sure you call Nancy And tell her to bring her
          lasso! We'll show you a great time!

Angle on Jackie's back. We see DWIGHT's reflection in the sink mirror.
Coming slowly out of the curtain behind Jackie.

                    JACKIE BOY
          I don't hear you making those calls. Don't do me like this,
          baby. This isn't funny anymore.

Over Jackie onto the approaching Dwight... a straight razor being lifted.

                    JACKIE BOY
          Answer me, damn it! I don't need this grief!

Dwight grabs Jackie by the hair. Razor held to his eye.

                    DWIGHT
          Hi. I'm Shellie's new boyfriend and I'm out of my mind.

View from inside the toilet.

                    DWIGHT
          You ever so much as talk to Shellie again -- you even think
          her name-- and I'll cut you in ways that'll make you useless
          to a woman.

                    JACKIE BOY
          You're making a big mistake, man. A big mistake.

                    DWIGHT
          You already made a big mistake yourself. You didn't flush.

PLUNGE! Dwight shoves Jackie face down into the toilet in front of camera.

Side view. Dwight holding him down. Front shot. Dwight holding him down. Top shot. Dwight holding him down.

Jackie lifts his head out of the toilet. GhAGG! Hukk. GHUKK.

Dwight is nowhere to be seen.

> JACKIE BOY
> Son of a bitch...
> (drawing gun)
> I'll blow you in HALF!

EXT. SHELLIE'S PLACE - LEDGE OUTSIDE BATHROOM - NIGHT

Dwight is outside the bathroom, on the apartment ledge.

> JACKIE BOY
> Huh? Where -- Oh, man -- I don't deserve this... TROOPS! Move it! We're outta here!

EXT. SHELLIE'S PLACE - NIGHT

Dwight's POV of them loading into the car down below.

> JACKIE BOY
> No questions! Damn it, don't any of you argue with me!

EXT. SHELLIE'S PLACE - LEDGE OUTSIDE BATHROOM - NIGHT

> SHELLIE
> What the devil did you do to him?

Shellie is leaning out the window of the bathroom. Police chopper overhead.

> DWIGHT
> I just gave him a taste of his own... medicine. I don't think he'll be bothering you again. It's wherever he's headed next that's got me worried. How's your jaw?

> SHELLIE
> I been slapped around worse. Dwight-- he was from a while

CLIVE OWEN ON GREEN SCREEN

"WHEN DOING GREEN SCREEN ON A DIFFERENT TYPE OF MOVIE, LIKE ONE OF THOSE BIG SPECIAL EFFECTS MOVIES, YOU'RE HAVING TO REACT TO THE THINGS THAT AREN'T THERE. BUT THIS IS VERY GROUNDED, BECAUSE ULTIMATELY WE'RE JUST TRYING TO CREATE THE IMAGES FROM THE GRAPHIC NOVEL, AND THE IMPACT THAT THEY HAVE. THE FIRST DAY IS A BIT UNUSUAL, YOU'RE SORT OF ACTING IN THE MIDDLE OF NOWHERE, YOU'RE SORT OF ACTING IN A BUBBLE OF NOTHING. BUT THEN I GOT USED TO IT VERY QUICKLY, AND IT FEELS NATURAL, AND YOU FEEL A REAL SENSE OF ACHIEVEMENT WHEN YOU FEEL THAT YOU'VE NAILED THE IMPACT OF AN IMAGE FROM THE BOOK. AND SOMETIMES YOU FEEL THAT'S JUST HOW THE BOOK IMPACTED ME, THAT IMAGE, OR THAT LITTLE BIT WAS EXACTLY HOW I FELT WHEN READING. IT'S VERY DIFFERENT, AND IT'S EXCITING."

back. Before you showed up again with that new face of yours. It was only cause I felt sorry for him. And it was onl once. I've done some dumb things.

> DWIGHT
> Seeing as how I'm one of those dumb things, I can't give you too hard a time about that, Shellie.

Close on Dwight.

> DWIGHT (CONT'D)
> But this guy -- he might kill somebody if I don't stop him. I'll call you later.

> SHELLIE
> No! Don't go!

Dwight leaps off the ledge.

EXT. SHELLIE'S PLACE - NIGHT

> DWIGHT
> (vo)
> Shellie shouts something I can't quite make out over the racket of a passing police copter. It sounds like "stop" But I can't be sure.

Dwight leaps into his convertible.

EXT. SHELLIE'S PLACE - BATHROOM WINDOW - NIGHT

Shellie in the window. Wind blowing the hair over her face.

> SHELLIE
> Damn it, Dwight. Damn it. You fool. You damn fool.

INT./EXT. DWIGHT'S CONVERTIBLE (MOVING) - NIGHT

Driving behind Jackie Boy. Two car distance between them.

DWIGHT
(vo)
I cut my caddy across the park to pick up Jackie Boy heading
like a bat out of hell up the hill. Speeding. It's a good way
to get yourself noticed. And if you're a murderer with a new
face who's one fingerprint check away from the fast track to
the gas chamber like I am, the last thing you want is to get
noticed.

Close on Dwight driving.

Close on Dwight's eye in rear view mirror, as a cop car flies up from behind
him. Sirens blaring.

DWIGHT (CONT'D)
(vo)
I don't have nearly enough cash on me to bribe this cop...

Cop car fast approaching...

DWIGHT (CONT'D)
(vo)
Do I try to talk my way out of this? Or do I take this cop
down and risk it all?

Jackie swerves his car and knocks a smaller VW off the road.

DWIGHT (CONT'D)
(vo)
Then Jackie Boy saves me a great, big steaming pile of
trouble.

The cop car chases JACKIE now.

DWIGHT (CONT'D)
(vo)
Then I realize where we're headed and my gut tightens up.
Jackie Boy's leading us straight to Old Town. Damn it!

EXT. OLD TOWN - STREET - NIGHT

We see a line of cars heading to Old Town. OLD TOWN GIRLS coming out to see
what the deal is.

133

FRANK MILLER ON BECKY

"BECKY IS QUITE YOUNG, AND SHE IS ONE OF THE GIRLS OF OLD TOWN, AND SHE'S A WORKING GIRL. BUT SHE COMES FROM THE COUNTRY, FROM SOMEWHERE IN THE SOUTHWEST, AND SHE HAS A MOTHER WHO LIVES OUT OF TOWN, WHO SHE'S IN CONSTANT CONTACT WITH, WHO BELIEVES THAT SHE'S A SECRETARY SOMEWHERE, AND HAS NO IDEA OF THE DARK WORLD SHE INHABITS. AND SO A LOT OF HER LIFE IS TRYING TO GET OUT OF THE WORLD SHE'S IN, AND ALSO TO KEEP DECEIVING HER MOTHER ABOUT WHERE SHE'S BEEN SPENDING THE LAST FEW YEARS."

> DWIGHT
> (VO)
> The cop shuts up his siren. He knows he's not the law. Not in Old Town. The ladies are the law here, beautiful and merciless. If you've got the cash and you play by the rules, they'll make all your dreams come true. But if you cross them, you're a corpse.

CLOSE on girls. Beautiful. Hard.

Close on the girl's silently pulling guns. Click CHAKK!

SCREEEECHHH! Cop car spins, and retreats.

INT. JACKIE BOY'S CAR (MOVING) - NIGHT

> BOZO 4
> That squad car's long gone!

> JACKIE BOY
> Did I call it? Was I right?

> BOZO 2
> You're always right, Jack. None of us ever doubted you for a second. But I heard things about these girls. Things they done to guys who got out of line.

> JACKIE BOY
> Who's out of line?

EXT. OLD TOWN - STREET - NIGHT

One of the ladies walks by their car. Dwight steps out of his car and heads toward them. We get a point of view from the building top that MIHO stands on. Miho walks the ledge.

> JACKIE BOY
> Hop in, Sugar. We'll get you there.

> BECKY
> Aw, sweetheart, I work the day shift and it's been a long day. Besides, I don't do group jobs.

134

                    JACKIE BOY
Get in the car, baby. We'll just talk. It'll be nice.

Dwight drops his back against a wall. Guns drawn. Ready.

                    BECKY
I don't do talk jobs, either.

                    JACKIE BOY
Baby doll. I've had me one hell of a bad day. I been beat up
every time I turn around. But the day I get turned down by a
hooker when I got good hard earned cash to pay her with ---
well, there's only so much a man can take!

Dwight is light on his feet as he sprints silent.

                    BECKY
Go try the Alamo, over on Dillon street. That's the Alamo,
not the Amigo. The Amigo's a fag joint.

                    JACKIE BOY
You're having a good time, doing me like this, aren't you?
Humiliating me for no damn reason at all!

EXT. OLD TOWN - GATED ALLEY/SIDE - NIGHT

An Uzi pointing at Dwight's face stops him in his tracks.

                    GAIL
That's far enough, Dwight. We've been on top of these
peckerwoods since they first showed up with that cop behind
them. Everything's under control. Enjoy the show.

                    DWIGHT
                    (vo)
There's no use arguing with her. The ladies are their own
enforcers.

                    GAIL
So how's the barmaid? You know, the one who never shuts up?

                    DWIGHT
Not right now, Gail.

FRANK MILLER ON MIHO

"I ADORED MIHO FROM THE MOMENT I FIRST STARTED DRAWING HER. SHE'S A CHARACTER WHO, IN A WAY, IS FROM A DIFFERENT REALM THAN *SIN CITY*. SHE'S A CHARACTER OF MAGIC MUCH MORE THAN THE OTHERS ARE. I DON'T MEAN SHE CAN FLY OR ANYTHING, BUT CLOSE TO IT. AND SHE IS ALSO A CHARACTER OF MYSTERY. IN *SIN CITY* EVERYBODY TALKS A LOT. MIHO NEVER SAYS A WORD, AND SHE'S COMPLETELY AND LITERALLY LETHAL. WORKING WITH DEVON HAS BEEN A REAL TREAT. IT WAS HARD FOR ME TO IMAGINE FINDING SOMEBODY WHO COULD BRING MIHO TO LIFE, BUT DEVON—WITH THOSE EYES, AND WITH THE SUPERB WAY SHE MOVES—I THINK WE'RE ONTO SOMETHING REMARKABLE."

Angle, higher. Gail pulls a smoke from a pack with her teeth.

> GAIL
> Wound up a little tight, aren't we? That's your whole problem, Dwight. You worry too much. That, and your lousy taste in women. Those clowns down the way-- they some of the barmaid's boyfriends?

> DWIGHT
> One of them thinks he is. He's out of control. I followed him here to make sure he didn't hurt any of the girls.

> GAIL
> (chuckles)
> Us helpless little girls.

She lights her cig. Angle. He eyes her.

> GAIL (CONT'D)
> Us girls are safe as we can be, Lancelot. But those boys in that Plymouth are one mistake away from seeing what MIHO can do. She's been aching for some practice.

EXT. OLD TOWN - GATED ALLEY - NIGHT

HIGH angle, Over Miho, looking down on the action.

> BECKY
> You're running out of alley, cowboy. Turn around. Save yourself and your buddies a ton of grief.

> JACKIE BOY
> You're a sassy little thing, but you ain't hardly in any kind of position to be making threats.

Close on Miho - her throwing star earrings dangling in the desert win RUMMMMBBLLLL KANK! KANK!

Two girls slam a gate shut.

> DWIGHT
> (vo)
> The trap is set, locked, and ready to spring. So what? They're scum. They deserve what's coming. So why this rotten feeling in my gut that something is awfully wrong?

EXT. OLD TOWN - GATED ALLEY/SIDE - NIGHT

Close on Dwight and Gail.

                    DWIGHT
          They haven't killed anybody I know about. It got pretty bad
          at Shellie's place, but they didn't kill anybody.

                    GAIL
          And they won't.

                    DWIGHT
                    (vo)
          Why this rotten feeling? Something Shellie said. I can't
          place it....

EXT. OLD TOWN - GATED ALLEY - NIGHT

Jackie still coasts besides the walking Becky.

                    JACKIE BOY
          ...Okay! Okay. I sounded off a little more than I should have.
          I'm just a little on edge.

                    BECKY
          It's not a woman you need, it's a good night's sleep. You
          couldn't handle a woman, the state you're in.

Camera inside the car looking over them to Sugar.

                    BOZO 2
          She's saying you ain't got what it takes, Jack!

                    JACKIE BOY
          You want to see it? You want to see what I got?

                    BECKY
          I seen all shapes. All sizes.

Jackie pulls a gun and aims it at her face. Camera still inside the car.

                    JACKIE BOY
          Seen this? Get in the car!

BECKY
Sugar. You just gone and done the dumbest thing in your
whole life!

Close on MIHO pulling a huge throwing star. It ricochets perfectly off the
side of the building, and strikes JACKIE BOY perfectly across his wrist.
Severing his gun hand. CHUNK!

SHING SHING! Miho's Two samurai swords are pulled.

JACKIE BOY
Oh Jesus, my hand.

Close on the hand on the street, still gripping the gun. The star embedded in
the ground.

JACKIE BOY (CONT'D)
My hand. Oh, Jesus. My hand. What's going on? What's going
on?

Jackie Boy is on his knees now holding his stump. Miho flies down from above
onto the top of the car. Her swords cut through the roof.

We see the swords come through the roof and 2 bozo's heads.

BOZO 2
Oh god no...

SHAK!

BOZO 2 (CONT'D)
Oh god...

Bozo 2 throws the car door open and makes a run for it. SHAK! His head gets a
lot further than his body.

His head bounces past a crawling Jackie Boy. KONK.

JACKIE BOY
This is crazy. This is crazy. Out of nowhere. For no reason!

Jackie aims his retrieved gun at Miho. She moves from side to side. Quick.
Taunting.

JACKIE BOY (CONT'D)
Go ahead! Dance around all you want to! I got you right
where I want you and you know it!

EXT. OLD TOWN - GATED ALLEY/SIDE - NIGHT

Dwight kicks into a crouch. Ready for action.

                    DWIGHT
          He's got the drop on her!

                    GAIL
          He's got squat. He's dead. He's just too damn dumb to know
          it. Don't get in her way.

EXT. OLD TOWN - GATED ALLEY - NIGHT

                    JACKIE BOY
          You got no idea what kind of mistake you and your sassy slut
          friend made, maiming me like this! This is a career ending
          wound. There's gonna be hell to pay!

High angle of Dwight sneaking up behind Jackie.

                    DWIGHT
          Watch your step, Jackie Boy.

Jackie Boy slips on his own bloody severed hand, butt first onto the upright
throwing star jutting out of the ground.

CHUNK! Close on Dwight's reaction. "Yeesh."

                    JACKIE BOY
                 (star poking out)
          Don't anybody laugh! This isn't funny!

He stumbles up to a standing position.

                    JACKIE BOY (CONT'D)
          I got friends you can't imagine! Every one of you is gonna
          burn! But first you're eating some bullets, you scrawny Jap
          whore!

Gail is approaching. High angle showing all involved.

                    DWIGHT
          Hang it up. She's just playing with you. You're only making
          it worse.

FRANK MILLER ON BENICIO DEL TORO

"WORKING WITH BENICIO WAS A LOT LIKE WORKING WITH MICKEY IN THAT THEY BRING AN AWFUL LOT TO THE ENTERPRISE, AN AWFUL LOT IS UNEXPECTED. NEITHER ARE BIG ON ADLIBBING, THEY'RE NOT COMING IN TRYING TO CHANGE THINGS SO MUCH AS BRING THEM TO FRUITION, BUT IN UNPREDICTABLE WAYS. BENICIO IS AN UNUSUALLY GIFTED PHYSICAL ACTOR. IN COMIC BOOKS YOU GO FROM A PANEL TO A PANEL, AND THERE'S THE WHITE GUTTER BETWEEN THEM, AND IN YOUR MIND YOU'VE MADE UP A HUNDRED IMAGES THAT I DIDN'T HAVE TO DRAW BECAUSE I JUST GIVE YOU THE KEY MOMENTS. BUT IN MOVIES YOU NEED TO FILL THOSE MOMENTS A BIT MORE. BENICIO WAS VERY GOOD AT FINDING PREPOSTEROUS AND WONDERFUL WAYS TO FILL THOSE GUTTERS. YOU KNOW, HOW DOES A MAN GET A GUN FROM HIS OWN SEVERED HAND? BENICIO CAME UP WITH THE OBVIOUS SOLUTION—HE USES HIS TEETH. HE'S FULL OF MOMENTS LIKE THAT, AND HE USES HIS FORMIDABLE PHYSICAL PRESENCE TO GREAT ADVANTAGE."

Close on Miho throwing a small pipe.

> JACKIE BOY
> You shut the hell up!

THUNK! The pipe lands right inside Jackie's barrel.

> DWIGHT
> Don't pull the trigger. She blocked the barrel. It'll
> backfire.

> JACKIE BOY
> I told you to shut up!

Jackie boy whirls around and fires at Dwight. Sure enough. BLAM! The barrel disassembles.

KUNK! The barrel of the gun flies back into Jackie's forehead. The barrel now juts out from his skull. He falls to the ground in a sitting position, back against the wall.

> JACKIE BOY (CONT'D)
> I can't see. What's happening? I can't hear anything.

> DWIGHT
> For God's sake, Miho. Finish him.

> GAIL
> Yeah, make it quick, will you?

SLASH!

> DWIGHT
> (vo)
> She doesn't quite chop his head off. She makes a Pez
> dispenser out of him.

Other armed girls step out of the shadows.

> DWIGHT (CONT'D)
> (vo)
> Then it's straight to business, stretching the corpses out on
> the alley floor and going through their pockets, divvying up
> cash when they find it.

Dwight searches Jackie. Stops at a discovery.

DWIGHT (CONT'D)
(vo)

I'm fishing around in Jackie-Boy's pants. His wallet is
packed. Mastercard. Discover. Platinum American Express.
Snapshots of two adorable strawberry blonde girls who
must be his kids. And nearly three hundred bucks worth of
twenties that I'm not too proud to stuff into my own pockets.
Then I find an atom bomb. Jackie boy, you son of a bitch.

BOOM! Lightening cracks the sky. Hard rain.

High angle as the rain falls over the corpse, Dwight, and the approaching
Gail.

DWIGHT (CONT'D)
(vo)

That rotten feeling in my gut. Something Shellie said when I
jumped from her window. There was a helicopter that kicked
up such a racket I couldn't quite make out what she said.

Gail approaches the wallet.

Dwight's POV. Close up on the BADGE. The girls looking on.

DWIGHT (CONT'D)
(vo)

I thought Shellie said "stop." She said "cop." Detective
Lieutenant Jack Rafferty. "Iron Jack," the papers call him.
A goddamn hero cop.

High angle shot. Gail sees it. "GODDAMN IT!"

DWIGHT (CONT'D)
(vo)

It's held for years, the shaky truce. The cops get a slice of
the profits and free entertainment when they throw a party.
The girls get to administer their own brand of justice.
They get to defend their own turf. If a cop blunders into
the neighborhood and he's not shopping for what the girls
are selling, they send him packing. But they send him back
alive. That's the rules. That's the TRUCE. The cops stay out.
That keeps the girls free to keep the pimps and the mob out.
This'd be a dream come true for the mob. Iron Jack Rafferty,
hero cop, tortured, mutilated, murdered by the girls of old
town. The Cops will come down on us like the wrath of God if
they find out. Old town will be left wide open. It'll be war.
The streets will run red with blood. Women's blood.

Close on the dying Jackie Boy.

FRANK MILLER ON GAIL

"MANY OF THESE CHARACTERS STARTED IN OTHER STORIES
IN *SIN CITY* AND THEN RESURFACED, ALMOST ON THEIR OWN.
GAIL STARTED AS A MINOR CHARACTER IN THE STORY, *THE
HARD GOODBYE*, THE FIRST EPISODE OF THIS MOVIE. AND
SOMETHING ABOUT HER JUST KEPT WORKING, AND SHE
ENDED UP BEING THE MAJOR LOVE INTEREST OF THE MIDDLE
SECTION, *BIG FAT KILL*. IT'S A VERY DEMANDING ROLE BECAUSE
SHE HAS TO BE MANY DIFFERENT THINGS. SHE HAS TO BE,
OBVIOUSLY, VERY SEXY, VERY ANGRY, FIERY, AND ALSO QUITE
A BIT FUNNY. ROSARIO SEEMS TO BE DOING ALL OF THIS IN A
WALK. ON AND OFF THE SET SHE IS SO ABLE TO PERSONIFY
GAIL, THAT MADE MY JOB WAS VERY, VERY EASY."

THE OLD TOWN GIRL WITH THE ZORRO MASK AND SIX GUNS IS PORTRAYED BY ROBERT RODRIGUEZ'S SISTER, PATRICIA VONNE. A NATIVE OF SAN ANTONIO, VONNE IS A SUCCESSFUL SINGER-SONGWRITER, WHOSE MUSIC HAS PREVIOUSLY BEEN FEATURED IN RODRIGUEZ'S *ONCE UPON A TIME IN MEXICO*.

DWIGHT (CONT'D)
(vo)
I shove the dead cop's badge inside my coat. It hangs heavy against my chest.

BECKY
The cops. The mob... things are gonna go back to the way they used to be...

Close on the different girls' reactions.

GAIL
The hell they will! We got guns. We'll fight the cops and the mob and any who try to move in on us! We'll go to war!

DWIGHT
Don't be stupid Gail, you wouldn't stand a chance. Get me a car. Make sure it's a hardtop with a decent engine. I'll hide the bodies.

High angle looking down on the scene.

GAIL
What, you forget that squad car that trailed them here? The cops know Rafferty came here! They'll check the river! They'll check the sewer! They'll find him and they'll come gunning for us!

Miho has her sword at the ready.

DWIGHT
I'll haul the bodies to the pits. The cops won't check the pits. Get that gun out of my face or I'll smack you.

Miho moves to my back. One word from Gail and she'll cut me in half. Gail leans in close. Her gun closer.

GAIL
They'll be watching the roads. They'll catch you! They'll come gunning. It'll be the bad old days all over again. The pimps, the drugs, the beatings. The rapes.

DWIGHT
They won't be watching the roads. Not yet they won't. Get me a damn hardtop! If I don't make it you can have your war. Get that gun out of my face, now!

142

SMACK! He swats Gail. Miho watches.

                    GAIL
     You bastard!

The other girls draw guns. Gail wipes her face.

                    GAIL (CONT'D)
     I forgot how quick you are.

They kiss. Swept up in the rain.

                    DWIGHT
                    (vo)
     My warrior woman. She almost yanks my head clean off.
     Shoving my mouth into hers so hard it hurts. Her kiss a
     savage thing, an explosion that blasts away the dull gray
     years between the now and that one fiery night when she was
     mine. My Valkyrie. There's no place in this world for our
     kind of fire. If I have to die for you tonight, I will.

Close on Dwight, face pelted by hard rain. Gail behind him.

                    DWIGHT (CONT'D)
     ... A hardtop. With a decent engine. And make sure it's got a
     big trunk!
                    (vo)
     Gail's eyes are burning into the back of my skull like a pair
     of laser beams. If that kiss was our last good-bye it was a
     damn good one and we'd both just as soon leave it that way.

EXT. OLD TOWN - GATED ALLEY - NIGHT

Top shot of the girls checking out the car. The bodies laid out nice and
neat.

                    DWIGHT
     Where'd you find that heap? Just look at that trunk! We'll
     never fit them all in!

                    GIRL
     It ain't like we had a lotta time.

                    BECKY
     Gail? Unless there's something you want me to do, you think

FRANK MILLER ON QUENTIN, MIHO AND THE BRIDE
"I THINK QUENTIN AND I ARE IN SOME SORT OF COLLISION OF
UNIVERSES THESE DAYS, ESPECIALLY WORKING WITH HIM ON
BIG FAT KILL. I DIDN'T EVEN KNOW IT, BUT THE SWORDS THAT
MIHO USES ARE THE SAME ONES THAT UMA USED IN KILL BILL.
SO, WHO KNOWS, MAYBE THEY MET ONCE."

maybe I could go home? All this blood and stuff, it's got me feeling kinda like maybe I'm gonna hurl.

                    GAIL
Sure, Becky. Go on home. But don't you talk to anybody, not even your Mom. You promise me.

                    BECKY
I promise.

SHANK! SHANK!

                    GAIL
Yeesh.

Dwight has his shirt off. Holding a body up by its ankles as Miho cuts them down to size. SHAKK SHAKK SHAKK! SHAKK!

EXT. OLD TOWN - PAYPHONE - NIGHT

Tak tak tak. Becky dials a payphone. Two other girls behind her.

                    GIRL 2
Hey! Becky -- Gail said no calls!

                    BECKY
I just wanna hear my mom's voice. I won't tell her nothing. Please don't say nothing to Gail.

INT./EXT. HARDTOP CAR - NIGHT

Hard rain falls on the car as it drives.

                    DWIGHT
                    (vo)
Dizzy dames. What were they thinking, sticking me with a beat-up bucket of bolts like this? Somebody oughtta take it out back and shoot it. It'd be a mercy.

Hard rain on the rooftop. Hard drops hitting Dwight.

Over JACKIE BOY, propped up in the passenger seat onto Dwight. The barrel still jutting from Jackie's skull.

ROSARIO DAWSON ON ALEXIS BLEDEL

"ALEXIS IS ALMOST SCARY. HER EYES, AS BIG AS THEY CAN GET. AND HER ENERGY. AND HER LITTLE PIGEON-TOED THING WHEN SHE STANDS. AND HER WHOLE BODY LANGUAGE. HER VOICE, EVERYTHING IS SO PERFECT. I ACTUALLY WANT TO JUST SQUEEZE HER, OR SLAP HER, OR SOMETHING. I'M JUST SO EXCITED BECAUSE SHE'S THE POLAR OPPOSITE OF GAIL, AND IT'S REALLY FUN TO WORK WITH HER. SHE'S REALLY VERY GOOD. THE CHANDELIER EARRINGS, AND THE EYES, AND HER VOICE. THERE'S SOMETHING SO SWEET ABOUT HOW NAIVE SHE IS, I JUST WANTED TO TAKE A BITE OUT OF HER NECK, THAT'S BASICALLY THE ONLY WAY I COULD PUT IT."

Dwight gigs into Jackie's pockets for some smokes.

                    DWIGHT (CONT'D)
                    (vo)
We were barely able to get the trunk to stay closed as it
was, we'd packed it so tight. There wasn't anything we could
do but pile Jackie in right next to me.

Close on cig pack.

On DWIGHT as he lights up. Over onto Jackie, who speaks.

                    JACKIE BOY
Gotcha smoking, huh, bud?

                    DWIGHT
Shut the hell up, Jackie. You're dead. I'm just imagining
this. So shut the hell up.

Over Jackie onto Dwight.

                    JACKIE BOY
Tells ya something about your state of mind, don't it? Your
nerves are shot. It's gotcha hearing things. It's gotcha
smokin.' You know, it's true -- nobody ever really quits. A
smoker's a smoker, when the chips are down. And your chips
are DOWN, pal. You're sucking sidewalk.

                    DWIGHT
I'm fine, you shut the hell up!

Something draws Jackie Boy's attention.

                    JACKIE BOY
Aw, will you look at that? Those hookers let you down, honey
bunch! What're you gonna do when you run outta gas. Call
Triple A?

Close on the gas gauge. Pegged at EMPTY.

                    JACKIE BOY (CONT'D)
You're a sucker for the babes. You ain't even gonna make it
to the pits, you schmuck!

                    DWIGHT
Shut the hell up! I'll make it!

ROBERT RODRIGUEZ ON QUENTIN TARANTINO

"QUENTIN AND I HAVE BEEN FRIENDS SINCE 1992, AND I KNEW THAT FRANK WOULD FALL INTO THE FOLD VERY QUICKLY; AND WHEN WE ALL FIRST GOT TOGETHER, FRANK FELT LIKE WE'D ALL BEEN SEPARATED AT BIRTH. I WANTED QUENTIN TO EXPERIENCE DIGITAL FILMMAKING BY HAVING HIM SHOOT A SEGMENT OF A MOVIE FOR ME, SO HE COULD SEE HOW IT'S REALLY ABOUT GOING FOR PERFORMANCE, AND NOT ABOUT THE TECHNICAL SIDE OF MAKING MOVIES. MOST PEOPLE THINK PERFORMANCE WOULD GET LOST ON A GREEN SCREEN, BUT THE WAY WE SHOOT, THAT'S ALL WE'RE CONCENTRATING ON. QUENTIN SHOT A SEGMENT OF *SIN CITY*, AND AT THE END OF IT TURNED TO ME AND SAID, 'MISSION ACCOMPLISHED. NOW I KNOW WHY YOU BROUGHT ME DOWN HERE. I WANT TO SHOOT A WHOLE MOVIE LIKE THIS NOW, BUT I WANT YOU TO PHOTOGRAPH IT.' IT WAS GREAT FUN HAVING HIM THERE DIRECTING WITH US, AND I EVEN STUCK HIM ON ONE OF THE CAMERAS TO OPERATE. THAT WAS A GREAT TIME. SITTING SIDE BY SIDE LIKE OLD SCHOOL CHUMS, MANNING CAMERAS AND DIRECTING *SIN CITY*. FRANK CAME UP TO ME AT THE END OF THAT FIRST DAY WITH QUENTIN AND SAID, 'THIS IS THE MOST FUN DAY I'VE EVER HAD IN MY LIFE.'"

FRANK MILLER ON QUENTIN TARANTINO

"IT WAS FASCINATING WORKING WITH QUENTIN BECAUSE I GOT TO SEE A COMPLETELY DIFFERENT STYLE THAN ROBERT'S. EVEN THOUGH THE THREE OF US SHARE SO MUCH IN TERMS OF A POP CULTURE SENSIBILITY, AND RATHER MACABRE SENSE OF HUMOR, IT WAS SHOCKINGLY HARMONIOUS, GIVEN THE ENORMITY OF THE THREE EGOS IN THE ROOM. WE ACTUALLY WERE JUST A BUNCH OF LITTLE KIDS IN A TREE FORT HAVING A BALL. SO THE DAY QUENTIN WAS ON THE SET WAS ALMOST LIKE A PARTY."

HONK! Dwight swerves, barely missing an oncoming truck.

                    JACKIE BOY
          This is great! Just like being in a buddy movie!

                    DWIGHT
Shut up!

EEEEEEEE!

                    JACKIE BOY
Told you so.

A COP BIKE rips up the road behind them.

                    JACKIE BOY (CONT'D)
You are SCREWED. YOU ARE OUT! You are finished! Stick a fork in it! You're swirling around the bottom of the bowl and nose-diving down the pipe! It's over! You're flushed!

                    DWIGHT
                    (vo)
This time I can't bring myself to tell him to shut up. Sure he's an asshole. Sure he's dead. Sure I'm just imagining that he's talking. None of that stops the bastard from being absolutely right. I don't have a prayer of outrunning him. Not in this heap.

High angle.

                    COP
PULL OVER!

                    DWIGHT
                    (vo)
The only question left is whether I'm gonna kill him or not. Tough call. For all I know he's an honest cop, a regular guy, a working stiff with a mortgage, a wife and a pile of kids. My hands move all on their own, sliding one of my guns to my lap and thumbing back the hammer. I don't know what to do.

                    JACKIE BOY
Oh, the angst! The torment! You're breaking my heart! You're making him mad. You better stop.

                    DWIGHT
        Whatever you say.

He hits the brake. The tires screech. Jackie Boy lurches forward, smashing
the barrel deeper into his head when he hits the dashboard. CHUNK!

EXT. STREET - HARDTOP - NIGHT

The cop walks up through the rain. Flashlight drawn.

Dwight readies his gun.

                    COP
        Your friend here party a little too hard tonight?

                    DWIGHT
        Yeah, I'm the designated driver.

                    COP
        Well, you're driving with a busted tail light. I'll let you off
        with a warning.

Close on EMPTY gauge. Turns red. The cop drives away.

                    DWIGHT
        What next?

EXT. TAR PITS - NIGHT

Lightning illuminates a Dinosaur of the Pits. Dwight is pushing the car.

                    DWIGHT
                    (vo)
        The tank goes dry a quarter mile from the pits. I shove the
        T-Bird the rest of the way. A couple million years ago, the
        Santa Yolanda tar pits trapped some of the dumber residents
        of the neighborhood, preserving the skeletons of cave men
        and woolly mammoths and a sabre tooth tiger or two. More
        recently, the county turned the pits into a theme park and
        found the goop could suck in money, too. Until a railing
        broke and somebody's grandmother fell in and had a heart
        attack before they could pull her out. There was nothing
        left to do but swallow the cost and shut the place down.

We see DWIGHT through the cross hairs of a scope rifle.

> DWIGHT (CONT'D)
> A few minutes more work and it'll all be over. I'll catch a
> train out of Sacred Oaks and go home and call it a night.

BLAM!!

> DWIGHT (CONT'D)
> GAAA!

Black out.

INT. OLD TOWN – TBD – NIGHT

A huge Man with in a chauffeur's hat grips a naked GAIL by the moonli
window.

> MANUTE
> Don't struggle. You'll only hurt yourself. We know
> everything. Soon the corpse of detective Rafferty will
> be in our hands. The truce between the police and your
> prostitutes will be shattered. There will be arrests. There
> will be deaths. My employer will seize what remains of this
> neighborhood. You will all be slaves. Nothing can stop this.
> But it is in your power to save many lives. By facilitating
> the process of transition. By negotiating the terms of Old
> Town's surrender.

> GAIL
> You son of a bitch. I know you.

She's on the floor now. He stands over her.

> MANUTE
> I have suffered your kind before. The dregs of Sin City. I
> serve a new master, now. Soon you and all your wretched
> kind will serve him as well. Get dressed. Shed a tear for
> Dwight McCarthy, if you must.

Angle on Gail

> MANUTE (CONT'D)
> By now he is surely dead.

EXT. TAR PITS - NIGHT

A group of Mercs surround the downed DWIGHT. He LOOKS dead.

> MURPHY
> I can't fathom these Americans.... always whinin' and
> going on about how they got it so bad. This is a fine, grand
> country. The guiding light of the modern world, it is.

> MAEVE
> You wouldn't consider doing the rest of us a favor and
> shutting your mouth and keeping it shut, now would you,
> Murphy?

> MURPHY
> The mouth on our dear little Maeve! That's American for you.
> Equal rights. Low taxes. The land of opportunity! Where else
> would one bullet buy the fortune we're getting for this?

> BIG GUY
> Sure beats the living hell out of blowing up airports and
> churches without a shilling to show for it.

Maeve sees Jackie in the front seat.

> MAEVE
> Yeesh.

> BIG GUY
> You find something Murphy?

Murphy is searching Dwight.

> MURPHY
> Looks to be our poor, dead cop's badge. But it's all bent up.
> There's something stuck in it.

Close on the badge.

> MURPHY (CONT'D)
> ... oh bloody hell, it's the bullet.

MICHAEL CLARKE DUNCAN ON MANUTE

"MANUTE IS THE BODYGUARD FOR A CHARACTER WHO
WE KNOW NOTHING ABOUT. ALL WE KNOW IS THAT MANUTE
CARRIES OUT ALL HIS ORDERS. MANUTE HAS A GANG THAT
HE'S OVER, AND HE DOESN'T TAKE ANYTHING OFF ANYBODY.
HE'S A NO-NONSENSE TYPE OF GUY. IF THIS WAS DAREDEVIL,
MANUTE WOULD BE THE KINGPIN'S ULTIMATE BODYGUARD,
AND TO ME IT WAS JUST THE ULTIMATE PRIZE TO PLAY THIS
GUY 'CAUSE I WAS A FAN OF FRANK MILLER FROM A LONG
TIME AGO. SO TO BE ABLE TO BE IN ANOTHER ONE OF HIS
WORKS AFTER BEING IN DAREDEVIL, AND LOOK TOTALLY
DIFFERENT, IT'S MIND-BOGGLING, REALLY. THIS GUY, HE GETS
SLICED UP, HE GETS SHOT, BUT HE KEEPS COMING BACK. AND
THE NEXT ONE, YOU'LL SEE HIM AGAIN. HE'LL PROBABLY DIE
IN THAT ONE, AND THE NEXT ONE HE POPS AGAIN. HE'S LIKE
A MYTHICAL CHARACTER THAT NOBODY UNDERSTANDS. HE'S
LIKE A PHOENIX. HE ALWAYS RISES FROM THE ASHES, AND YOU
CAN'T DEFEAT HIM."

DWIGHT
(vo)
Jackie boy's badge. Slapping against my chest. Right over my heart.

Dwight is rising, two guns aimed. BLAM BLAM! He takes out Murphy and Big Guy, then runs to the driver side of his car.

MAEVE
You son of a bitch! Bastard!

BREK BREKK!! BUDDA! They fire at him. Dwight fires bullets through Jackie's head and hits Maeve and the other guy. Dead.

DWIGHT
(vo)
They weren't cops, these four. They were mercenaries. And if they were hired by who I think they were, the bad times haven't even started yet.

Something heavy lands in the grass beside him.

DWIGHT (CONT'D)
(vo)
And here everything seemed to be going so well.

KABOOM! The car flies. The bodies fly. The trunk is blasted open in the explosion, sending severed body parts flying.

Dwight floats in the tar muck.

EXT. TAR PITS - NIGHT

More mercenaries talk.

BRIAN
..sure I got hold of this Copper well enough, Ronnie, but we'd be needing us a friggin CRANE to pull the bastard outta this soup.

RONNIE
It's not like we gotta deliver every last inch of the man, Brian.

BRIAN
You got a point there, Ronnie. Lend me your knife.

We see Ronnie standing atop the half submerged car. The other body parts floating in the muck along with Dwight.

RONNIE
Should I take me a nap while I'm doing all this waiting?

BRIAN
I'm at the bone, all right?

Brian lifts the severed head of JACKIE BOY into frame.

BRIAN (CONT'D)
Here we go. You ever seen anything so pretty in your life?

Close on Dwight, as the two mercenaries pass three others.

RONNIE
We'll be back for the three of you. If anybody happens by here --

MERCENARY
We know what to do, Ronnie. It's not like you're talking to a pack of nuns, now is it?

Dwight sinks into the abyss. Face, then hand... fingers... he floats downward.

DWIGHT
(vo)
Silence, now. No sound but Jackie Boy's laughter. No sound. No light. No air to breathe. Only the horrid oily tar taste, creeping up my nostrils. Let it in. Let it fill your lungs. You're finished. They were counting on you and you blew it. Suck it in and choke on it and die like a man.

EXT. TAR PITS - NIGHT

Close on a woman's hand through the muck. Reaching for his.

DWIGHT
(vo)
Skinny, steely fingers at my wrist.

A chain fastened to a car. Miho's foot wrapped to the chain.

>   DWIGHT (CONT'D)
>   (vo)
> Miho. You're an angel. You're a saint. You're Mother Theresa.
> You're Elvis. You're God. And if you'd shown up ten minutes
> earlier, we'd still have Jackie Boy's head.

Miho and Dwight. Covered in tar. An Old Town girl pokes her head from the
car.

>   DALLAS
> Dwight! They got Gail!

>   DWIGHT
> It's a cinch you got yourselves a spy in old town. A stoolie
> who sold you out to the mob. We gotta find out who that is
> and rescue Gail. But first we gotta get our hands on Jackie-
> Boy's head before it gets to wherever it's going and this
> whole situation blows wide open.

Dwight stands over Miho.

>   DWIGHT (CONT'D)
> Miho, I hope to hell you left one of them alive enough to
> talk.

She points. We see a mercenary hanging upside down from a dinosaur. Dwight
stands before him. Big KNIFE in his hand.

>   DWIGHT (CONT'D)
>   (vo)
> I let him know I'm not fooling around. We talk.

The knife is now jutting out off the mercenary's belly.

INT./EXT. DALLAS' CAR (MOVING) - NIGHT

DRIVING FAST.

>   DWIGHT
>   (vo)
> Stay smart. Stay cool. It's time to prove to your friends
> that you're worth a damn. Sometimes that means dying.
> Sometimes it means killing a whole lot of people.

The mercenary van on the move as we descend a hill.

DALLAS
There they are! Whatta we do?

DWIGHT
We stop them, Dallas.

She floors it.

DALLAS
This'll stop em damn good!

They sideswipe the van.

DWIGHT
(vo)
Crazy broad! She'll get us all killed! I should've known--
her nerves are shot --

The car crash sends everything flying.

DWIGHT (CONT'D)
(vo)
Jackie Boy's head so close to me I could almost reach out
and grab it right then and there.

EXT. STREET - NIGHT

Jackie's head crashing through the windshield, flying through the air.
DALLAS dances an ugly death dance and curses the sons of bitches even as
their bullets rip the life from her.

MERCENARY
Get the head!

MERC 2
I got it -- I got it --

The throwing star flies through the air. Merc 1 loses the top half of his
head to the star.

MERC 2
Suck on this, you stupid slag!

153

He hurls a grenade at her. BOOOM! Miho flies.

> DWIGHT
> (vo)
> I can't tell if Miho is alive or dead. But I'm feeling on my
> feet and every ounce of me wants to get some killing done.

SPANG! We see the head of Jackie being taken down into a sewer. Dwight runs over to the hole in the ground.

> MERC VOICE
> Come on down, sweetheart. You want the head now don't you?

INT. SEWER - NIGHT

Dwight leaps down the hole, firing all the way down. SPLASH! He falls into the sewage.

> MERC VOICE
> Brave lad. I coulda put a bullet straight down your ear just
> now if I hadn't got my revolver all wet and useless.

Dwight aims at the merc holding Jackie's head like a football.

> MERC VOICE (CONT'D)
> You got the drop on me, love. I'm helpless as a baby.

POOM! CHIKK! Merc detonates a grenade under Dwight.

> MERCENARY
> I gotta come clean with you sweetheart. It was an outright
> LIE I was giving with, about my revolver being wet. Y'see,
> I'm not too fond of shooting. It's my preference to blow
> things up. Once you've blasted the roof off a pub and seen
> all the parts flying off people -- a little bang bang's never
> gonna match the sighta that! And here I got me all these fine
> grenades and such a sweet beauty of a remote. State of the
> art, it is.

Dwight floats face down in the sewage.

> MERCENARY (CONT'D)
> But it's my knife I'll be doing you with. You killed my mates.
> Somebody shoulda' told you never to give an Irishman good
> cause for revenge.

SHAKK!! Merc freezes. Blade out of his face.

>   DWIGHT
>   (vo)
>   Deadly little Miho. You won't feel a thing unless she wants
>   you to. She twists the blade. He feels it.

EXT. HILL - NIGHT

Miho and Dwight run through the rain. The storm kicks up.

>   DWIGHT
>   (vo)
>   I hate the rain. It makes it so damn hard to think straight.
>   I grab poor Dallas' car phone and make the most important
>   call of my life. I tell Miho what we're gonna do and how
>   we're gonna do it. First we gotta rescue Gail. Then comes
>   the kill... the big fat kill...

EXT. BUILDINGS - NIGHT

Dwight in the rain. Checking out the buildings.

INT. OLD TOWN - BUILDING - GAIL TORTURE ROOM - NIGHT

Wide on the buildings. Closer and closer. Till we too hear it. Shadow on the
wall of Gail being tortured. Two thugs stand against the wall watching.

>   THUG 1
>   Yeesh... do we gotta just stand here and watch this?

>   STUKA
>   You kidding, man? I could watch old Davis do his thang all
>   night long and not get tired of it. The man's an artist.

>   DAVIS
>   He's right, you know. Takes an artist just using hands and
>   not leaving any marks. You're as pretty as when you got
>   here. And I haven't even opened my toolbox yet.

ROSARIO DAWSON ON RODRIGUEZ

"ROBERT'S CALMNESS IS WHAT MAKES ME FEEL REALLY COMFORTABLE DOING ALL THE GREEN SCREEN, BECAUSE HE'S JUST SO EXCITED. HE PLAYS GUITAR HALF THE TIME, WALKING AROUND GOING, 'IS THIS COOL? ISN'T THIS GREAT? OKAY, WE'RE JUST GOING TO TURN YOU ALL AROUND, NOT THE CAMERAS, NOT ANYTHING AROUND, JUST TURN ALL OF YOU ALL AROUND, AND NOW WE'RE GOING TO SHOOT AGAIN. EXCELLENT, THAT WAS REALLY GOOD. NEXT.' AND HE JUST GOES SO QUICKLY, AND IT JUST KIND OF KEEPS THE ENERGY UP, AND MAKES IT REALLY FUN. IT FEELS A LITTLE DANGEROUS, AND IT FEELS A LITTLE OFF-KILTER, AND IT JUST FEELS REALLY FUN. IT'S DEFINITELY HIS THING THAT'S GOING ON. I DON'T KNOW IF I COULD NECESSARILY TRUST ANYBODY ELSE WITH THE WAY HE'S DOING THIS, BUT HE'S BEEN DOING IT FOR A LONG TIME, SO I THINK HIS RESUME IS REALLY HELPFUL IN MAKING YOU FEEL COMFORTABLE."

MICHAEL CLARKE DUNCAN ON RODRIGUEZ

"I HAD NEVER DONE A WHOLE MOVIE ON GREEN SCREEN. I THOUGHT YOU'D DO CERTAIN SEQUENCES, BUT TO ROBERT AND HIS CREW'S CREDIT, THEY MOVE VERY QUICKLY, AND SHOTS THAT YOU WOULD NORMALLY HAVE TO WAIT FOR THE SUN TO GO DOWN, WAIT FOR THE CLOUDS TO CLEAR, OR WAIT FOR THIS TYPE OF SUNLIGHT, YOU DON'T EVEN HAVE TO DO ALL THAT. WE CAN PUT THAT IN LATER. SO YOU KNOW WHAT? IT'S GONNA BE FUNNY GOIN' BACK AND DOING A REGULAR MOVIE, BECAUSE NOW I'VE JUST BEEN USED TO DOING THIS AND IT'S VERY QUICK. PRETTY SOON ALL MOVIES WILL BE DONE THIS WAY, AND I THINK ROBERT JUST PUT HIS FINGER ON A GOLD MINE."

BECKY
Just give them what they want, Gail.

GAIL
Becky?

Becky steps in.

BECKY
It's over, Gail. There's no fighting them. Dwight's dead. They got what's left of that cop we killed. The mob's gonna turn it over to the police chief. We gotta cut a deal.

GAIL
You little bitch. You sold us out.

BECKY
I didn't have any choice! They was gonna hurt my mom! You gotta cut a deal with these people. It's selfish, you holding out like this. You're gonna get a lotta girls killed and for no good reason.

Manute walks in.

GAIL
It wasn't your Mom. We could've protected her and you know it. It was the money, you little bitch.

BECKY
Sure there's money! Sure you coulda moved my Mom into old town and let her know her daughter's a goddamn whore! They offered me what you couldn't never offer me! A way out! I hadda watch out for my own neck!

GAIL
Your neck. Your precious scrawny little neck.

CHOMP! Gail lunges and bites into Becky's neck. FAP!

Manute swats Gail off Becky.

BECKY
Crazy! You're crazy! Coulda ripped my throat out you crazy whore!

                    MANUTE
Enough! Davis. Fetch your tools. Stuka, kill this one.

                    BECKY
No! I was promised!

                    GAIL
Stupid little bitch. You deserve worse.

                    STUKA
I knew there was a reason I got outta bed this morning!

ho standing atop the tractor. Letting loose an arrow from her bow. THUNK!

e arrow has gone through the window and THROUGH STUKA.

                    THUG 2
Hey...

e other thugs rush to the window.

                    THUGS
Nobody! I don't see nobody!

                    STUKA
Will ya look at that? It's right through me. Guys. Look.

                    THUG 3
There's something wrapped around it. Some kind of note.

                    MANUTE
Give it to me.

                    STUKA
Guys. This is starting to really hurt. It's poked a hole right
through me. Guys?

e note in foreground, Stuka yacking in the back. The Note: THE COP'S HEAD
R THE WOMAN. OUT BACK. YOUR PAL, DWIGHT.

                    MANUTE
McCarthy you fool.

                    STUKA
    Don't you think somebody oughtta call a doctor for me or
    something? This isn't the kind of thing you just ignore,
    guys.

                    MANUTE
    Out back. Everyone. Bring the women.

They leave.

                    STUKA
    Guys?

Miho lets another arrow fly. KTANNG! SPAK THUNK! The glass shatters again.
The arrow goes through Stuka's throat.

                    STUKA (CONT'D)
            Aw...

EXT. BUILDING - OUTSIDE ALLEY - NIGHT

OUTSIDE

Dead bodies everywhere. Arrows through their eyes and hearts.

Manute leads a small army out the back door.

                    DWIGHT
                    (vo)
    Dozens of them. Armed to the teeth.

Dwight stands with the head atop a pile of trash between the walls of a
narrow alley.

                    DWIGHT (CONT'D)
                    (vo)
    I'm outnumbered. Outgunned. But the alley is crooked. Dark.
    And very narrow. They can't surround me. Sometimes you can
    beat the odds with a careful choice of where to fight.

He holds Jackie's head up high. Manute's army point their guns at him as they
close in.

                    BECKY
    Hey wait a minute.

GAIL
Dwight, don't do this.

DWIGHT
You can have old town. I don't care. Just give me the woman.

BECKY
Wait a minute, something's not right.

THUG 1
Shut up or I'll plug you.

MANUTE
Of course, Mr. McCarthy. A fair trade. She's all yours.

Manute takes the head.

MANUTE (CONT'D)
Now perhaps you'll explain why we shouldn't blow you both to
pieces.

GAIL
(running into his arms)
Dwight-- what have you done?

BECKY
No! It's not right! There wasn't no tape over his mouth! How
come there's tape over his mouth?

Close on Jackie's head. Tape over his mouth. Dwight lifts his hand while
holding Gail tight. He clicks the detonator.

POOM! Jackie's head explodes.

MANUTE
Cute trick McCarthy. But it will do you no... NO! McCarthy
you SHIT!

Above the alley is the armed girls of OLD TOWN.

DWIGHT
(vo)
Where to fight counts for a lot. But there's nothing like
having your friends show up with lots of guns.

On the girls as their guns rip the night.

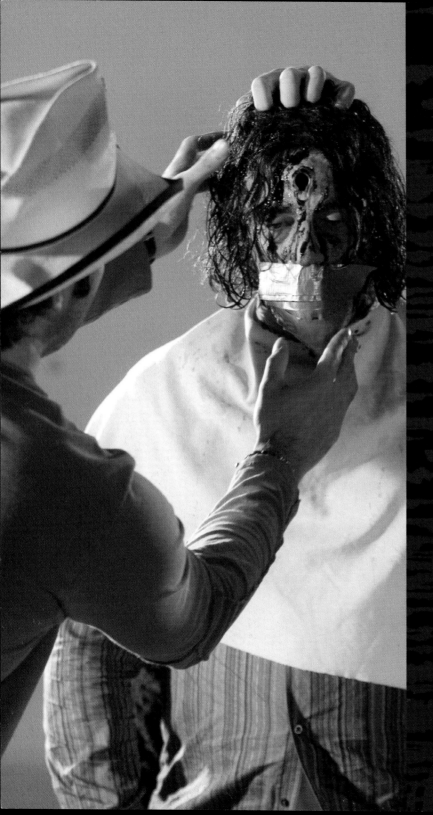

DWIGHT (CONT'D)
(vo)
The girls all know the score. They know what we gotta do. No escape. No surrender. No mercy. We gotta kill every last rat bastard one of them. Every last one.

Angles on Manute's gang getting ripped to shreds with gunfire. Becky manages to crawl away with only a few wounds.

DWIGHT (CONT'D)
(vo)
Not for revenge. Not because they deserve it. Not because it'll make the world a better place. There's nothing righteous or noble about it. We gotta kill them because we need them dead. We need a heap of bloody bodies so when mob boss Walenquist looks over his charts of profits and losses he'll see what it cost him to mess with the girls of Old Town.

Close on Dwight and Gail tearing up the night.

DWIGHT (CONT'D)
(vo)
The thunder doesn't stop. We fire and reload and fire and reload and fire and watch their heads explode and their guts fly like butcher's scraps and the alley walls get caked with wet wads of skin and meat and the smoke gets so thick that the things we're pumping bullets into are nothing but twisted toppling screaming smudges of movement. The Valkyrie at my side is shouting and laughing with the pure hateful bloodthirsty joy of the slaughter... and so am I.

NEW
DWIGHT
LOOK - INFORM
KNB - *FM*

THE FOLLOWING PAGES CONSIST OF DRAWINGS FROM
FRANK MILLER'S SKETCHBOOK CREATED DURING THE
PRODUCTION OF *SIN CITY*. MANY WERE DRAWN ON SET AND
USED AS STORYBOARDS TO ASSIST IN THE PLACEMENT
OF ACTORS AND POSITION OF THE CAMERA.

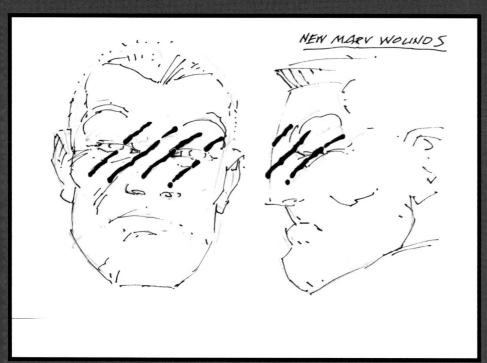

NEW MARV WOUNDS

← CAR

163

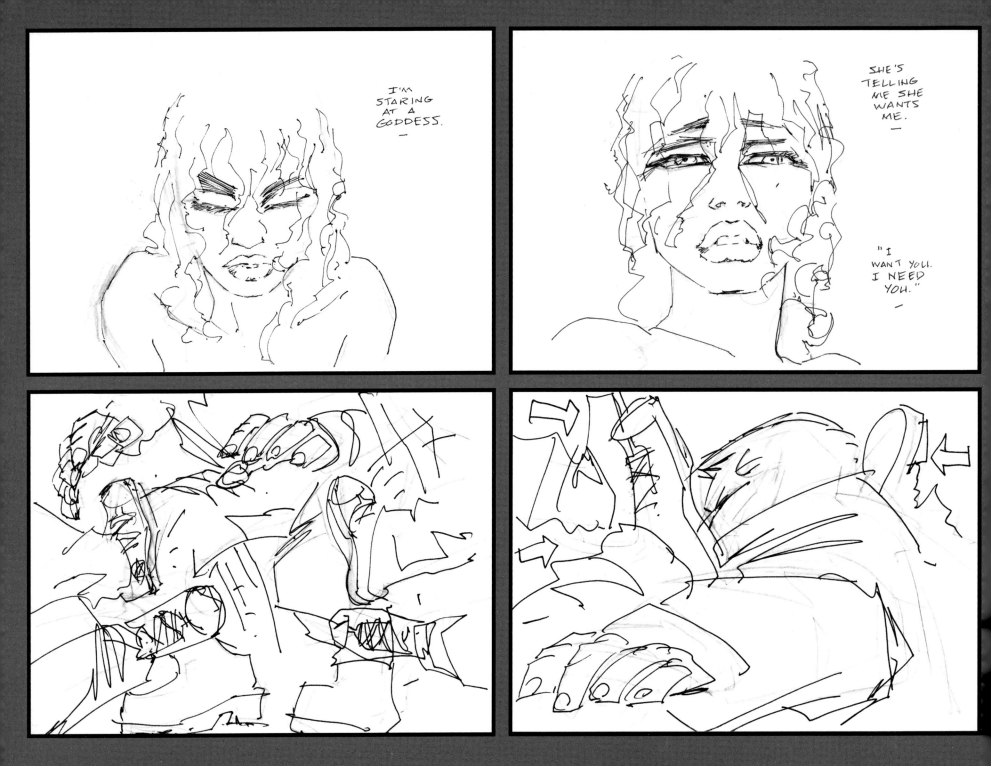

167

GOONS AT END OF ALLEY HAVE "OH, SHIT!" MOMENT TO END ALL "OH, SHIT!" MOMENTS — THE MOTHER OF ALL "OH, SHIT!" MOMENTS —

LOW ANGLE

MIHO.

OH, SHIT...

TAK TAK

WAY LOW ANGLE

DWIGHT V.O. =

... SHE'S BEEN DYING FOR SOME PRACTICE.

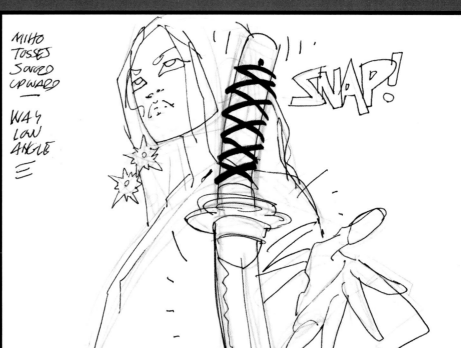

MIHO TOSSES SWORD UPWARD

WAY LOW ANGLE

SNAP!

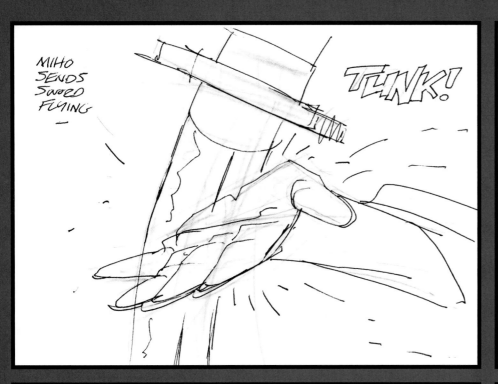

MIHO SENDS SWORD FLYING

THUNK!

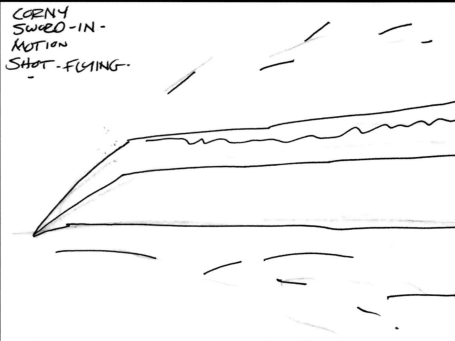

CORNY SWORD-IN-MOTION SHOT - FLYING.

SWORD SKEWERS FIRST THREE GOONS.

THUNK! THUNK! THUNK!

MIHO REVEALS BIGASS DOUBLE-BLADED STAFF. SHE BRANDISHES IT, LETTING THEM KNOW WHAT THEY'RE IN FOR —

WAY, WAY LOW ANGLE!!!

170

"It's very exciting. I don't think anything like this has ever been done. I was excited the very first day. I had no idea what we were doing, and when I saw the work we did that day, it was just amazing. I seldom ever e-mail Robert and say 'Hey, good job,' but after the first day of shooting I e-mailed him and said, 'It's just amazing!' The whole black and white process is incredible. I don't think that a graphic novel like this has ever been done. I don't think that the audiences have ever seen this type of movie. I just think it's going to be really exciting, I really do."

"Frank's been very supportive. Early on we met about every character, and as we got more and more into the story, it was harder to get his opinion. I really got the feeling that he basically trusted me at some point to do the characters right. During production we had a hiatus, and everyone went away. The costume department continued to work because we had to prepare for the next story, and I was a little worried because Frank wasn't here, and Robert wasn't here, and I was preparing for all these characters. Frank actually didn't get back in town until the day before we were filming, and there

were a million things that needed his attention at that point, so he really didn't see some of the characters until the day they were shooting. He was very pleased with them. Frank and Robert both pretty much at this point trust me to come up with the correct look for them, and I do try to follow his work as close as possible. But it's been great—the collaboration between the three of us has just been great."

GAIL

PROCTOR ON ENTERING SIN CITY

"I'm always astounded by what Robert throws at us, I love the challenge, and we've worked together enough now that he can throw things at me, and I know what he's talking about. When we started this project, I got an e-mail and it said 'I need a guy in a black tuxedo, and I need a woman in a dress.' And that was all the information he gave me. I had about three days to pull this off. It ended up looking great. I always try to give him choices, and then we pick out our favorite and discuss why I like the particular one better than the other one. Marley Shelton in that red dress actually ended up looking phenomenal. The red dress was just such a big payoff. It had glitter, and we had no idea that the glitter would do what it did when it went to black and white, the dress was just alive! It was a little surprising to get this e-mail on a Tuesday evening, letting me know that we were going to film this

thing on Saturday. I don't have actors, I don't know who they are, and had to just get out there and try to come up with some good selections and work with the cast once I had them, you want to make them happy. You want to do what's right for the character. We've had some incredible actors on this. Everyone has been so into the characters that we've really been able to go very close to the graphic novel, even with the women. They've really been excited about some of the things that I've done. I mean, the character of Gail is literally in belts and fishnet, and she was so excited about wearing it, we were able to construct it in a way that she feels totally comfortable wearing it. There's really no nudity there, though there's still the hint of nudity. She has shoes that come all the way up to the top of her leg, literally, with spikes and belts. That was a fun character to design."

PROCTOR ON A BLACK AND WHITE WORLD

"*Sin City* has been a great project to work on. Thanks to Frank, the illustrations are already there, and my job has been to bring those illustrations to life. Obviously, you can draw things moving in ways that fabrics, leathers and materials can't really move. It's been a big challenge making the wardrobe as big as it is in the *Sin City* books. It's been a blast doing the wardrobe for the guys. They all have these trenchcoats. It's a huge trenchcoat show. The character Marv has three different trenchcoats throughout his part of the story, and it was a challenge coming up with trenchcoats that look different from each other, so it doesn't look like he's wearing the same coat all the time. We had to be really creative and come up with different styles, so the audience would know that he is indeed taking these coats from other people. Later on, we get into the Hartigan story, and Hartigan is also in two different trenchcoats. I kept Marv in dark fabrics and put Hartigan in grays. In fact, I started him in a really light gray because, since he's saving the little eleven-year-old Nancy, he really is a knight in shining armor. When he gets out of prison he goes into a darker gray. When we got to the Dwight character, we 'cowboyed' up on him. It's a duster look, but we put in some browns."

"Working with black and white, you have to study a lot. I look at everything through a black and white viewfinder. It's all about the value of color and not about the color itself. You still want it to be pleasing to the eye, because when the directors or the actors look at it, it needs to look good, and they're not looking at it in black and white. That was another challenge. But we've used a lot of silver studs on black leather, which helps with the contrast."

Nancy:
Age 11

NANCY

PROCTOR ON HER BIGGEST CHALLENGE

"The biggest challenge was coming up with the Nancy costume. That was a lot to ask an actress to do. She had to wear chaps, and work a rope, and spin six-guns. At one point she had the cowboy hat on, and the ropes, and so she had to be totally comfortable within her costume, and because it was chaps, I didn't want her to have to think about her wardrobe, because she had so many things going on."

"Jessica Alba was an angel. Nancy is the sweet girl in the stories, so there was a real fine line there of trying to make the costumes sexy without going too far, or not going far enough. And I think we finally came up with a very comfortable place, and she looked like an angel, and she didn't have to think about her costume when she was working the ropes and twirling the guns."

PROCTOR ON THE CHARACTER BOARDS

"I TOOK EACH CHARACTER AND MADE BOARDS FOR THEM. THE BOOKS WERE TOO MUCH TO WORK WITH DIRECTLY. IF YOU FLIP THROUGH THE BOOK, THERE'S INFORMATION EVERYWHERE. I REALLY HAD TO BREAK IT DOWN INTO A MUCH SMALLER WORLD. WE WOULD COPY PAGES FROM THE BOOKS AND CUT OUT IMAGES OF THE CHARACTERS. WE DID BOARDS THAT JUST HAD IMAGES OF THE MARV CHARACTER, OR THE DWIGHT CHARACTER, OR THE GAIL CHARACTER, AND DIDN'T HAVE ANY IMAGES OF THE OTHER CHARACTERS. OTHERWISE, IT WOULD JUST GET TOO CONFUSING. YOU WOULD GET LOST IN ALL THESE THOUGHTS BECAUSE THERE'S SO MUCH GOING ON IN THE BOOK. THE BOARDS WERE REALLY VERY HELPFUL. WHEN THE ACTORS CAME IN, I PUT THEIR BOARD IN THE FITTING ROOM, AND IT WAS REALLY EASY FOR THEM TO SEE HOW THE CHARACTER LOOKED. WE HAD ALL THE INFORMATION RIGHT THERE FOR THEM TO LOOK AT."

Opposite page: Michael Madsen as Bob
This page: Nina Proctor's character boards

MARV

PROCTOR ON MICKEY ROURKE

"I tried to stress to the actors, when I spoke to them, that we were trying to go as close to the graphic novel as we could. With Mickey, I told him, 'In your story you get three different trenchcoats. Pretty much everything else is the same.' He stayed in the same shirt and the same pants. He would just see a coat and take it. We custom built his first coat, so that it was really Marv's coat. In the beginning he owns that coat, so that it's not taking it from someone. I made it a little more special. It has these really massive shoulders and this skirt that would billow, so that it was almost like a Superman cape (in fact, a lot of people on set called it a cape, but it was indeed a coat). Then this coat gets a little bit torn up so when he sees another coat, he takes it away from the guy, saying 'Nice coat,' his signature line.

Mickey was very easy to work with. He was in leather pants, and we had to have just the right shoes. We did go through a couple of different boots that he really liked, and they did look a little bit like they belonged in the book, but they didn't have treads on them, and it was really important that they do. You see the bottoms of the boots a few times in the comics, and they had all these great treads on them. He actually ended up wearing just your basic army boot. He was a good guy; very pleasant to be around, and got really excited when he got into his wardrobe. Of course, he had two hours of make-up every day, but he was still a trouper about wearing all those heavy coats."

Opposite page: Gail's panties; This page (clockwise from upper left) : Lucille's bra, Dwight's shirt, Marv's boxers, Dwight's boxers, Nancy's panties, Nancy's nightgown, Lucille's robe, Dwight's jeans, Lucille's panties

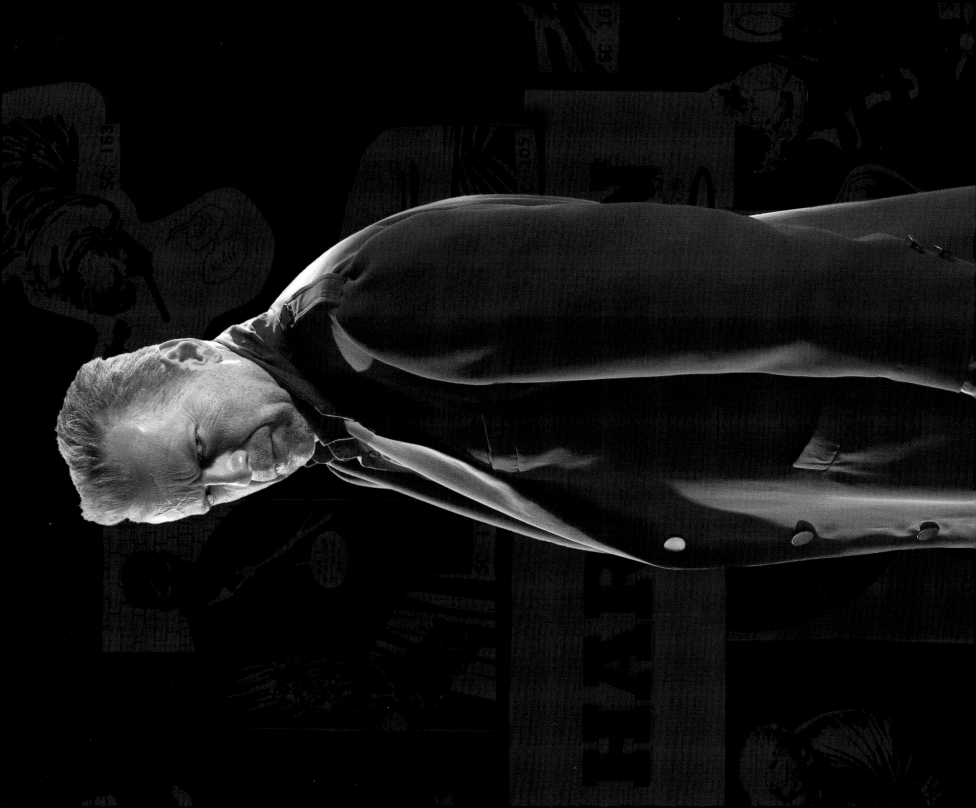

HARTIGAN

PROCTOR ON BRUCE WILLIS

"Bruce Willis was great. I had a conversation with his people before he got here. I offered to go out and meet with him, but both of us felt pretty secure after we had talked. The first time I met him was at Robert's house for a fitting. Bruce loved his wardrobe. He literally put the first coat on and said, 'I want one of these. Can I have this? I want one of these to take home. I want some pants made like that.' His coats were much lighter weight than Mickey Rourke's, more tailored. He seemed to really enjoy his wardrobe."

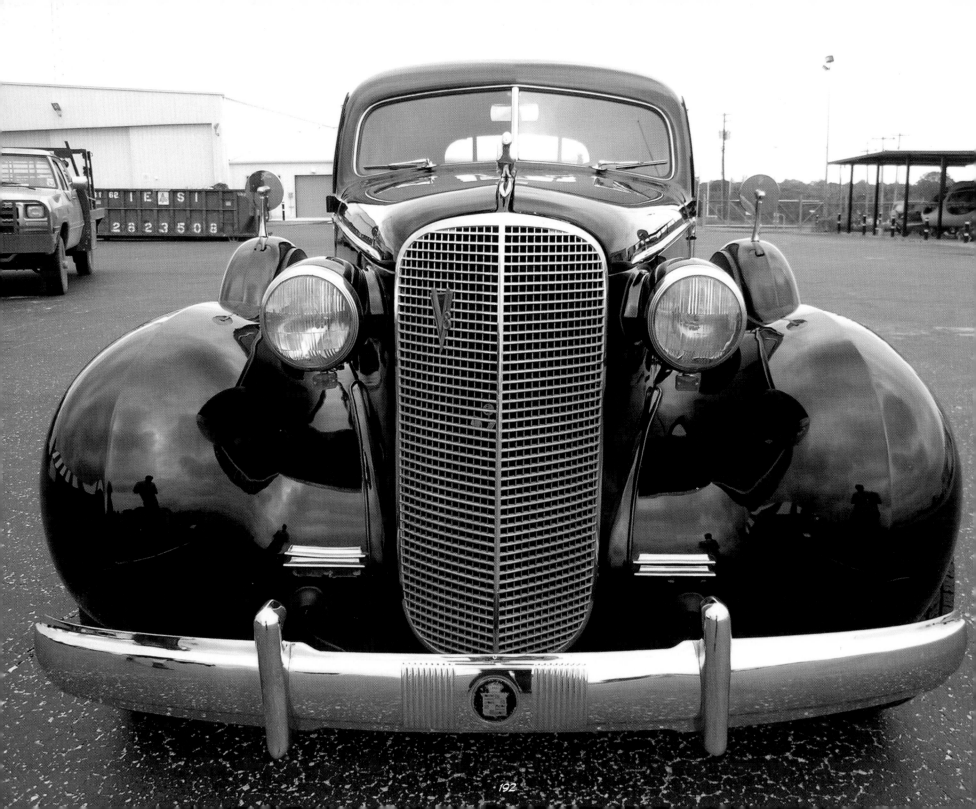

TRANSPORTATION COORDINATOR CECIL EVANS ON THE CARS OF SIN CITY

"When I got the three books we were going to film, the first thing I did was go through and identify all the cars. I went down to the newspaper, took out an ad. I contacted all the various car clubs in town. Then I called Ron Chambers and Bobby Sconce, gave them pictures of all the cars and said 'okay, let's go find them.' I thought the only place the Yellow Bastard's car existed was in Frank Miller's mind, because it just did not look like anything I was familiar with. It could possibly pass for a kit car that someone put together. That evening, when we met back at the office to see what we had accomplished, Bobby Sconce came up and said, 'you

know that car you said only existed in Frank Miller's mind? It's a Bugatti.' I said, 'well, what in the hell is a Bugatti?' I went over to see (Visual Effects Artist) Alex Toader. Through his internet expertise we found this Bugatti. It's an Atlantic 57 C. Through a little more research I found out they made one in 1936, one in 1937 and one in 1938."

"It was a popular looking car and they made replicas. So we tried to find a replica. The first one we found was in Germany. And we found out Jay Leno had one. I told Robert we were going to book him on the Jay Leno

show and he could ask Jay in front of America if the Yellow Bastard could borrow his car for a few weeks."

"We did eventually find one in L.A. It was going to cost us one hundred thousand dollars a week plus shipping, which would have been two hundred and thirty thousand dollars to use the car for essentially three to four days of filming. When I gave Frank, Robert and (UPM) Bill Scott this story, they decided to pick another car. I found a 1936 Cadillac Limo that looked like a big old gangster car. We decided to use that one for the Yellow Bastard."

FRANK MILLER ON THE CARS OF *SIN CITY*

"This whole production has been astounding to me because I've seen such expertise and dedication. And all from pages I drew with no intention of having them translated into any other medium; it was a graphic novel, that was its final fate. Of course, I did a lot of research at the time, hunting things down. I used some pretty obscure sources. Take the cars, for example, which are such important characters in *Sin City*. I have several hundred die cast metal cars, and I'm always finding new ones. When I came to the set, these people had hunted down all these cars. Now they're being driven across the lot in my movie. That's just stunning, but it's also a little creepy, because what I had in mind, I'd never seen in reality. I'd never seen the real, live big cars, and had only been to car shows occasionally. And yet, here they were."

EVANS ON WENDY'S PORSCHE

"We found hundreds of cars, took pictures and had them on the board before Frank ever got here. We could tell he loved the classic look of the 1950's and early '60's. This was the big thing."

"We used about 95 percent of the cars in the show that were pictured in the books - the three graphic novels we shot. An exception was Wendy's Porsche, which in the book was about a 1946. We found a '55 Spyder Convertible. They liked the look of it better."

"What was Frank's favorite car? Every car. Frank went crazy over every car. He loved the Jaguar, the Nomad. He was crazy over the '59 Cadillac. He was crazy about the '55 Porsche. He said that was going to be the top car until we brought in the next one. And then he loved it more."

Frank checked to make sure the prop department had the license plates for Wendy's car true to his ink. LEV 311 are his wife's initials and birth date.

EVANS ON DWIGHT'S CADILLAC

"DWIGHT'S CAR WAS A '59 CADILLAC CONVERTIBLE. IN OUR SEARCH WE FOUND TWO NORTH OF FORT WORTH AND TWO IN HOUSTON. WE KEPT LOOKING. WE JUST KNEW THERE WOULD BE ONE HERE (AUSTIN). BOBBY SCONCE (OUR PICTURE CAR WRANGLER) WAS HOME ONE WEEKEND MOANING AND GROANING ABOUT THE CARS HE COULDN'T FIND. HE SHOWED A PICTURE TO HIS SISTER-IN-LAW WHO WORKS AT A COUNTRY CLUB HERE IN TOWN. SHE SAID A DOCTOR DROVE ONE TO THE GOLF COURSE ALL THE TIME. WE FOUND OUT WHO THAT DOCTOR WAS, MADE A DEAL WITH HIM, AND WHEN WE PICKED UP THE CAR IT STILL HAD HIS CLUBS AND SHOES IN THE TRUNK. HE AND A REAL ESTATE DEVELOPER BOUGHT THAT CAR, WENT TO CALIFORNIA, GOT ON ROUTE 66 AND DROVE AS FAR EAST AS ROUTE 66 WENT. NOW THE DOCTOR DRIVES IT TO AND FROM THE GOLF COURSE."

PICTURE CAR WRANGLER
BOBBY SCONCE ON DWIGHT'S CADILLAC

"WHEN I BROUGHT IN THE '59 CADILLAC, FRANK ALL BUT RAN THROUGH THE GATE. HE SAID, 'MY GOD I HAVEN'T SEEN ONE IN A LONG TIME. I FORGOT THESE CARS WERE THIS BIG.' ROBERT LOVED THE GRILL, WITH ALL THE CHROME AND, OF COURSE, THE RED HAD A LITTLE BIT TO DO WITH IT TOO. AS A MATTER OF FACT, THAT CAR HAD A LITTLE HISTORY. IT WAS USED IN A MOVIE YEARS AND YEARS AGO CALLED *VIVA LAS VEGAS*."

SCONCE ON DALLAS' CAR

"DALLAS' CAR WAS PROBABLY ONE OF MY FAVORITES BECAUSE I LOVE THAT ERA. THE LITTLE '41 CHEVROLET WAS ONE THAT REALLY IMPRESSED ME. IT WAS ALL VINTAGE. EVERYTHING IN IT WAS EXACT. AS FAR AS THE WORKMANSHIP, IT WAS PRETTY CLOSE TO BEING A PERFECT CAR. IT WAS A 1941 MODEL BUT YOU'D DRIVE IT, AND IT WAS LIKE DRIVING A BRAND NEW CAR. THERE WAS NO ROAD NOISE. IT WAS DEFINITELY A HIGH-END CAR."

"IF I HAD TO TAKE A GUESS, TO COMPLETELY RESTORE THAT CAR WOULD COST IN THE $30,000 RANGE. IT WAS IN FAIRLY DECENT SHAPE. THE GENTLEMAN WHO OWNED THE CAR STRIPPED IT AND STARTED FROM SQUARE ONE. IT WASN'T JUST A PAINT JOB. HE REDID IT DOWN TO THE WEATHER STRIPPING, THE ENGINE, EVERYTHING. HE COMPLETELY WENT FROM ONE BUMPER TO THE OTHER. IF MEMORY SERVES ME, I THINK HE WORKED FIVE OR SIX YEARS ON THIS CAR."

This page from upper left: Schlump's 1989 Ferrari 348TS Targa, 1992 Kawasaki Kz1000 Police Motorcycle, Nancy's 1957 Chevy Nomad Stationwagon, Dallas' 1941 Chevy, "Mercenary Van" 1965 GMC Carry-All, The Priest's 1990 Mercedes, Dwight's 1959 Cadillac, Hartigan's 1955 Buick, "Body Transfer Car" 1957 Ford T-Bird, Jackie Boy's 1957 Chrysler Imperial, Yellow Bastard's 1936 Cadillac, Roarke Jr's 1963 Jaguar XKE, Lucille's 1974 Volkswagen Convertible, Wendy's 1955 Porsche Spyder, 1949 Chevy Taxi Cab; Opposite page: "Police Car" 1955 Chevy

INT. HARTIGAN'S CAR (MOVING) - NIGHT

HARTIGAN, mid 60's. Driving hard.

> HARTIGAN
> (vo)
> Just one hour to go. My last day on the job. Early
> retirement. Not my idea. Doctor's orders. Heart condition.
> ANGINA, he calls it. I'm polishing my badge and getting
> myself used to the idea of saying Good-bye to it, it and the
> thirty odd years of protecting and serving and tears and
> blood and terror and triumph it represents. I'm thinking
> about Eileen's slow smile, about the thick, fat steaks she
> picked up at the butcher's today... and I'm thinking about
> one loose end I haven't tied up. A young girl who's out there
> somewhere, helpless in the hands of a drooling lunatic.

Over Hartigan onto his partner Bob. Frustrated. As usual.

EXT. DOCK - HARTIGAN'S CAR - NIGHT

Hartigan charges out of his Chevy convertible. Bob follows him.

> BOB
> Damn it, Hartigan-- I won't let you do this! You'll get
> yourself killed! You'll get us both killed and I won't let you!
> I'm warning you!

> HARTIGAN
> Let go my coat, Bob.

Bob pulls Hartigan around.

> BOB
> You're dragging me down with you! I'm your partner! They'll
> kill me too! I'm not putting up with that! I'm getting on the
> horn and calling for back-up!

> HARTIGAN
> Sure, Bob. And we'll sit on our hands while that ROARK
> brat gets his sick thrills with victim number four. VICTIM
> NUMBER FOUR. Nancy Callahan. Age Eleven. She'll be raped

and slashed to ribbons. And that BACK-UP we're waiting on will just happen to show up just LATE enough to let Roark get back home to his US Senator Daddy. And everything will be fine until junior gets the itch again.

> BOB
> Take a deep breath Hartigan. Settle down and think STRAIGHT. You're pushing sixty. You've got a bum ticker. You're not saving anybody.

> HARTIGAN
> You've got a great attitude, Bob. A credit to the force, you are.

> BOB
> Eileen's home waiting for you. Think about EILEEN.

They are standing on a dock.

> HARTIGAN
> Heck, Bob, maybe you're right.

> BOB
> I'm glad to hear you finally talking sense.

Hartigan slugs Bob hard. Bob goes down.

> HARTIGAN
> (vo)
> Hell of a way to end a partnership. Hell of a way to start my retirement.

Hartigan's eyes wander the dock.

> HARTIGAN (CONT'D)
> (vo)
> Nancy Callahan. Age eleven. For all I know she's dead already.

INT. DOCK - NANCY'S CELL - NIGHT

A door opens. A shadow looms over Nancy, hands tied behind her back t chair.

                    VOICE

You've been a very good girl, Nancy. You've been very quiet.
Don't be scared. If we were going to hurt you, we would've
done that already. You understand that, don't you?

Close on Nancy. Her eyes.

                    VOICE (CONT'D)

Of course you do. Now don't you worry Nancy. We'll be taking
you home really soon. But first we're going to introduce you
to somebody. He's a very nice man.

EXT. DOCK - ALLEY - NIGHT

Hartigan storms through an alley. Toward the lights.

                    HARTIGAN
                    (vo)
Halfway to the warehouse where they took her and it hits.
Wicked spot of indigestion. At least that's what I pray it is.

Hartigan doubles over. Leaning against the alley wall. Hartigan hears the
voices of KLUMP and SHLUBB offscreen.

                    SHLUBB
Your unflagging rigidity in regard to this matter we
now discuss bespeaks caution beyond all measure of
reasonableness, Mr. Klump. I seek only the most light-
hearted and momentary digressions -- the briefest
indulgement in automotive pleasure.

                    HARTIGAN
                    (vo)
That tip from Weevil was solid. I know these clowns. They're
as rotten as they are stupid.

                    KLUMP
And for cheap thrills of such short-lived durability, Mr.
Schlubb, you would risk engendering ILL WILL on the part
of our employers...

OVER HEAD SHOT of Hartigan hiding off the side of the men.

                    SHLUBB
I seek only the briefest of spins Mr. Klump.

211

BRUCE WILLIS ON FRANK MILLER

"IF YOU READ FRANK'S WRITING, WITHOUT LOOKING AT THE
PANELS, IT STANDS ALONE AS TRUE FILM NOIR WRITING. IT'S
VERY POETIC, VERY DARK, AND IT'S GOT THAT HARD-BITTEN
FILM NOIR STYLE, OF WHICH I'VE ALWAYS BEEN A HUGE
FAN."

KLUMP

Not to be considered, Mr. Shlubb. This jaguar you so
pinheadedly covet, temporarily remanded to our custody
though it may be, remains property of the son of Senator
Roark. A single dent, the merest scratch thereupon and the
beforementioned CONSEQUENCES of which I so recently made
mention shall surely be ATHWART us!

HARTIGAN
(vo)

Burt Shlubb and Douglas Klump, aka "Fat man and Little
Boy," tow any-dirty-job-there-is thugs with delusions of
eloquence.

Hartigan reaches for a pipe from the ground.

HARTIGAN (CONT'D)
(vo)

Gotta keep this quiet. Take them down fast.

Konnk! "UrF! "Hnh?

Shlubb is felled with the pipe. Klump pulls his gun. WHOOF! GURGG! KONK.
Klump is down.

HARTIGAN (CONT'D)
(vo)

Take a second. Settle down. Catch your breath. Give your
heart time to slow down. But it won't slow down. Pounding.
Vicious pain. Across my chest. In my jaw. In my teeth. Like
they're getting yanked out all at once. My heart won't slow
down. Don't panic. Don't panic.

Hartigan grips the pipe. Tightens his fists. Fights the pain.

HARTIGAN (CONT'D)
(vo)

No. Not a heart attack. Not now.

INT. DOCK - FOYER - NIGHT

Nancy Callahan is surrounded by three men.

LENNY

We're all done here, Benny. Let's give them some time
together. Give them some privacy.

BENNY

with you in a minute, Lenny. I'm just making sure they get
ong really well.

ROARK

at kind of beast couldn't get along with a precious young
dy like this? You boys just run along. Me and little Nancy
ll get along just fine. Poor thing. You must be awfully
ared right now.

s to one knee.

ROARK (CONT'D)

t you've got nothing to be scared of. All we're going to do
have a nice talk. That's all. Just a nice talk. Just you
d me.

way a tear from her eye.

ROARK (CONT'D)

n't you cry, now.

- ALLEY - NIGHT

HARTIGAN
(vo)

. Not a heart attack. Angina. The doctor said it'd be like
is. Take the pill he gave you.

s the pill in his teeth.

HARTIGAN (CONT'D)
(vo)

et over it. She needs you. Nancy Callahan. Age Eleven.

unsteady at first. Then Strong. He pulls the gun.

HARTIGAN (CONT'D)
(vo)

need to play it quiet. Not anymore. Settle down. Think
ke a cop.

NICK STAHL ON ROARK

"ROARK JUNIOR IS THE SON OF SENATOR ROARK, A VERY
CORRUPT MAN WHO CONTROLS *SIN CITY*, AND HE'S PRETTY
MUCH A CHIP OFF THE OLD BLOCK. HE'S A SPOILED KID, HE'S
WEALTHY, AND HE GETS WHAT HE WANTS. EACH CHARACTER IN
THIS STORY HAS THEIR OWN SENSE OF CORRUPTION, I THINK,
BUT ROARK JUNIOR IS KIND OF A SICKO. HE'S NOT A GOOD
GUY."

FRANK MILLER ON BRUCE WILLIS

"WORKING WITH BRUCE WILLIS IS LIKE BEING AROUND A BRILLIANT SURGEON. HE COMES IN WITH SUCH EXPERIENCE AND POLISH THAT FIRST YOU'RE OF COURSE DAUNTED, BUT THEN AS YOU SEE HIM USE HIS INSTRUMENT TO ATTACK MATERIAL, IT'S A TRANSFORMATION THAT HE UNDERGOES. HE TRANSFORMS THE MATERIAL TOO. OF COURSE, I'M THINKING, 'MY GOODNESS, HE'S BRUCE WILLIS, I'M A FIRST-TIME DIRECTOR, AND HE'S GOING TO MOP UP THE FLOOR WITH ME.' INSTEAD, HE CAME IN WITH LOVE FOR THE MATERIAL. HE WAS AN ABSOLUTE DREAM TO WORK WITH, AND FED INTO IT CONSTANTLY. HE UNDERSTOOD ALL THE REFERENCES FROM FILM NOIR, HE UNDERSTOOD THAT THE CHARACTER HAD A LOT OF RAYMOND CHANDLER IN HIM, AND HE CERTAINLY UNDERSTOOD CHANDLER'S THEORY ABOUT THESE CHARACTERS BEING KNIGHTS. HE BROUGHT BEAUTY TO THE PERFORMANCE. IF MICKEY WAS OUR DIONYSUS, HE WAS OUR APOLLO."

He opens up the hood of the Jag.

> HARTIGAN (CONT'D)
> (vo)
> If Junior gets past you, he'll get to this jag of his. And there's no catching up with this machine.

He takes the spark plugs. Close on his hand.

> HARTIGAN (CONT'D)
> (vo)
> Breathe steady, old man. Prove you're not completely useless. Hell, go out with a bang. He likes to hear them scream. I've seen his victims and their twisted little faces, frozen in their last horrible moment of living, not a trace of tape from a gag on their lips.

He listens.

> HARTIGAN (CONT'D)
> No screams. Either I'm just in time-- or I'm way too late.

INT. DOCK - FOYER - NIGHT

He crashes through the door. BOOM BOOM. He blows away Goon 1 and Goon 2. H reaches for his heart.

> HARTIGAN
> (vo)
> Not chest pains again. Not now.

Junior steps into the room and shoots Hartigan. He carries Nancy with him as he makes for the door.

> HARTIGAN (CONT'D)
> (vo)
> It's nothing. Barely a flesh wound. On your feet, old man. Junior's got a hostage.

EXT. DOCK - JAG - NIGHT

Junior leaps into the jag with Nancy.

HARTIGAN
(vo)
Go ahead, Junior. You keep trying that engine. Keep turning that key and cursing the world, you spoiled brat psycho son of a bitch.

ROARK
Nothing, nothing! Just had it tuned, and I'm getting nothing! That cop, Hartigan. On my ass. All the time. He killed my car.

Roark makes a run for it, carrying Nancy. Hartigan is waiting.

HARTIGAN
ROARK! Give it up. It's over. Let the girl go.

ROARK
You can't do a goddamn thing to me, Hartigan. You know who I am. You know who my father is! You can't touch me, you piece of shit cop!

BOOM! Roark crumples to the ground, a bloody mess.

ROARK (CONT'D)
Look at you! You can't even lift that cannon you're carrying!

HARTIGAN
Sure I can.

Hartigan shoots off Roark's ear.

HARTIGAN (CONT'D)
Close your eyes Nancy, I don't want you watching this.

Roark pulls out a gun in the meanwhile. Fires. Piece of Hartigan's shoulder comes off.

HARTIGAN
Lousy shot, Junior. Didn't even hit any meat.

Hartigan walks over and shoots off ROARK'S GUN HAND.

HARTIGAN (CONT'D)
(vo)
I take his weapon's away...

215

MICHAEL MADSEN ON BOB

"BOB IS A CYNICAL MAN, AND A BACK-SHOOTER, BUT I THINK
THAT HE FEELS JUSTIFIED IN HIS ACTIVITIES BECAUSE HE'LL
EVENTUALLY MAKE THE ULTIMATE SACRIFICE FOR THE RIGHT
REASON, WHATEVER THAT IS."

Hartigan blasts Roark's crotch.

> HARTIGAN (CONT'D)
> (vo)
> Both of them.

BOOM! BOOM! Hartigan spasms as gunfire blasts from behind.

> HARTIGAN (CONT'D)
> (vo)
> Then there's thunder from behind me and lightning bolts
> punching holes through my chest. I guess I won't be having
> that steak I was looking forward to, after all. My last day
> on the job. Hell of a way to start my retirement.

Bob appears behind him, gun smoking.

> BOB
> Damn it, Hartigan. I warned you.

> HARTIGAN
> (vo)
> Hell of a way to end a partnership. My blood is hot. My skin
> is cold. The breeze is warm. I don't fall down.

Hartigan is doubled over. Bleeding.

> BOB
> For God's sake. Stop FIGHTING it. Don't make it any worse.
> Don't make me kill you!

> HARTIGAN
> I'm doing fine, Bob. Never better. Ready to kick your ass.

Hartigan turns to Bob now.

> HARTIGAN (CONT'D)
> That's right. I'm gonna kick your flabby ass. Bastard.
> (vo)
> Keep him talking. Buy time. Just a few more minutes. Just
> till the back-up gets here. Keep his mind off the girl.
> Skinny little Nancy. He can't kill her once the back-up gets
> here.

> BOB
> Sit down and stay down, Hartigan, I'll kill you if I have to!

216

ROARK
God.. Oh god...

HARTIGAN
Junior's squealing like a stuck pig. You see me blow his
balls off? Bet that hurts!
              (vo)
Still no sirens. Getting dizzy. Running out of time. Gotta
get her out of here.

HARTIGAN (CONT'D)
Run home, Nancy. Run for your life.

BOB
Don't listen to him. He's a crazy man. You stay right where
you are.

HARTIGAN
              (vo)
Poor kid. Frozen in her tracks. Still no sirens. Hold on.
String him along. Keep him ANGRY.

View from the water. Over Hartigan, at dock's edge.

HARTIGAN (CONT'D)
Tough man you are. A real mensch! First you shoot your
partner in the back-- now you try to scare a little girl!
Goddamn pansy is what you are! And I'm gonna kick your
pansy ass!

BOB
You're doing nothing! I'm through being nice about this!

HARTIGAN
Maybe I'll reach down and grab my spare ROD from off my
ankle and plug you a couple times just to show you how it's
done.

Nancy looks on, frozen.

BOB
Don't try it. You're bluffing and you're not fooling anybody!
We coulda worked something out but you've blown that! Sit
down or I'll blast you in half!

Overhead shot looking down.

MICHAEL MADSEN ON RODRIGUEZ AND MILLER

"ROBERT STRUMS HIS GUITAR. HE'S VERY SOOTHING. HE HAS A
CALMNESS ABOUT HIM THAT MAKES EVERYBODY ELSE CALM
DOWN, AND I DON'T KNOW IF HE'S AWARE OF IT, BUT HE
SEEMS TO BE GENUINE. FRANK, MEANWHILE, IS MENTALLY
DISTURBED, AS YOU COULD TELL BY READING HIS BOOKS.
IT'S INTERESTING THAT HE'S ON THE SET AND THAT HE'S SUCH
A COLLABORATOR ON THIS WHOLE THING BECAUSE WHEN I
DID RESERVOIR DOGS I ALWAYS THOUGHT IT WAS GREAT
THAT QUENTIN WAS DIRECTING HIS OWN MATERIAL. SO TO
HAVE FRANK AROUND WITH ROBERT IS GREAT BECAUSE HE'S
GETTING TO SEE HIS COMIC STRIP COME TO LIFE, WHICH MUST
BE FASCINATING FOR HIM. I CAN WATCH HIS FACE WHILE WE'RE
SHOOTING IT. YOU CAN TELL THAT HE'S PRETTY AWESTRUCK,
BUT NOT SO MUCH SO THAT HE'S LOSING PERSPECTIVE. HE'S
RIGHT THERE WITH IT."

         HARTIGAN
Right here. Right on my ankle. You're so slow, I'll have all the time in the world.

         BOB
Don't try it! Damn it, you sit down!

         ROARK
God....

Hartigan reaches for his ankle gun.

         HARTIGAN
         (vo)
Just a few more seconds... And she'll be safe.

BLAM! BOB fires. Hartigan goes down. Hartigan clings to the dock post. Bob unloads more bullets in his back. Nancy screams. Hartigan falls to the dock. Bob blasts him again. In the chest.

         HARTIGAN (CONT'D)
         (vo)
I finally sit down, just like he told me to. The sirens are close, now. She'll be safe.

KHAFF. Nancy runs up to him, kneels beside him and puts her tiny hand in his. She curls up in his arm.

Close on Hartigan.

         HARTIGAN (CONT'D)
         (vo)
Things go dark. I don't mind much.

Side view of dock, silhouette in the dark.

         HARTIGAN (CONT'D)
         (vo)
No pain now. Getting sleepy. That's okay. She'll be safe.

Nancy in his arms as he sleeps.

         HARTIGAN (CONT'D)
         (vo)
An old man dies. A little girl lives. Fair trade.

T. DOCKS - PIER - NIGHT MONTAGE

p cars swarm the area.

T. STREET - AMBULANCE - NIGHT MONTAGE

bulance surrounded by police escorts on every side.

T./EXT. HOSPITAL - NIGHT MONTAGE

rtigan wheeled into hospital.

T. HOSPITAL - OPERATING ROOM - NIGHT MONTAGE

army of surgeons huddled around an operating table.

T. HOSPITAL - HARTIGAN'S ROOM - NIGHT

large unsavory looking character stands at the foot of Hartigan's
covery bed. Smoking a big cigar.

                    SENATOR
        Evening, Officer. I don't have to introduce myself, do
        I? You're a good, responsible citizen. You keep yourself
        informed. You read the papers. This being an election year,
        you've seen plenty of my picture. You know what I can do.
        And I'm doing you, Hartigan. Cold and hard, I'm doing you.

leans in close.

                    SENATOR (CONT'D)
        Oooh... I know that look in your eyes. Like some piss ant
        rookie legislator out to save the world who's just gotten his
        first lesson in how things actually work. Yeah. I like that
        look. Hell, I LIVE for that look. I seen it a thousand times
        and I never get enough of it. Right now you're wishing you'd
        died back on that dock, aren't you, you goddamn PIECE OF
        SHIT cop?

walks around tubes hanging down into Hartigan's arms.

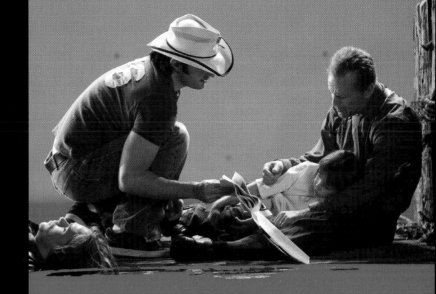

BRUCE WILLIS ON THE PRODUCTION

"THE BEST WAY I COULD DESCRIBE THE SOUND STAGE WOULD
BE LIKE WORKING ON A *PLAYHOUSE 90* SET. THERE WAS A
REAL DOCK, THERE WAS A REAL STAIRCASE, THE CARS WERE
ALL REAL, THE PROPS WERE REAL; OTHER THAN THAT IT ALL
HAD TO BE IMAGINED. IT WAS ALL JUST A BIG GREEN STAGE.
SO YOU HAD TO IMAGINE WHAT WAS THERE."

"IN THAT KIND OF ACTING, YOU REALLY HAVE TO RELY ON A
CERTAIN AMOUNT OF SENSE MEMORY. THE WAY THEY SHOOT
WITH THE BRAND NEW DIGITAL CAMERAS, THEY NEVER CUT. SO
IT'S A MUCH FASTER PROCESS. I WORKED TEN DAYS SHOOTING
ON THIS FILM, AND WITH A REGULAR FILM CAMERA I THINK
THAT WOULD BE THE EQUIVALENT OF ABOUT SIX WEEKS OF
SHOOTING. THEY NEVER CUT, THEY NEVER STOPPED ROLLING.
THAT OFFERS A LOT OF CHALLENGES. YOU HAVE TO BE
PREPARED, YOU HAVE TO KNOW WHAT YOU WANT TO DO WITH
THE CHARACTER. I RELY A LOT ON BOTH ROBERT AND FRANK.
IT WAS GREAT HAVING FRANK THERE. AFTER ALMOST EVERY
TAKE YOU KNOW, ROBERT WOULD ASK FRANK, 'IS THAT WHAT
YOU WANTED? IS THAT WHAT YOU THOUGHT? IS THAT WHAT YOU
HAD IN MIND FOR THIS CHARACTER?'"

"I THINK ALL THE ACTORS FELT THAT IT WAS OUR JOB TO
NOT ONLY PAY HOMAGE TO THE BOOKS, AND TO THE FILM
NOIR STYLE, BUT ALSO TO FRANK'S WRITING. I DON'T THINK
ANYBODY CHANGED ANY LINES. FRANK DID, AND HE WOULD
SUGGEST CUTTING A LINE, OR CHANGING A LINE, AND I ALWAYS
ARGUED WITH HIM. 'NO, NO, LET'S DO THE EXACT TEXT IN THE
BOOKS.'"

SENATOR (CONT'D)
Oh, you're a piece of work. A real tough guy. Too stupid to take a hint and lay off my boy! Even when I had your car blown up you couldn't take the hint! I was gonna have you snuffed! It's tricky business, snuffing a cop with a record clean as yours -- but you wouldn't have been my first! Then I heard about your heart condition. Your forced retirement. I almost threw a party. You were gone! You were out of the picture!

He leans in again.

SENATOR (CONT'D)
But No! You still wouldn't let up! You kept after my boy! You blew his ear off! You blew his arm off! You even blew his nuts and his pecker off! He's in a coma right now! They say he might never come out of it! My boy, he coulda been the first Roark to become President of the United States! And you went and turned him into a brain-damaged, dickless freak! Did that make you feel powerful? Well let me tell you a thing or two about power!

He lifts a gun up.

SENATOR (CONT'D)
Power doesn't come from a badge or a gun. Power comes outta lying big and getting the whole damn world to play along with you. Once you got everybody agreeing with what they know in their hearts ain't true, you got em trapped. You're the boss. You can make a saint out of a gibbering nutcase like my high and mighty brother.

He aims the gun at Hartigan.

SENATOR (CONT'D)
There's what, maybe five hundred people in this hospital? And every blessed one of them would hear it if I was to pump you full of bullets. I could be standing here laughing and holding a smoking gun and I wouldn't even be arrested. They'd all lie for me. They'd have to, otherwise all their own lies-- everything that runs SIN CITY -- it all comes tumbling down like a pack of cards.

He points the gun straight down.

SENATOR (CONT'D)
It's really getting damn near impossible to resist at least blowing your nuts off.

220

His fat face lifts back as he bellows a laugh. "hahaHAH HA"

                    SENATOR (CONT'D)
                    (taking a drink)
But I want you firm and fit and healthy. I'm even putting up
cash of my own to get you more surgery -- to fix that heart
condition of yours. You're gonna keep on living a long time.
You're gonna be convicted of raping that little brat and
shooting my boy. You're gonna spend the rest of your life in
prison. Disgraced. Destroyed. Alone.

His face edges closer.

                    SENATOR (CONT'D)
Your wife? You tell her the truth and she's dead. You tell
anybody the truth... and they're dead!

BLACK

INT. HOSPITAL - HARTIGAN'S ROOM - NIGHT

Hartigan's wife is standing at his bed now.

                    WIFE
Just tell me it isn't true, John. What they're saying about
you and that child -- It can't be true. Just tell me they're
lying and I'll stand by you. You know I will. You've never
been able to lie to me. Damn it, John I'm begging you! Say
something.

Hartigan says nothing.

                    WIFE (CONT'D)
If you ever want to see me again -- say something now!

She cries.

                    WIFE (CONT'D)
Oh God. Damn you. Damn you to hell.

FRANK MILLER ON NANCY

"WHEN WE WERE CASTING ALL THESE PARTS, STRANGE THINGS STARTED HAPPENING. PEOPLE SHOWED UP WHO LOOKED LIKE MY DRAWINGS. THEN OTHER PEOPLE SHOWED UP WHO FELT LIKE THEM. AMONG THEM WAS THE PRECIOUS CHARACTER OF NANCY CALLAHAN WHO WE SEE AT TWO STAGES OF HER LIFE— AS AN ELEVEN-YEAR-OLD GIRL, AND THEN AS A NINETEEN-YEAR-OLD WOMAN, A VASTLY TRANSFORMED WOMAN. SHE'S A CRITICAL CHARACTER BECAUSE IN MANY WAYS SHE'S THE SYMBOL OF *SIN CITY*, THE COWGIRL. WHEN YOU GO INTO THIS BAR IN *SIN CITY*, YOU STUMBLE INTO THE SALOON WITH ALL THESE LOSERS LOUNGING AROUND, AND THE PLACE IS FULL OF SMOKE, AND THEY HAVEN'T CLEANED IT IN YEARS. YOU LOOK AROUND AND YOU EXPECT TO SEE SOME DISGUSTING SHOW ON THE STAGE, AND AN ANGEL COMES OUT DANCING. THAT'S REALLY THE HEART OF *SIN CITY*, AND NANCY IS ITS SYMBOL. AT EACH STAGE I THINK SHE'S PLAYED BEAUTIFULLY. MAKENZIE AND JESSICA ALBA WERE BOTH WONDERFUL."

INT. HOSPITAL - HARTIGAN'S ROOM - NIGHT

Hartigan's attorney now stands at the bed.

> ATTORNEY
> We're looking at your basic mountain of DNA evidence...
> The testimony of your own partner.... corroboration by six
> eyewitnesses and that's just so far... And there's your own
> silence... I'll do what I can, but... Leave us say you are good
> and screwed.

INT. HOSPITAL - HARTIGAN'S ROOM - NIGHT

Hartigan's superiors stand by the bed now.

> MORT
> Come on, Hartigan! What's holding you back? What's shutting
> you up? This whole thing stinks to high heaven-- and I'm not
> the only one on the force who smells it! Say the word and
> we'll back you all the way, damn the consequences! But you
> gotta say the word!

> CHIEF
> Forget it, Mort. He's got nothing to say to us.

INT. HOSPITAL - HARTIGAN'S ROOM - NIGHT

The nurse is now at his bedside.

> NURSE
> Sure, I'll rinse out your bedpan and wipe your butt. That's
> my job. But don't expect any friendly chit-chat outta me,
> mister. I heard what you done to that girl. I hope they throw
> away the key.

INT. HOSPITAL - HARTIGAN'S ROOM - NIGHT

Out of the darkness... Nancy appears at his bed.

> NANCY
> They won't let me testify! I told the cops how you saved
> my life and they just acted like I was crazy and talked

my parents into keeping me away! They're saying you done
things you didn't do! They got it all backwards! I hadda
sneak down my fire escape just to come visit!

          HARTIGAN
You shouldn't have come here. You gotta go home. It's very
important you stay quiet.

She gets closer to him.

          HARTIGAN (CONT'D)
You speaking up won't do me or anybody any good. There's no
saving me and no point in you getting hurt or killed trying
to.

          NANCY
I told them you saved me from that Roark creep! But they
wouldn't even check me out and see I'm still a virgin! Still a
virgin and still alive -- thanks to you!

          HARTIGAN
Sometimes the truth doesn't matter like it oughtta. But
you'll always remember things right. That means a lot to me.
But they'll kill you if you don't stay away. Don't visit me.
Don't write me. Don't even say my name.

          NANCY
Maybe you won't let me visit-- but I'm gonna write you,
Hartigan, and there's nothing you can do to stop me. You
say they'll kill me. But I'll be smart. I'll sign my letters
"Cordelia." That's the name of a cool detective in books I
read. I'll write you every week. For forever.

          HARTIGAN
Sure, kid. Now run on home, it's not safe for you here. Bye,
Nancy.

Nancy goes to the door.

          NANCY
I love you.

BLACK

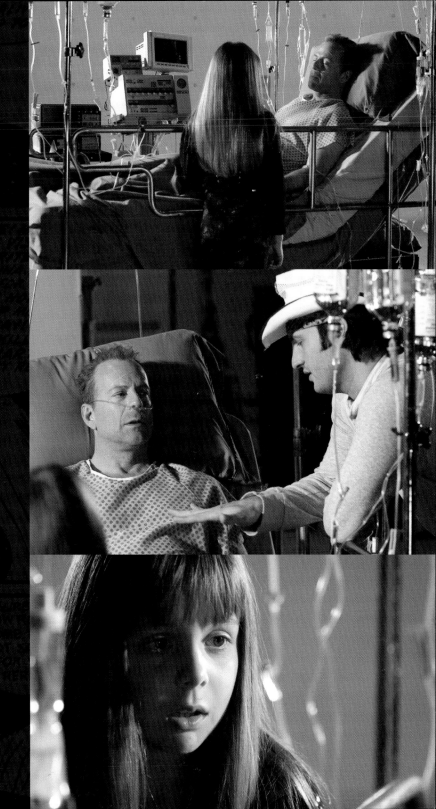

223

INT. HARTIGAN'S CELL - NIGHT

> HARTIGAN
> (VO)
> Weeks slide into months until time has no meaning, none at
> all. The dull gray haze of post-surgery anesthesia gives way
> to even more deadening process of legal this and legal that.
> I'm interrogated and accused and spat on and slapped around
> and indicted for a crime I didn't commit. This is nothing
> but a price I promised myself I'd pay and I'm paying it. You
> don't save a little girl's life, then turn around and throw
> her to the dogs. Not in my book, you don't.

Hartigan sits in a dark room, hands tied behind his back. Standing over
him is a block of a man, and two others. One is a woman. Liebowitz beats
Hartigan senseless. Face a mess.

> LIEBOWITZ
> John Hartigan. Mister law and order. Mister by the book.
> Mister high and mighty. Always looking down your nose at
> real cops like me and my pals, like we was something that's
> been sitting in the back of the refrigerator for too long.

Liebowitz turns.

> LIEBOWITZ (CONT'D)
> I gotta give you credit for being such a straight arrow for
> so damn many years without it catching up with you. But it's
> catching up with you now, friend-of-mine. It's catching up
> with you but good.

Liebowitz bunches up a fist, KRAK sending blood flying.

KRAK KRAK. Hartigan lies slumped over in his chair. Only the ropes keeping
him up. Blood pours from his face.

Overhead shot of Liebowitz, fists pour blood onto the floor along with
Hartigan.

Tammy, a way too sexy nurse, steps in.

> TAMMY
> Maybe I oughtta check him out. He's not looking too good.

> LIEBOWITZ
> (lifting Hartigan's mangled face)
> Aw, he's hale and hearty, Tammy. See? He's a picture of
> health.

224

Liebowitz shows Hartigan to Tammy.

                    LIEBOWITZ (CONT'D)
          That Tammy there, she's fine, isn't she? I rented her outta
          OLD TOWN-- and not just for medical services. I wanted to
          show you what you won't be getting any of, not in prison.
          You hear me, Hartigan? Stop being stupid and start playing
          along with us, you might just get some of Tammy. I'll pay for
          it myself.

Tammy shudders at the thought. He's is in his ear now.

                    LIEBOWITZ (CONT'D)
          HAH! You see that? She FLINCHED! You make her sick! She
          heard about you and that little girl!

Skinny steps up with his two cents.

                    SKINNY DUDE
          Ahem. There are other advantages to your signing the
          confession, Mr. Hartigan. I was successful in securing
          certain assurances from the district attorney himself
          regarding the conditions of your incarceration.

Skinny brings the paperwork over. Floats it in front of Hartigan. Hartigan's
blood trickles down his handcuffs.

                    HARTIGAN
                    (vo)
          All I've gotta do is nod my head and Liebowitz will stop
          punching me and the cuffs will come off. They're gonna
          convict me anyway. There's no reason on earth to keep
          standing my ground. There's nothing to gain. Nothing but
          more pain.

Hartigan and the paperwork.

                    SKINNY DUDE
          Worked my butt off, putting it together-- and he won't even
          look at it. I'm going home.

                    HARTIGAN
                    (vo)
          They want a confession. They won't get it.

Liebowitz throws another punch. BLACK OUT.

INT. HARTIGAN'S CELL - NIGHT

Overhead shot of a cell. Graphic. Hartigan in his tiny cell.

> HARTIGAN
> (vo)
> There's a letter from Nancy waiting when they put me
> in solitary. She calls herself "Cordelia," Just like she
> promised. She makes no mention of anything that'd give
> her away. At first, I figure she'll send another note or t
> before her young mind moves on to better things. But eve
> Thursday another one arrives.

INT. HARTIGAN'S CELL - NIGHT

Hartigan reading the letter.

> HARTIGAN
> (vo)
> What a sweet kid. She rockets through high school, a rea
> bookworm. Every single Thursday. I do my best to keep my
> hand from shaking when I reach for it.

INT. HARTIGAN'S CELL - NIGHT

Reaching for another letter.

> HARTIGAN
> (vo)
> Every Thursday. Before I know about it, she's had her hea
> broken for the first time. She writes about it poignantly
> beautifully. She could get this stuff published. She's the
> only friend I've got, the daughter I never had. My sweet
> "Cordelia." Skinny Little Nancy Callahan.

INT. HARTIGAN'S CELL - NIGHT

Hartigan in his cell.

> HARTIGAN
> (vo)
> Eight years pass. Then comes a Thursday when I bound fr

my cot. Excited as a kid at Christmas, only to find myself
staring at the damn floor of my damn cell. Looking for a
letter from Nancy that isn't there. Then another Thursday,
with no letter. Is she all right? Did something happen to
her? Nothing.

INT. HARTIGAN'S CELL - NIGHT

He passes his cell.

> HARTIGAN
> (vo)
> Two months now-- and not a word from Nancy. Did they find
> her? Did they get to her?

He realizes. His head leans back, facing upwards.

> HARTIGAN (CONT'D)
> Of course! Stupid old man...
> (vo)
> Laughter explodes from me, long and bitter and dry as
> sand. Stupid, crazy, pathetic old man! Do your math. Nancy's
> nineteen years old. How long did you expect her to keep
> writing? She was a saint to keep it up as long as she did.

He curls up on the floor.

> HARTIGAN (CONT'D)
> (vo)
> She's forgotten you, old man, you're alone. Alone.

He turns at a noise. A new prisoner entered his cell. Greenish yellow skin,
shaved head.

> HARTIGAN (CONT'D)
> (vo)
> This guy smells awful. Like bad food. Like a corpse left in a
> garbage dumpster in the middle of summer.

Hartigan stands. So does the creep.

> HARTIGAN (CONT'D)
> (vo)
> He stinks so bad I want to throw up.

FRANK MILLER ON YELLOW BASTARD

"YELLOW BASTARD IS A VILLAIN IN THE TRADITION OF THE
JOKER AND THE OTHER *BATMAN* VILLAINS, WHO ORIGINALLY
WERE TERRIFYING CHARACTERS. IT WAS ONLY THE OLD TV
SHOW, AND THEN THE MOVIES, THAT HAVE MADE THEM MORE
CLOWNISH. AND I THINK THAT YELLOW BASTARD IS GOING
TO REMIND PEOPLE HOW SCARY THAT STUFF CAN BE. IT'S
ALSO GOING TO REMIND PEOPLE HOW SCARY A COMIC BOOK
CAN BE, AND I HOPE TO HELL IT REMINDS PEOPLE OF A
TIME BEFORE PEOPLE STARTED THINKING COMIC BOOKS WERE
JUST FOR KIDS. BECAUSE THEY NEVER REALLY HAVE BEEN,
BUT MAYBE *SIN CITY* CAN HELP MY OTHER FIELD STAND A BIT
TALLER."

CHOK! The Yellow Bastard punches Hartigan so hard he falls.

INT. HARTIGAN'S CELL - NIGHT

                    HARTIGAN
                    (vo)
          Practically knocked my head off, the bastard. When I come
          to, I see it - the same kind of envelope Nancy always uses.

An envelope.. Blood soaked.

                    HARTIGAN (CONT'D)
                    (vo)
          But there's no letter inside of it. Something soft. Something
          that oughtta be alive. A hunk of meat and bone that oughtta
          be the index finger of the right hand of a nineteen-year old
          girl. Nancy.

He holds up the bloody finger.

                    HARTIGAN (CONT'D)
                    (vo)
          How the hell did they find her? She was so careful. She
          never gave away where she lives or where she works. She
          never revealed a single thing that could possibly lead them
          to her, over all these years. I've got to get out. Got to help
          her. Nothing else matters. Not my life-- and not my pride,
          either. There's only one final surrender they want. You got
          me, Roark. You beat me.

EXT. LUCILLE'S APARTMENT BUILDING

It looks the same as when Marv scaled the walls.

                    HARTIGAN
                    (vo)
          I call Lucille. Before I got sent up, she told me she could
          help. She begged me to let her help. I pray she's still a
          sucker for hard-luck cases like me.

INT. BEDROOM - NIGHT

Claire wakes next to Lucille.

> **LUCILLE**
> I'll get it, Claire. It's gotta be Marv. Never sleeps, and he's
> always getting himself in deep...
> (answers phone)
> Yeah? What? Who? Say again? Hartigan, my god it is you. Yes,
> yes. I'll get right on it. Right this second. I'll be there by
> noon, I promise.

EXT. LUCILLE'S CAR - NIGHT

She drives like a bat.

> **LUCILLE**
> Hartigan! Hot damn.

INT. CELL BLOCK - NIGHT

> **HARTIGAN**
> (vo)
> She shows up an hour early, breathless, looking like she's
> just run a mile. Melting snow glinting in her hair, wild
> sparks dancing in her eyes. The first woman I've seen in
> eight years. I manage to stand up without making a fool of
> myself.
> (alternate)
> Lucille. She wouldn't give up on me, back before the trial.
> She almost slugged me when I stopped her from hiring me a
> new attorney. When I refused to plead innocent, she did slug
> me. And when she hears what I'm going to do, she'll probably
> slug me again.

Lucille and a guard escort Hartigan down a hall.

> **LUCILLE**
> It's like they were waiting for my call. They're ready to
> deal. Hell, they're practically begging for a deal. They're
> scared of something. One of them as much as promised me
> you'd be out on parole if you'd confess and express regret
> and all that other dumb crap that of course we won't go for.
> No, we're getting you out of time served with no strings

CARLA GUGINO ON LUCILLE

"IN THE STORY WITH BRUCE WILLIS' CHARACTER HARTIGAN,
LUCILLE HAD BEEN HELPING DEFEND HIM AT THE BEGINNING
OF HIS TRIAL, HE ENDS UP GOING TO JAIL FOR THINGS HE
DIDN'T DO. HE'S CALLED HER UP AND ASKED HER TO COME
BACK AND HELP HIM, AND IT'S GOING TO BE THE BIGGEST
OPPORTUNITY OF HER PROFESSIONAL LIFE. AND SHE'S GOING
TO HELP SAVE THIS GUY WHO NEVER ASKS FOR ANY HELP.
ULTIMATELY THOUGH, SHE REALIZES HE'S GOT SOMETHING
COMPLETELY DIFFERENT THAT HE'S GOING FOR, AND SHE'S
VERY DISAPPOINTED BY IT. SHE'S KNOWN FOR PUNCHING MEN
WHEN SHE GETS ANGRY, BUT IT'S OUT OF LOVE. SO SHE'S
KIND OF A TOUGH-LOVE BROAD."

attached -- then we're turning right around and suing those
sorry sons of bitches for false prosecution. You're gonna
be exonerated, and you're gonna be a very rich man.

                         HARTIGAN
          This isn't like you think it is.

They walk up stairs.

                         LUCILLE
          The hell it isn't! It doesn't take a genius to figure out who
          framed you -- but even Senator Roark isn't God. We'll use the
          law. We'll use the press. He'll never know what hit him.

                         HARTIGAN
          I'm going to confess.

Lucille gives him a long, hard look.

                         LUCILLE
          Excuse me? John Hartigan, crawling on his belly in front
          of a parole board -- confessing to raping a little girl and
          blubbering for mercy, nah. Doesn't work.

                         HARTIGAN
          That's exactly what I'm going to do.

                         LUCILLE
          Count to ten. Count to ten... It's the isolation. Eight years
          is a long time. You've snapped your cap. There's no way John
          Hartigan would go chicken. John Hartigan had guts.

                         HARTIGAN
          I'm going in there and telling them I'm a twisted, wretched
          child molester. I'm agreeing to anything they want from me.

Another long hard look. Then KRAK! She whacks him.

                         LUCILLE
          Alright. You son of a bitch, let's get this over with.

INT. HEARING ROOM - NIGHT

They are escorted into the hearing room.

>   HARTIGAN
>   (vo)
> Do this right, Hartigan. You've rehearsed it a hundred times.
> Don't get proud. Think about Nancy.

He stands in the streaks of light.

>   HEARING BOARD PERSON
> Mr. Hartigan, we're ready for your statement.

>   HARTIGAN
>   (vo)
> I say everything they want to hear, just the way they want to
> hear it. I love you, Nancy.

EXT. PRISON - NIGHT

He walks out a free man. Breaths in the cold air.

BOB is standing by his car.

>   BOB
> It's a lot of miles to town, Hartigan. Care for a ride?

>   HARTIGAN
> Sure. Bob-- as long as you stay in front of me.

>   BOB
> Prison's made you paranoid. Talk about water under the
> bridge. Christ, Eight years.

We're inside the YELLOW BASTARD'S car, looking out the windshield over his
yellow hand and steering wheel.

>   HARTIGAN
> Sorry, I guess I'm not used to being treated like a human.

>   BOB
> You did your time. You made parole. You had your reasons for
> handling things like you did. As did I. Let's go.

The Yellow Bastard follows.

NICK STAHL ON RODRIGUEZ AND MILLER

"ROBERT HAD A CERTAIN PASSION FOR THIS STORY, BUT I THINK HE ALSO RECOGNIZED THE FACT THAT IT'S FRANK'S PROJECT, AND THAT IF ANYONE WAS GOING TO BRING IT TO LIFE IT WOULD BE HIM. I THINK IT'S REALLY HELPFUL THAT BOTH FRANK AND ROBERT WILL GIVE NOTES. THEY NOTICE DIFFERENT THINGS, INCONSISTENCIES, AND THEY BOTH GIVE DIRECTION, AND SO I THINK IT'S ACTUALLY REALLY HELPFUL TO HAVE TWO SETS OF EYES WATCHING."

EXT. BOB'S CAR - NIGHT

                    HARTIGAN
          Any word from Eileen?

                    BOB
          Yeah, she remarried four years ago. She's had two kids.
          Sorry, John.

                    HARTIGAN
          Don't be. I'm glad. She always wanted kids. She'll make a
          good mother. Like you said, Bob. Water under the bridge.

INT. HARTIGAN'S ROOM - NIGHT

Hartigan is in his room. Thumbing through a phone book.

                    HARTIGAN
                    (vo)
          Right here in the phone book. Cordelia Callahan. An address
          on North Culver. It's a sure bet Bob's got a man staked out
          down in the lobby.

EXT. FIRE ESCAPE - NIGHT

He climbs out the fire escape. Sees the name: Nancy Callahan. An address on
North Culver.

                    HARTIGAN
                    (vo)
          I leave the same way any other criminal would.

EXT. STREET- HARTIGAN'S PLACE - NIGHT

He cuts in front of the Yellow Bastard's car.

EXT. NANCY'S CONDO - FRONT - NIGHT

A cab waits outside a condo.

> HARTIGAN
> (vo)
> I take a twenty-minute ride to a smart collection of condos squatting low on the hills. Not bad. Nancy's done okay for herself. And no wonder. She's a sharp kid. I see her open window and for a few seconds there I can't breathe at all.

INT. NANCY'S CONDO - NIGHT

He walks into an open porch door. Examines books/papers.

> HARTIGAN
> (vo)
> Nothing. Not a sound. No sign of life. The place is a mess.
> (examines room)
> Has Roark gone to all this trouble just to torture a broken old man? Like a kid poking at a fly when he's already torn his wings off? What has he done to Nancy?
> (examines papers)
> Books, papers scattered everywhere. It's like all she ever does is read and study and write. Almost nothing personal. No diary. No phone numbers or addresses written down anywhere. The closest thing to a clue is a pack of matches from a lousy saloon.

Close on matchbook for Kadie's Club Pecos.

> HARTIGAN (CONT'D)
> (vo)
> It's a longshot, but maybe she's got some friends there.

INT. KADIE'S CLUB PECOS - NIGHT

Hartigan walks in.

> HARTIGAN
> (vo)
> One look at the joint and my heart sinks. A dead end. Nancy wouldn't have anything to do with a pack of drunks and losers like this. But if there's anything to be found here-- the faintest lead to wherever Nancy is or to whoever kidnapped her and mutilated her and did God knows what else to her... Pretend you're still a cop. Stay calm. Stay smart.

He walks up to a waitress.

HARTIGAN (CONT'D)
Excuse me, Miss. I wonder if you could help me. I'm looking
for somebody.

SHELLIE
Cold night like this, everybody's looking for somebody,
stranger. Good luck.

HARTIGAN
It's not like that. It's a friend. Her name's Nancy. Nancy
Callahan.

SHELLIE
Everyone's looking for Nancy. Eyes to the stage, Pilgrim.
She's just warming up.

Nancy on stage. Hartigan can't take her eyes off her. He doesn't see
behind him is Yellow Bastard.

HARTIGAN
(vo)
Skinny little Nancy Callahan. She grew up. She filled out.

She uses ropes and a western getup.

HARTIGAN (CONT'D)
(vo)
Nancy Callahan. Nineteen years old.

Nancy Dances something fierce.

HARTIGAN (CONT'D)
(vo)
And here I was expecting a skinny little bookworm, maybe a
bit too shy for her own good. How little she told me about
herself, in all her letters, over all those years. How the hel
did they find her? Then it hits me.

He looks around.

HARTIGAN (CONT'D)
(vo)
They DIDN'T. They were bluffing. They were counting on me t
be so addled after eight years in solitary I'd fall for their
crummy bluff. And I did. I've led them straight to her.

234

HARTIGAN (CONT'D)
(vo, eyeing bar)
Stupid Old Man! If they followed you here --- you've led them
straight to her!

He spins.

HARTIGAN (CONT'D)
(vo)
From right behind me-- That SMELL...

We see him eyeing the Yellow Bastard. Drinking a shot. Slow and deliberate.
Yellow Bastard raises his gun slightly from his jacket. A customer leans
over and pukes.

HARTIGAN (CONT'D)
(vo)
Stay steady, old man. Stay sharp. You haven't quite managed
to completely screw everything up. Not yet. She hasn't
spotted you yet. You're just a horny ex-con watching an
exotic dancer. Stay calm. Turn around and walk out the door
-- and she'll be safe.

Yellow Bastard follows Hartigan out.

HARTIGAN (CONT'D)
(vo)
Lead the creep outside. Get that Beretta away from him --
somehow-- and kill him. Walk steady. Stay calm. Just a few
more seconds... and she'll be safe.

Nancy sees him from the stage. Stops dead. Close on Hartigan.

HARTIGAN (CONT'D)
(vo)
No, Nancy. Don't notice me. Don't recognize me.

She leaps from the stage. Hartigan can't do anything. Yellow Bastard watches
intently. She runs into his arms and kisses Hartigan. A long embrace.

HARTIGAN (CONT'D)
Nancy.. There's no time to explain. I've made a terrible
mistake. I've put you in terrible danger. We've gotta get out
of here. Right this second.

NANCY
Whatever you say, Hartigan, I'll throw some clothes on.

ROBERT RODRIGUEZ ON BRUCE WILLIS

"IT WASN'T UNTIL I WAS LOOKING AT *SIN CITY* AS A MOVIE THAT I STARTED THINKING OF CASTING, BECAUSE WHEN YOU FIRST READ THE BOOKS, YOU JUST TAKE THE CHARACTERS AS THEY'RE DRAWN. BUT WHEN I LOOKED AT THEM IN CASTING TERMS, I KNEW RIGHT AWAY BRUCE WILLIS WOULD HAVE TO BE HARTIGAN. I'D SEEN AN OLD *MOONLIGHTING* EPISODE, THAT I KEPT ON TAPE FOREVER, WHERE HE PLAYED A HARD-BOILED DETECTIVE. IT WAS A COMEDIC TONE, BUT HE PLAYED IT VERY STRAIGHT, AND HE LOOKS GREAT IN BLACK AND WHITE, SO I THOUGHT BRUCE WILLIS WOULD BE GREAT. HE'S A LITTLE YOUNG TO PLAY HARTIGAN, BUT WE CAN AGE HIM UP WITH MAKEUP EFFECTS, AND HE'S PERFECT FOR THE PART."

She turns to leave.

> NANCY (CONT'D)
> And here I figured you'd forgotten all about me. Me and my dumb letters.

> HARTIGAN
> They kept me going. Kept me from killing myself. Hurry up, will you?
> (vo)
> She tosses me a wink that'd make a corpse breathe hard. Then minutes crawl by. No sign of the creep. That comforts me not a bit.

> NANCY
> Let's go.

EXT. KADIE'S CLUB PECOS - PARKING LOT - NIGHT

She leads him by the hand out to her car.

> HARTIGAN
> (vo)
> Maybe I oughtta drive.

> NANCY
> (with a look)
> Not a chance. Nobody but me can keep this heap running.

INT./EXT. NANCY'S CAR - BASTARD'S CAR - STREET - NIGHT

Driving.

> NANCY
> Besides, from the sound of things, you might have to shoot somebody.

> HARTIGAN
> I don't have a gun.

Another look from Nancy.

NANCY
Under the seat.

He pulls up the gun. Close on gun.

HARTIGAN
Yeah. This'll do.

NANCY
It's loaded, and it works. I've taken it to the range a few times. Kicks like a mule. Hartigan -- there's so much I've wanted to say to you. You've never been far from my thoughts. I've lain awake NIGHTS. Thinking about you.

HARTIGAN
What are you talking about.

SPAK! The back window cracks open with a bullet. The front windshield follows.

HARTIGAN (CONT'D)
Damn!

NANCY
(losing control of car)
Aaaa! Oh my God! Oh my God!

HARTIGAN
Keep driving, Nancy! Keep driving and stay on the road!

SPUKK! Her car hits a post and goes sliding off and then back onto the road.

Yellow Bastard hangs out the window. Gun in hand.

HARTIGAN (CONT'D)
What are you doing? Keep driving!

They fly down the road.

HARTIGAN (CONT'D)
(vo)
She's counting on you old man. Prove you're still worth a damn.

He hangs completely outside the open car door, aiming his gun, even as they fly off road.

He gets tagged in the arm. Still shooting.

          HARTIGAN (CONT'D)
          (vo)
    He's a decent shot-- he's got skill. But he's in too much of a
    hurry. Throwing away bullets like they were candy-- doesn't
    know to take his time-- aim careful -- look the devil in the
    eye --

Hartigan aims carefully.

          HARTIGAN (CONT'D)
          (vo)
    --show him HOW, old man-- Nancy's counting on you. Take
    your time -- aim careful.

Yellow bastard fires yet again.

Hartigan let's loose a savage return shot.

CASH! The windshield cracks, Yellow Bastard recoils.

Yellow Bastard's car flies off the small cliff.

          HARTIGAN (CONT'D)
    Stop the car, Nancy. I gotta confirm the kill.

          NANCY
          (terrified)
  What?

          HARTIGAN
    NANCY! STOP THE CAR!

          NANCY
    Stop the car. Confirm the kill.

She stops.

          NANCY (CONT'D)
    Sorry. I got a little rattled.

          HARTIGAN
    Sit tight. I'll be right back.

NANCY
No! My love, let me stay close! Nothing can happen to me when
I'm with you! Let me stay close.

EXT. HILL - NIGHT

Close on Hartigan lifting up yellow blood on his fingertips.

HARTIGAN
(vo)
The stink. I almost gag. His blood smells even worse than he
does. And it's all over the place. But the creep himself --
he's gone. He couldn't have gotten far.
(vo)
Sirens. I used to welcome the sound.

HARTIGAN (CONT'D)
We're out of time. Let's go.

EXT. MIMI'S MOTEL - NIGHT

MIMI'S NIGHT FLIGHT VACANCY Motel Cafe

They pull into the motel.

HARTIGAN
(vo)
There's nothing to do now but find a place to hole up for the
night. Get Nancy calmed down and figure out what on earth
I'm going to do next. The STINK. Somehow it stays with us all
the way to the hotel.

INT. MIMI'S MOTEL - ROOM - NIGHT

Inside the hotel.

HARTIGAN
Nancy -- I went to your apartment. Your window was thrown
wide open. Your rooms were almost empty. That's why I was so
sure you'd been kidnapped.

239

NANCY
My window? Robbed again! That's the third time this year! I swore if I ever saw you again I'd show you I grew up strong. But there I was, just like before. Scared, helpless. I'm such an asshole.

HARTIGAN
You need to sit down, Nancy. You'll feel a little better if you sit down.

EXT. MIMI'S MOTEL - ROOM - NIGHT

Yellow Bastard rises up from the back seat of their car. Peering into their window.

YELLOW BASTARD
Kheff... Khurff..

HARTIGAN
(vo)
Nancy calms down-- and the real trouble starts. Her eyes go tearful, Radiant.

INT. MIMI'S HOTEL - ROOM - NIGHT

NANCY
It's always been you, Hartigan. All these years. I had a couple of boyfriends -- but it was never right. It was always you.

They are sitting on the couch.

HARTIGAN
That's just nerves, making you say things like that. You're exhausted. You need to sleep.

NANCY
(closer)
Sleep with me.

HARTIGAN
Stop it, Nancy.

EXT. MIMI'S MOTEL - ROOM - NIGHT

Yellow bloody footprints in the dark asphalt. The Yellow Bastard spews
yellow blood from his neck as he stumbles to the hotel door.

INT. MIMI'S MOTEL - ROOM - NIGHT

          NANCY
    Eight years. Why do you think I kept writing you those
    letters? It wasn't just gratitude. I tried to fall in love with
    boys. I even thought I did, once or twice. But I was already
    in love-- with you.

          HARTIGAN
    That's enough, Nancy. I'm old enough to be your grandfather.
    You're scared and it's got you talking crazy.

Nancy gets even closer.

          NANCY
    I'm not scared.

He turns his face aside. She kisses his cheek.

          HARTIGAN
    No...

He turns back. They kiss. He pulls away.

          HARTIGAN (CONT'D)
    There's wrong and there's wrong, and there's this. For God's
    sake, you're just a kid.

          NANCY
    I love you.

          HARTIGAN
    I love you too. With all my heart.

She smiles.

JESSICA ALBA ON NANCY AND TRUE LOVE

"I BELIEVE IN LOVE, I BELIEVE IT'S POSSIBLE TO FIND
SOMEONE THAT YOU CONNECT WITH ON THAT OTHER LEVEL,
AND SOMETIMES WE BURY THAT VERY HOPE IN ORDER TO
EMOTIONALLY SURVIVE IN THE WORLD, BUT NOT NANCY. SHE
JUST WEARS HER HEART ON HER SLEEVE, SOMETHING I WISH
I COULD DO MORE. THAT'S WHY THIS IS KIND OF A FANTASY
TO PORTRAY A CHARACTER SO SINCERE, SO SOFT, AND SO
VULNERABLE, DESPITE THE SIDE OF HER THAT'S REALLY
STRONG AND CONFIDENT ON STAGE. HARTIGAN IS HER KNIGHT
IN SHINING ARMOR. SHE WAS KIDNAPPED, HE SAVED HER, AND
GAVE UP HIS LIFE FOR HER. SO HE COMES BACK AND SHE
THINKS THAT FOR THAT MOMENT, EVERYTHING IS POSSIBLE,
AND NOTHING'S GETTING IN HER WAY OF LOVE AND HAPPINESS.
THEY GET TO SPEND SOME MOMENTS TOGETHER WHERE THEY
TRULY GET TO JUST BE, AND THAT'S IT. HE THINKS IT'S ALL
BEHIND THEM, THE PLAN FOILED, BUT SOON REALIZES HE'S
BEEN USED TO TRACK HER AGAIN. IT'S AN AMAZING AND
CLASSIC TRAGEDY."

INT. MIMI'S MOTEL - SHOWER - NIGHT

He's taking a shower now.

> HARTIGAN
> (vo)
> Cold shower. It helps.

CLACK CLACK CLACK.

> HARTIGAN (CONT'D)
> No, Nancy.

KRAK! The Yellow Bastard throws a savage swing through the curtain, connecting with Hartigan's jaw. KRAK!

> HARTIGAN (CONT'D)
> (vo)
> No. Not Nancy.

> YELLOW BASTARD
> Recognize my voice, Hartigan? Recognize my voice, you piece of shit cop? I look different, but I bet you can recognize my voice. I'd be really insulted if you didn't recognize my voice.

Hartigan on the floor of the tub. Yellow Bastard's foot squeezing his head down.

> HARTIGAN
> Sure. I recognize your voice, Junior.

                                                    CUT TO:

INT. MIMI'S MOTEL - ROOM - NIGHT

Hartigan is in a noose, now. Hanging by the neck.

> HARTIGAN
> (vo)
> Everything's gone right straight to hell. I've been suckered right into betraying the only friend I've got and putting her in the hands of a giggling psychopath. Suckered by a spoiled brat son of a Senator. Suckered by a murdering rapist I thought I'd put down for good. It's all gone to hell.

> YELLOW BASTARD
> (on phone)
> Koonz. It's me. I got a dead man who needs to be fetched --
> and I want you to set me up for a party.

Nancy is bound and gagged. Junior removes the syringe.

> HARTIGAN
> (vo)
> Nancy. I was a fool. A damn old fool. I'm sorry.

Hartigan is standing on his toes atop a flimsy table. The only thing keeping
him from snapping his neck in the rope.

> YELLOW BASTARD
> Tonight. I've already got the girl, you dumb shit! You just
> get things ready. And don't screw anything up, this time.

> HARTIGAN
> (vo)
> Like hot pokers shoved up my legs. Can't hold out much
> longer. Every twitch-- every wobble-- and the noose pulls
> tighter.

Close on toes. Teetering table.

> YELLOW BASTARD
> Everything's got to be perfect or I'm calling my Dad! All my
> tools better be clean and sharp! Right! It better be ready---
> and it better be perfect!

He hangs up and laughs.

> YELLOW BASTARD (CONT'D)
> Hahahah. I get to do whatever I want! However I want!
> Whenever I want it!

He has a hand around Nancy's neck, at his feet. He sits on the couch. The
Yellow blood flowing from around his neck.

> YELLOW BASTARD (CONT'D)
> My dad! I'd love him, if I didn't hate him. He spent a fortune,
> hiring every expert on the planet to pull me out of that
> coma you put me in -- and to grow me back the equipment you
> blew off from between my legs, so the old fart can hold out
> some hope of having a grandson.

BRUCE WILLIS ON SIN CITY

"I WAS WORKING NIGHTS ON A FILM CALLED *HOSTAGE*,
AND I GOT A CALL FROM MY OFFICE SAYING THAT ROBERT
RODRIGUEZ WANTED TO COME TALK TO ME ABOUT A FILM HE
WAS DOING, AND THAT HE HAD A DVD THAT HE WANTED TO
SHOW ME. ROBERT CAME OUT TO THE HOUSE WITH FRANK, AND
WE STARTED WATCHING THE DVD. THE CLIP THAT HE HAD WAS
FOUR OR FIVE MINUTES LONG, BUT ONCE I STARTED WATCHING
IT - AND ABOUT A MINUTE IN - I SAID, 'HANG ON A SECOND,'
AND I HIT PAUSE. I SAID, 'WHATEVER ELSE I SEE ON THIS I
JUST WANT YOU TO KNOW THAT I'M IN, I WANT TO DO THIS.'
AND WE WATCHED THE REST OF THE CLIP. IT WAS THAT SIMPLE.
THE CLIP WAS THE MOST STARTLING PIECE OF FILM FOOTAGE
THAT I'VE EVER SEEN. I'D NEVER SEEN ANYTHING QUITE LIKE
THIS. I THINK ROBERT HAS INVENTED A NEW TECHNOLOGY
THAT NO ONE'S EVER SEEN BEFORE. EVERYTHING YOU SEE IN
THAT FILM WAS NOT THERE ON THE DAY WE SHOT EXCEPT FOR
THE BAR SCENE. IT'S JUST RIVETING. IT WAS JUST REALLY
VISUALLY STARTLING AND REALLY STUNNING."

He flaunts.

> YELLOW BASTARD (CONT'D)
> It was those gene wizards who put me back together, God bless em -- Though there were, as you can see, a few side effects. Not that I'm complaining. With you out of the picture, I've been having the time of my life. And now you've led me back to sweet little Nancy.

He grips her face.

> YELLOW BASTARD (CONT'D)
> Your darling "Cordelia." We wondered who wrote all those letters. She left not a clue. Clever girl. And so pretty.

He sniffs her face..

> YELLOW BASTARD (CONT'D)
> A little old, for my taste. But I can forgive that, this once.

> HARTIGAN
> Nancy. Don't scream. Whatever he does to you-- don't scream.

> YELLOW BASTARD
> She'll scream. I'm gonna take all night doing dear old Nancy -- and you're gonna die knowing it's all your fault!

He throws her over his shoulder.

> YELLOW BASTARD (CONT'D)
> They've all screamed Hartigan! Dozens of them! Maybe a hundred! Eight years worth and every one of them screamed! If there weren't so many people hereabout, I'd show you how I'm gonna make old Nancy scream. It's gonna be one hell of a show.

He looks up at Hartigan, with false sadness.

> YELLOW BASTARD (CONT'D)
> I guess this is goodbye.

KAK! He kicks the legs out from the table.

GLAKK! The rope tightens. Feet kicking.

HARTIGAN
(vo)
This is it. No way to fight it now. No hope left. No chance.
This is it. This is... the end.

Blackout. Credits begin to roll.

INT. MIMI'S MOTEL - ROOM - NIGHT

Hartigan's eyes open. Credits retreat.

HARTIGAN
(vo)
NO. Give it a shot, old man! Keep your neck tight. Stay
conscious. Move. The window, maybe there's an alarm. The
window.

He starts to swing.

HARTIGAN (CONT'D)
(vo)
Keep your neck tight. Stay conscious. Stay conscious.

His feet crack through the window.

HARTIGAN (CONT'D)
(vo)
No alarm. Doesn't matter. Find a way. The glass.

Close on feet, gripping a shard of glass with bloody feet.

HARTIGAN (CONT'D)
(vo)
Get it to your hands. Cut the rope. You can do it. You can do
it.

INT./EXT. FANCY CAR - STREET (MOVING) - NIGHT

Fancy car rips down the road. Familiar voices prattle on inside.

KLUMP
It is inclement upon me to comment with marked displeasure
on your rash impulsiveness in selecting such an eye-

catching and impractical car to heist, MR. Shlubb.

>   SHLUBB
> Protest though you might, Mr. Klump, you must nonetheless
> admit to the sheer, phallic magestry of said Ferrari's
> performance. An engine of cyclopean power throbs beneath
> this steel stallion's hood!

>   KLUMP
> Point readily conceded, Mr. Shlubb. But this vehicular
> structure on which you so amorously fixate could garner us
> attention of the law-enforcement variety- and is plainly
> ill-suited for the mission at hand.

>   SHLUBB
> Be this as it might-- the thrusting manhood of this
> automotive juggernaut has transformed our tawdry task into
> an experience as profound as it is ejaculatory. Which leads
> me to ponder, MR. Klump... Is there no poetry in your soul?

EXT. MIMI'S MOTEL - FANCY CAR - NIGHT

They pull into MIMI's Night Flight Motel Cafe.

>   KLUMP
> A relevant to said mission is the following query I now
> put forth to you-- said query concerning matters strictly
> spacial in nature. Wherein this most streamlined and
> trunkless of transports boner-inspiring though it may be...
> wherein are we to reposit our recently deceased cargo?

INT. MIMI'S MOTEL - ROOM - NIGHT

They walk in and find Hartigan's severed rope dangling form the lamp. But
no Hartigan.

>   KLUMP
> I can only express puzzlement that borders on alarm.

Slam! KONK KONK! Hartigan slams Klump's head through the window.

>   HARTIGAN
> Tell me where Roark takes the girls or I'll cut your damn

head off. In plain English, creep.

                    KLUMP
              (through bleeding teeth)
     The answer you seek is rural-- even agrarian. The farm.

INT./EXT. FANCY CAR - STREET (MOVING) - NIGHT

Driving.

                    HARTIGAN
                    (vo)
     The farm. That's all I need to hear. Every cop on the force
     knows about the Roark family's farm and to stay away from
     it. I stick to the side roads like any ex-con driving a stolen
     car would.

Guns on the side seat.

                    HARTIGAN (CONT'D)
                    (vo)
     Shlubb and Klump were packing an arsenal. Once things get
     loud, I'll probably have use for the cannons. But at first
     it'll have to be quiet.

Snap! a switchblade.

                    HARTIGAN (CONT'D)
                    (vo)
     Quiet and nasty.

INT./EXT. FANCY CAR - ROAD TO FARM - NIGHT

He pulls over a new area.

                    HARTIGAN
                    (vo)
     I've lost so much time. I pray she's still alive.

We see out his windshield. A parked car.

JESSICA ALBA ON RODRIGUEZ

"WHEN YOU FIRST MEET HIM YOU THINK, BECAUSE HOLLYWOOD IS SO DISINGENUOUS, IT'S A LITTLE WEIRD BECAUSE HE'S SO NICE, COOL AND NORMAL. HE'S JUST CREATED AN ENVIRONMENT IN AUSTIN THAT'S A FAMILY ENVIRONMENT, WHERE HE CAN THRIVE CREATIVELY. MOST PEOPLE IN FILM ARE UPROOTED FROM A FAMILIAR PLACE, AND THROWN INTO L.A. AND IT'S LIKE 'OKAY, NOW BE CREATIVE.' AND IT'S HARD. YOU KIND OF LOSE YOUR MIND, AND I THINK THAT CREATES A LOT OF CRAZINESS, AND THE REASON I THINK A LOT OF DIRECTORS ARE BANANAS IS BECAUSE IT'S SUCH A STRUGGLE. BUT HERE ROBERT IS COMFORTABLE, HE KNOWS EVERYONE, EVERYONE'S PART OF THIS UNIT, AND THAT ALLOWS HIM TO JUST BE FREE, AND EXPLORE, AND TRY NEW THINGS. IT'S SO INSPIRING, REALLY."

                    HARTIGAN (CONT'D)
                    (vo)
         Nancy's car. Six miles from the farm.

He slows as he passes the car.

                    HARTIGAN (CONT'D)
                    (vo)
         "Nobody but me can keep this heap running," she told me.
         Good girl. The car stalled out on that yellow bastard and
         you didn't tell him how to start it up again. You kept your
         mouth shut. I'll bet junior was furious.

Hartigan rips the Ferrari over a hill.

                    HARTIGAN (CONT'D)
                    (vo)
         I'll bet he slapped you around something fierce. But you
         stayed strong. Good girl. You bought a few extra minutes.
         There's still a chance. Don't scream.

Close on Hartigan. His eyes. Burning.

EXT. FARM - WOODS - NIGHT

                    HARTIGAN
                    (vo)
         I ditch the car a mile or so from the farm and make my way
         through the woods. I'm not halfway there when it hits.

He leans against a tree. Clutching his heart.

                    HARTIGAN (CONT'D)
                    (vo)
         No. No. Not my heart. It can't be my heart. I was cured. The
         doctors said I was cured.

KHAFF! A bad cough. Blood in it.

                    HARTIGAN (CONT'D)
                    (vo)
         Doesn't matter. I don't have to stay alive that much longer,
         anyway.

EXT. FARMHOUSE - NIGHT

Hartigan sneaks up behind a guard. MNFF. Knife into neck.

>   HARTIGAN
>   (vo)
>   Rotten way to kill a man. But it's quiet. Hate yourself later.

He looks up at the sound of a whip CRACK! Top room in the farmhouse is lit.

INT. FARMHOUSE - TOP ROOM - NIGHT

>   YELLOW BASTARD
>   You're only making this worse for yourself, you stupid cow!

Crack! Crack! Crack!

>   YELLOW BASTARD (CONT'D)
>   You think I'm tired, is that it? You think I'm getting tired?

Nancy has her hands tied up as Yellow Bastard lays her back open with the whip.

>   YELLOW BASTARD (CONT'D)
>   Stupid, ugly cow! I don't get tired! No-- you're the one who's
>   gonna wear down. You can't take much more of this. Nobody
>   could! You'll crack! (Huff huff) You'll crack!

The speedo wearing, repulsive Yellow bastard stands over her with the bloody whip.

>   YELLOW BASTARD (CONT'D)
>   You'll cry and beg! You'll SCREAM! Oh, yeah, you'll scream you
>   big, fat, ugly cow! You'll scream!

WHIP! CRACK!

>   YELLOW BASTARD (CONT'D)
>   You'll SCREAM!

He leans into her face.

>   YELLOW BASTARD (CONT'D)
>   You thinking the whip was the worst I can do? That was

foreplay.

                    NANCY
Hartigan was right about you. You can't get it up unless I
scream. You're pathetic.

                    YELLOW BASTARD
It's not wise at all to make fun of me like that.

He lifts a savage knife.

                    YELLOW BASTARD (CONT'D)
It brings out the worst in me.

EXT. FARMHOUSE - TOP ROOM - NIGHT

BREKK. SHPLUKK! Hartigan recoils outside and falls onto the ground
shoulder shot off by a guard.

                    HARTIGAN
                    (vo)
Stupid old man! In too much of a hurry-- wasn't careful.

INT. FARMHOUSE - TOP ROOM - NIGHT

                    YELLOW BASTARD
Damn! It can't be...

He drags Nancy with him as he goes to the window.

EXT. FARMHOUSE - NIGHT

                    HARTIGAN
                    (vo)
Charging in like Galahad just like I told myself I wouldn't.
Stupid old man!

                    GUARD 1
Tagged him good!

GUARD 2
Don't take no chances. Perforate the fool!

Hartigan rolls over. Guns blazing.

HARTIGAN
Good advice.

BRAK BOOM!GAKK! SPUKK! Right through the skulls.

HARTIGAN (CONT'D)
(vo)
No. Not now. Can't breathe. No. Not now.

KHAFF KHAFF! He strains. HGGNN. He stands.

HARTIGAN (CONT'D)
(vo)
Get over it, old man. Get sharp. Get smart. She needs you.

He crawls to the farmhouse.

INT. FARMHOUSE - NIGHT

Descending the ladder up to the loft is Yellow Bastard carrying Nancy.

HARTIGAN
Give it up, Junior. It's over. Let her go.

The huge knife at her throat.

YELLOW BASTARD
Hah! You're dreaming, Hartigan. This is better than I hoped!
I get to see your eyes while I fillet the woman of your
dreams right in front of you! Sit down and enjoy the show!
You've had it! You're about to keel over! You can't even lift
that cannon!

HARTIGAN
Sure I can.

He tries to lift it. It falls to the ground. He falls to his knees.

                    HARTIGAN (CONT'D)
          Nancy, I'm sorry.

Nancy, wide eyes. Yellow Bastard grins. THUD. Hartigan falls over.

                    YELLOW BASTARD
          You gave me a scare for a second there, old man! I'm taking
          no chances with you. First I soften you up -- then it's
          showtime.

He shoves Nancy aside. Raises the knife high.

                    YELLOW BASTARD (CONT'D)
          Here it comes! It's gonna hurt.

                    HARTIGAN
          You're right about that.

Snap!

                    HARTIGAN (CONT'D)
          Sucker.

The switchblade juts out of the Yellow chest. KRUNCH! The big knife flies as
Hartigan snaps some yellow bones.

                    HARTIGAN (CONT'D)
                    (vo)
          I take his weapon away.

                    YELLOW BASTARD
          No...

Hartigan grips Yellow Bastard's balls. And RIPS.

                    HARTIGAN
                    (vo)
          Both of them.

Hartigan tears into Yellow Bastard with a flurry of flying fists. Yellow
blood gushes and flows like rivers of gore.

                    HARTIGAN (CONT'D)
          Eight years you son of a bitch!
                    (vo)
          After a while. All I'm doing is pounding wet chunks of bone

into the floorboards. So I stop.

                    HARTIGAN (CONT'D)
So long, Junior. It's been a pleasure.

Shot from above. The bloodied corpse. Hartigan carries Nancy.

                    NANCY
                    (weak)
I didn't scream. Not once, Hartigan. I didn't scream.

                    HARTIGAN
I know it, darling. You grew up strong.

EXT. FARM - WOODS - NIGHT

Outside the Ferrari.

                    HARTIGAN
                    (vo)
By the time I get her to the car, Nancy's stopped shaking.
Her skin is warm again. She's herself again. She'll be all
right.

                    NANCY
Thanks for remembering my coat-- and for all the little
things, like saving my life twice. Hartigan - John - it's over
now, isn't it? The whole thing, I mean. You're finally free for
real?

                    HARTIGAN
It's almost over. You better get rolling.

                    NANCY
You're not coming along?

                    HARTIGAN
Hell no! I've got friends on their way - to collect evidence.
I'm gonna blow this whole sick mess wide open. I'm gonna
clear my name-- and get Senator Roark thrown behind bars,
where he belongs.

Close.

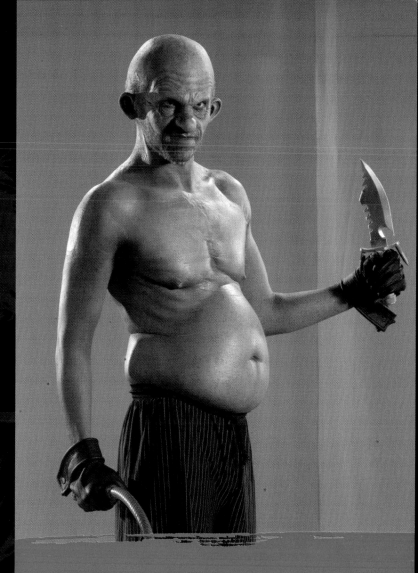

PROPERTY MASTER STEVE JOYNER ON NICK STAHL

"NICK IS AMAZING AS YELLOW BASTARD. I CAN'T THINK OF
NICK AS YELLOW BASTARD BECAUSE WHEN I SEE THIS GUY
WHO PLAYS YELLOW BASTARD IT DOESN'T LOOK LIKE NICK AT
ALL. KNB TURNED NICK STAHL, THIS WONDERFUL HANDSOME
YOUNG MAN, INTO THIS MONSTER. AND THEN WE GAVE HIM HIS
CREEPY PROPS. HE HAD THIS AUSTRALIAN BULL WHIP; HE HAD
THIS AMAZING SILVER KNIFE THAT HE THREATENS NANCY WITH.
HE HAD, OF COURSE, HIS YELLOW SYRINGE OF JUICE WHICH
HE USES ON HER, AND IT'S PRETTY TERRIFYING. THAT YELLOW
BASTARD IS DEFINITELY A BASTARD."

> NANCY
> Be careful. I can't lose you. Not again.

> HARTIGAN
> You'll never lose me.

They kiss. Light snow.

> HARTIGAN (CONT'D)
> (vo)
> Nancy Callahan. The love of my life.

The Ferrari drives away.

EXT. FARM - WOODS - NIGHT

> HARTIGAN (VO)
> Shame to lie to her. I hope she forgives me for it. Get
> Senator Roark behind bars? Sure, and maybe after I've pulled
> off that miracle, I'll go and punch out God. No, The game is
> rigged. There isn't a prosecutor in the state who'll go after
> Senator Roark. And he'll never stop. I killed his only son.
> He'll use all his power to get his revenge on me. He'll go
> after me through Nancy. He'll find her again. There'll be
> no end to it. She'll never be safe. Not as long as I'm alive.
> There's only one way to beat him.

Hartigan holds the gun up to his head,. Yellow blood drops on his gloved
hand.

> HARTIGAN (CONT'D)
> (vo)
> An old man dies. A young woman lives. Fair trade. I love you
> Nancy.
> BOOM

Hartigan's body lays in the snow. Smoke coming from the gun, and from his
head.

                                                        CUT TO BLACK

ON POSTER ART

"After Dimension Films and Troublemaker Studios approached BLT & Associates about creating the print campaign for *Frank Miller's Sin City*, something extraordinary happened in our offices. Before we could even think about assembling a team to work on this film, a passionate crew organically formed itself. Seemingly everyday a new designer, art director, and at least one very anxious copywriter personally asked to join this project. Unbeknownst to us, many of those die-hard Robert Rodriguez fans we work with on a daily basis were crazy for Frank Miller too. Everyone brought in their favorite Frank Miller comic books. We reread them and studied them all over again to better understand the visual language that Frank had created in each panel."

"Next we copied, cut, and scanned in our favorite visual images from the relevant *Sin City* stories. This collection of poses, layouts, designs, and graphic techniques became a visual bible for each character and major location. During this process, photographer Rico Torres sent over 2000 photographs taken on set from special shoots and unit photography. We pored through every single beautiful shot with the same attention we applied to the comics. Along the way, we made oodles of notes, while comparing and contrasting the original characters to their now real-life counterparts."

"Finally, it was time to play. Robert and Dimension's Josh Greenstein encouraged us to explore every possible path we could think of. We had a ball. In that first round, some posters were born entirely from Frank's artwork with only the tiniest hint of live photography to be seen upon close inspection. Other posters used full photography against backgrounds created from the smoke, shadows, windowpanes, and cold rain of the original stories. Some designers focused more on color palettes and discovered stark new combinations for black, white, red, and yellow."

"After countless rounds of group critiquing and even more late-night tweaking, the presentation was hand-delivered to Robert's home studio in Austin, Texas by Rick Lynch, a founding partner and a graphic artist on the project, and me, account executive for all Miramax/Dimension projects. We had worked with Robert previously on *Spy Kids* and found him to be the rarest of filmmakers. Robert actually rolls up his sleeves and works with us on the artwork, using his own computer and vision. In that first meeting, some approaches were eliminated while other styles were combined in electrifying new ways. Many poses and photographs were vetoed outright while others seemed destined to go straight to the theater. That threatening, yet sexy shot of Rosario Dawson, as she seductively licks her lips, was a unanimous favorite from the very start. Everyone also agreed that there would be a Nancy poster featuring Jessica Alba and her lasso; but no one knew which of the thirty looks presented would be the final version. We also decided that all poster copy would come directly from Frank's original dialogue and narration. If *Sin City* was to be the most faithful translation of a comic book series on the silver screen – its posters would have to be inspired by the original work in the purest way possible."

"With Robert's contagious energy and enthusiasm fueling us, Phase Two began in earnest. The agreed upon new concepts would display attitude, danger, and complete conviction. This tone would inform any one poster and greatly enlarge when experiencing two or more posters together. A second trip to Austin, weeks later, proved to be just as fun but twice as difficult. Hard choices had to be made. A final pose for each character had to be selected. Additionally, a final poster look had to be chosen for the overall direction that unifies each piece to the larger campaign."

"After that meeting, a family of posters was determined and the tough task of detailing, tinting, resizing, final rendering, and production eclipsed all previous creative efforts. The last major decision made was Robert's preference to turn Marv around and have him walking towards the viewer and unforgettably into our lives, his back tragically turned against the one town he knows he can never truly leave."

"Over the next few pages you'll find posters never seen before by the general public (pages 260-263), the rare 2004 Comic-Con International: San Diego teasers (pages 264-265), and the final campaign (pages 266-267). Each piece here was absolutely someone's favorite. All of these posters make us thrilled to be mixed up with one of the coolest movies ever made. Our best efforts come from collaboration. And when you have some of the toughest heavies in the business riding shotgun with you, we're all bound to hit something really good."

-Steven M. Gold
BLT & Associates

The BLT "Sin City" team: Rick Lynch, Steven Gold, Ronnie Blumenberg, Michael-Paul Terranova, Christian Aagaard, Will Ragland, Jeff Barnett, Kevin Ramos, Joseph Escareno, Mick Chase, Jose Perez and Anthony Bozzi

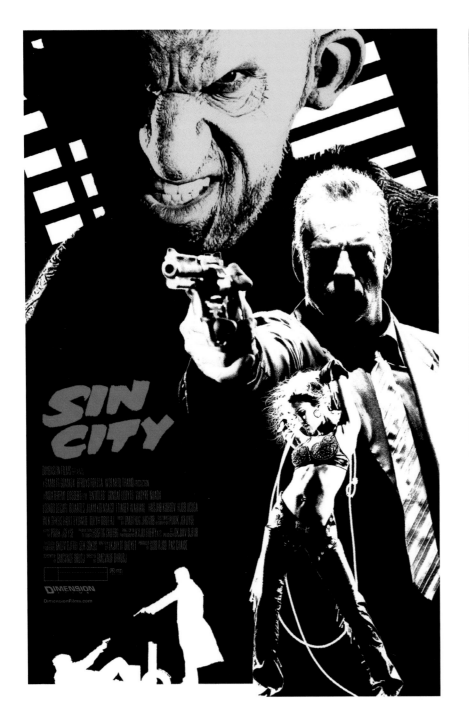

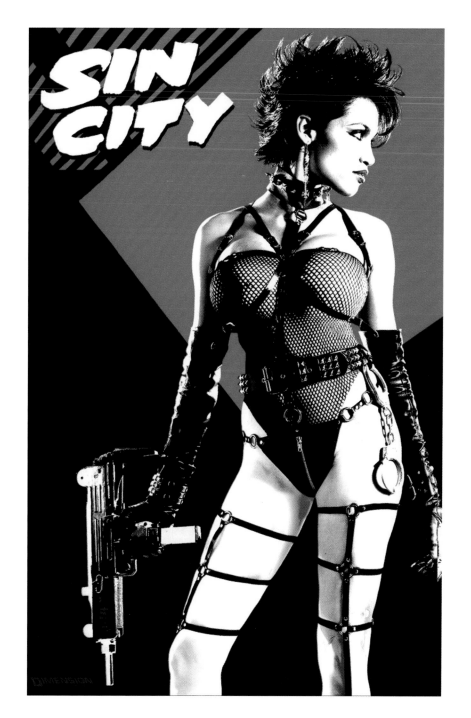

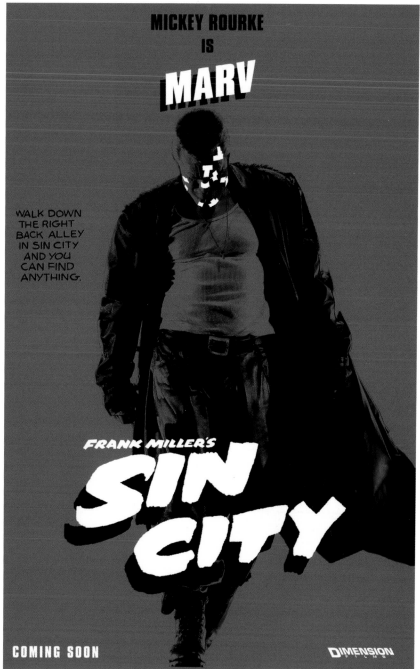

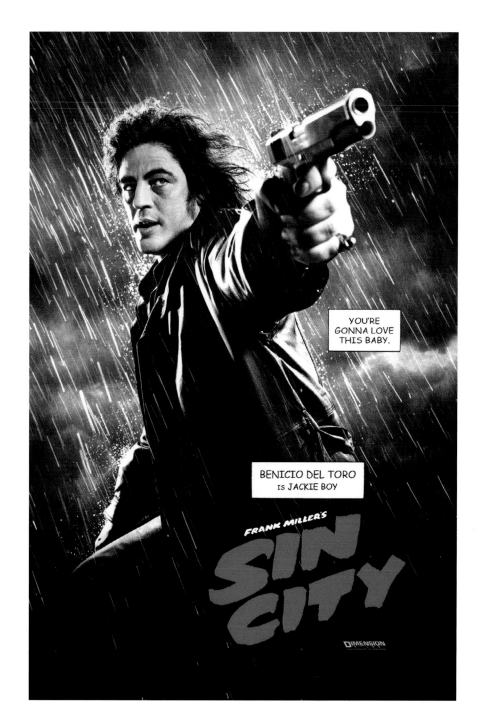

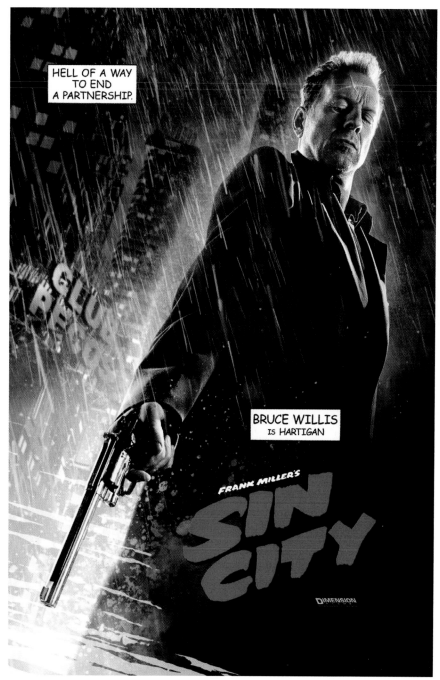

INT./EXT. HI-RISE HOTEL
                    SULTRY VOICE

Walk down the right back alley in Sin City and you can find anything.

BECKY, still having escaped the BIG FAT KILL finds her way into a hotel.
We've seen this hi-rise before. She takes an elevator. She selects the
Penthouse floor.

INT. HI-RISE HOTEL - ELEVATOR - NIGHT

One other occupant is in there with her. The MAN from the opening scene.
Dressed to kill, as usual.

He eyes her. She gives him a smile.

                    MAN
          Care for a smoke?

The elevator doors close.

                    CUT TO BLACK.

SULTRY VOICE

Anything....

Special thanks to all the people that made this movie possible

Chris Abeyta
David Michael Ableman
David Ackerman
Jeffrey Acord
Deepa Agarwal
J. Antonio Aguilar
Jaremy Aiello
Jance Allen
Jeff Allen
Mélissa Almeida
Tim Amyx
Kenny Anderson
Velvy Appleton
Steve Arguello
Chad Atkinson
Marc Aubry
Marie-Claude Aubry
Mariosé Auclair
Elizabeth Avellán
Joaquin Avellán
Kevin Baillie
Montell Baiochi
Allison Gay Baker
Dawn Baker
Bill Ball
Bob Barker
Jeff Barnes
Patrice-Alain Barrette
Michel Barrière
J.P. Barrow
Peter Baustedter
Romain Bayle
Olivier Beaulieu
Patrick Beaulieu
Jessica Becker
Ramiro Bélanger
Caroline Bélisle
Michaël Bentitou
Howard Berger
Louise Bertrand
Brian Bettwy
Vlad Bina
Kamar Bitar
Andrew Bland
Benoit Blouin
Kelly Bogdan
Mark Boley
Brendan Bolles
Cédric Bonnaffoux
Linda Borgeson
Maryse Bouchard
Marc Bourbonnais
Xavier Bourque
Maria Bowen
Mike Bozulich
Kirstin Bradfield
Michael Breymann
Jack Bricker
Caroline Brien
Wayne Brinton
Juan Bronson
Dawn Brooks
Bart Brown
Rodney Brown
Ali Brown
Rodney Brunet
Daniel Bryant
Roy Burger

Lyndsey Burr
Everett Burrell
Buzzy Burwell
Kris Bushover
Daniela Calafatello
Brandon Campbell
Paul Campion
Virginia Capobianco
Lee Carlton
Kit Casati
Carrie Cassada
Irfan Celik
Brenda Chambers
Billy Chambers
Ron Chambers
Matthieu Chatelier
John Cherico
Steve Cho
Youjin Choung
Tom Christopher
Danielle Ciccarelli
Andy Cockrum
Sandra Condito
Scott Conn
Cecilia Conti
Chryssa Cooke
Jacynthe Côté
Pierre Couture
Kevin Coyle
Michael Cozens
Doug Cram
Tracy Craytor
Gino Crognale
Billy Cude
Amanda Curry
Sébastien Dalphond
Jeff Dashnaw
JJ Dashnaw
Kathleen Davidson
Thadd Day
John Debney
Ronan Debrun
Thierry Delattre
Steve Dellerson
Peter Demarest
Luc Desmarais
Mitch Devane
Alex Diaz
Domenic DiGiorgio
Justin Ditter
Tim Dobbert
Gregg Domain
Loring Doyle
Christina Drahos
Valery Dubov
Michael Dudash
Laflèche Dumais
Bill Dunagan
Scott Duncan
Greg Dunn
Sean Dunn
Mathieu Dupuis
Joe Dye
David Ebner
Jody Echegaray
Caylah Eddleblute
Sheila M. Eitson
Troy Engel

Brad Engleking
Trina Espinoza
Cecil D. Evans
Jane Evans
Marcia Evers
Simon Eves
Paula Fairfield
Crystal Falkner-Paysse
Nathan Fariss
Doug Field
Arin Finger
Mike Fischer
Brian Fisher
Joe Fiske
Matt Fliehler
Brian Flora
Natalie Flores
John Ford
Tamara Ford
Joe Forlini
Steve Fossler
Karen Foster
Xavier Fourmond
Robert Freitas
Joe Gallien
Steve Gallien
Kathi Galloway
Jake Garber
Yanick Gaudreau
François Gendron
Stephan Gervais
Roger Gibbon
Phillip Giles
Mike Gillespie
Sandy P. Gilzow
Daniel Gloates
Jeff Goldman
Rainer Gombos
Jimmie S. Goodman
John B. Goodman'
Scott Gordon
David-Stern Gottfried
Lucas Granito
Victor Grant
Caroleen (Jett) Green
Todd Green
Tony Griffin
Rudy Grossman
Ben Grossmann
Peggy Grounds
Manuel H. Guizar
Mark Gutierrez
Debbie Haber
David Hack
Dwayne Haevischer
Asa Hammond
Scott Hankel
Trevor Harder
Jonathan Harman
Trevor Hazel
Erica Headly
Matthew Hendershot
Craig Henighan
Alex Henning
Pierre-Simon Henri
Dave Heron
Diana Hinek
Lucinda Hinton-Schwan

Joe Hoback
Sean "Huggy Bear" Hoessli
Grady Holder
Nadine Homier
Jean-François Houde
Jessica Hsieh
Wendy Hulbert
Cliff Hunt
Dale Hunter
Tony Hurd
Michael L. Hutchinson
Garrett Immel
Vange Ingan
Edward Irastorza
Chris Jack
Edison Jackson
Robyn Jacobs
William Jacobs
Robert Janecka
Julie Jang
Michael Janov
Susana Jasso
Jennifer Jasso
Sarahjane Javelo
Steve Jaworski
Matthew Cope Jones
Grzegorz Jonkajtys
Steve Joyner
Maxine Jurgens
Mike Justus
Thomas Karl,Jr.
Joseph Kasparian
Sean Kennedy
Michael Kennen
Joshua Kersey
Mina Kim
Sungrae Kim
Yoon Bae Kim
Laura J. King
Garry Kirks
Jeffrey D. Knott
Paul Kolsanoff
Kurt Kornemann
Margo Kornemann
Derek Krauss
David Kroach
Derek Krout
Sanghun Kwon
Alain Lacroix
Joshua A. Lacross
Jocelyn Lahaie
Mathieu Lalonde
David Lam
Franck Lambertz
Ivan Landau
Kevin Laneave
Nicolas Langlois-Demers
Jerry Laporte
Marcus Laporte
Julie Lauzon
Brian Lavin
Evelyne Leblond
Chris Ledoux
Daniel Leduc
François Leduc
Woei Hsi Lee
Joel Lelièvre
James Leonard

May Leung
Votch Levi
Jimmy Lillard
Jimmy Lindsey
Ann-Sophie Linteau
Randy Little
Joe Llanes
Peter Lloyd
Ting Lo
Tim Lobdell
David Lombardi
Jennifer Long
David Long
Sophia Longoria
Harrison Lorenzana
Martine Losier
Jeffrey Louie
Ron K. Lussier
Jeff Luther
Anastacia Maggioncalda
Steven G. Maggioncalda
Jay Mahavier
Jocelyn Maher
Stéphane Maillet
Ethan Maniquis
Nick Marra
Richard Martin
Stu Maschwitz
Szymon Masiak
Elspeth Mason
Elizabeth Matthews
Ian McCamey
Mike MCcarty
Annette McCaughtry
Andy McCauley
J.W. McCormick
Jay McCuin
Jill McCullough
Joe McCusker
Luke McDonald
Nicholas McDowell
Josh McGuire
Kirk McInroy
Shannon McIntosh
John McLeod
James McLoughlin
Ed Mendez
Justin Mettam
Scott Meyers
Paul Mica
Jocelyn Miller
Whitney Miller
Kelly Mitchell
Lucy Moncada
Brian Montgomery
Robert Moodie
Richard Moore
Anouk Deveault Moreau
Josh Morehead
Jared Morgan
Christian Morin
Shelly Morrow
Phillip Moses
Simon Mowbray
Tim Mueller
PK Munson
Michel Murdock
Carla Murray
Nicholas Katsumi

Nakadate
Leah Nall
Daniel Naulin
Chris Nelson
Greg Nelson
Toby Newell
Will Nicholson
Greg Nicotero
Vanessa Nirode
Natalie Nolan
Mark Norrie
Luke O'Byrne
Laura O'Keefe
Kyle Obley
Henry Ochel
Chris Olivia
Kym Olsen
Brian Openshaw
Akira Orikasa
Desi R. Ortiz
Ellery Ortiz
Ermahn Ospina
Olivier Painchaud
Mike Pangrazio
Jonathan Paquin
John Parenteau
Jaewook Park
Darren Patnode
Brett Paton
Amanda Peeples
Steve Pelchat
Martin Pelletier
Edward Scott Perez
Ron Perkins
Jeff Peterson
Monika Petrillo
Eric Pham
Patrick Piché
Dagan Potter
Alex Prichard
John Pritchett
Ralph Procida
Gabriel Proctor
Nina Proctor
Peter Profetto
Tom Proper
Tim Rakoczy
Erin Randall
Pavani Rao
Graeme Revell
Dav Mrozek Rauch
Pierre Raymond
Nathan Reidt
Robert Rendon
Shalimar Reodica
Sergio Reyes
Donis Rhoden
Aaron Rhodes
David Ridlen
Sébastien Rioux
Larry Rippenkroeger
Ben Rittenhouse
Joe Rivera
David Roberts
Dawn Robinette
Shawn Robinson
Ruben Rodas
Bernardo Rodriguez

Omar Rodriguez
Felix Rosales III
Jonathan Rothbart
Neil Rubenstein
Jesse Russell
James Ryan
Marc Sadeghi
Paul Sadeghi
Antoinette Sales
John Sandau
Pascal Sauvineau
Marie-Chantale Savard-Côté
Kathy Savoie
Jennifer Scheer
Ron Schmidt
Scott Schofield
Sissy Schriber
Jeff Schwan
Bobby Sconci
Bill Scott
Jeanette Scott
Guillaume Seers
Roman Ziad Seirafi
Stan Seo
Beth Sepko
Alan Serotta
Sharron Sever
Nanci Severs
Shannon Shea
Mike Sheeren
Joshua Sherrett
Mayumi Shimokawa
Dong Yeop Shin
Ferrell Shinnick
Emmanuel Shiu
Nicole Sieber
Mark Siew
Rob Simons
Rebecca Skelton
Todd Smiley
Travis Smith
Charles Ewing Smith
Mirin Soliz
Carsten Sørenson
Eddie Soria
Nelson Sousa
Michael Spaw
Nic Spier
Laurent Spillemaecker
Frédéric St-Arnaud
Paul Steele
Sheila Steele
Edward Steidele
Mylan Stepanovich
Romy Stevenson
Danny Stewart
Scott Stewart
Pete Stockton
Scott Stoddard
Sean Stranks
Cynthia Streit
Randall Stuckey
Christopher Stull
Geordie Swainbank
Sylvie Talbot
Frank Tarantino
Rodrigo Teixeira
Chris Telles

Mike Terpstra
Rob Tesdahl
Philippe Théroux
Gaétan Thiffault
Larry Thomas
Vanessa Thomas
Rhonda Thompson
Alex Toader
Steve Toh
Dino Tomelden
James Toole
Rico Torres
Daniel Torres
Veronica Torres
Vincent Toussaint
Quan Tran
Timothy Travis
Gabriel Tremblay
Marco Tremblay
Chris Trent
Jerry Trent
Charmaine Tuason
Ryan Tudhope
Trevor Tuttle
Leslie Valentino
Kristi Valk
Gabriel Vargas
Joe Vasquez
Sebastian Vega
Jean Frédéric Veilleux
Jessy Veilleux
Mary Vernieu
Brent Villalobos
Kurt Volk
Anh Vu
Jenny Wallace
Carl Walters
Alex Wang
Jonathan Wank
Mary D. Ward
Vicki Galloway Weimer
O.D. Welch
Jack Wells
Ron White
Melissa Widup
Yanick Wilisky
Dennis Wilkins
Tyler Williams
Tom Williamson
Steve Wilson
Sarah Witt
Richard Wood
Victoria Wood
Sean Wright
Tiffany Wu
Jeremy Yabrow
Radost Yankova
Grand Master Yi

SIN CITY

Photo collage by Rico Torres

Art on pages 3, 4, 9, 10, 14, 15, 17, 19-21, 23, 25-27, 29, 33-75, 79, 82, 83, 85, 88-90, 92-94, 97, 98, 106,

125-160, 162-171, 174-178, 180-185, 188, 189, 193, 196, 201, 202, 209-254 courtesy of Frank Miller, Inc.

Photos on pages 18, 32, 34-36, 38-49, 51, 52, 54-56, 58-60, 62-66, 68, 70-75, 78, 81, 83, 84, 88, 90, 91,

102, 109, 112, 115, 121, 124, 126, 128, 131-134, 136, 140-143, 146, 147, 149-153, 156-161, 176, 177,

179-182, 184, 185, 188, 189, 194, 203, 211-223, 226, 227, 230-232, 234-236, 239, 240, 243, 244, 246,

248-250, 252, 253, 255, 268, 271 by Rico Torres

Photos on pages 186-187 courtesy of the *Sin City* Wardrobe Department

Photos on pages 78, 79, 83, 85, 87, 89, 92-99 courtesy of the *Sin City* Property Department

Photos on pages 104, 105, 107, 108, 110, 111, 113, 114, 116-120 courtesy of KNB

Photos on pages 192, 197-200, 204 courtesy of Troublemaker Digital Studios

Photos on page 183 by Sebastian Vega